Educational
Ministry
of a
Church

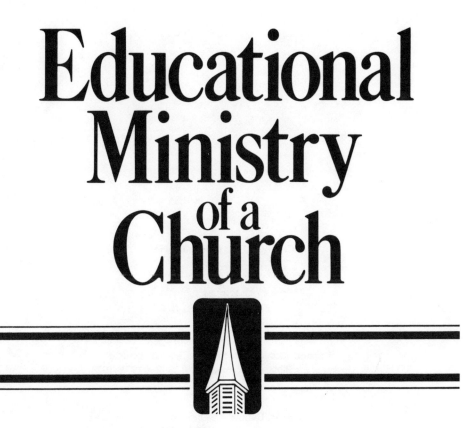

Educational Ministry of a Church

Charles A. Tidwell

Broadman Press
Nashville, Tennessee

©Copyright 1982 ● Broadman Press
All rights reserved.

4232-31
ISBN: 0-8054-3231-0

Scripture quotations are from the Revised Standard
Version of the Bible, copyrighted 1946, 1952, ©1971, 1973.

Dewey Decimal Classification: 268
Subject heading: RELIGIOUS EDUCATION
Library of Congress Catalog Card Number: 81-68922
Printed in the United States of America.

Preface

Early in 1980 Dr. Raymond M. Rigdon, executive director of the Seminary Extension Department and the Seminary External Education Division of the Southern Baptist Convention, asked me to consider preparing a new study guide for use in a course on educational administration. I agreed. The assignment began to grow, and I was asked if I might consider writing the teacher's guide as well as the student's study guide. Again I agreed. It also was agreed that a new textbook for the course was needed. The question came: would I consider writing the textbook? For the answer to that question I needed some time. I gave the answer, obvious to the reader, a few weeks later.

There is more to this evolving story. In October 1980 Broadman Press hosted an invitational meeting of religious education professors to identify textbook needs in the field of religious education, as part of Broadman's continuing plan to supply textbooks in major fields for college and seminary use. At this meeting many needs for textbooks surfaced. The need for a textbook on the educational ministry of a church ranked higher than any other. This volume resulted from these discussions.

It is our hope that *Educational Ministry of a Church* will not only meet the needs of the course in the Seminary Extension centers (now numbering more than three hundred), but also in other institutions where college or beginning seminary students are being introduced to the administrative dimensions of the educational ministry of a church. Further, we hope that many persons who lead in churches presently—pastors, ministers of education, other church staff personnel, and lay leaders—might find help herein for this vital area of a church's ministry.

There are some limits intentionally placed upon this volume. No attempt is made to present a complete philosophic rationale for the educational ministry of a church. Our approach is intentionally more general. Hence in Part I, "Necessity," the focus is upon biblical examples and commands that a church educate; the historical affirmation of the place and value of education in the church; the needs of persons for religious education; the imperative—growing out of its nature and mission—that a church educate; and the conditions and trends of our world which demand that a church educate.

In Part II, "Basic Components," rather than examining theoretically what should comprise this ministry, several components assumed to be basic in almost all churches are presented: Bible teaching and learning; discipleship training; mission education and action; music education and performance; and ministries of enrichment and support, in which only major illustrations of such ministries are included. The components are among those commended to churches affiliated with the Southern Baptist Convention by leaders in the agencies of that denomination whose responsibility is to make such suggestions, and to provide assistance in implementing the ministries of the churches accordingly.

For persons not of the Southern Baptist denomination, it is our hope that this presentation will be taken as an illustrative model, and certainly not as an exclusive design within which the author conceives that all valid educational ministries must operate. The bias is explained simply: the author has been a Southern Baptist from childhood, and has been educated and experienced in the practice and teaching offered by churches and institutions of higher education which are Southern Baptist related. Even so, not all churches of the Southern Baptist persuasion would be expected to find their complete model in this book!

Part III, "Leadership Personnel," identifies the roles of the pastor, the minister of education, other staff leaders, and volunteer leaders in the educational ministry of a church. Leadership through group processes is advocated as ministers and others work together to lead a church in its educational ministry. Definitions of various leadership theories are intentionally not extensive, but are left to the further study by the reader of other sources.

In Part IV, "Vital Processes," the emphasis is intended to be functional and practical. Planning and organizing to meet needs; discovering, recruiting, and training workers; providing resources; and implementing and evaluating are the major concerns. For some, these processes are the sum of administration. One of the secondary hopes is that persons would come to see that, as vital as the "how to" processes are to administration, they are necessarily associated with not only "what to" but with "why to" and "who to." ("When to" and "where to" would complete the scope of administrative concerns, but even these items must be left for other times and places.)

Educational administration is far more than doing that which is predetermined by some individual or group. Vital to both the educational and the administrative aspects of the term is participation with genuine meaning in all levels of leadership activity by all who need to be included. As should become clear to the reader, such an approach to leadership in the church's educational ministry is part of the ministry itself.

It also should be clear to the reader that the involvement of both men and women as leaders and participants in the educational ministry of a church is encouraged. Regarding the use of pronouns in this volume, sometimes both genders are referenced; at other times *man, he,* or *him* are used generically.

Grateful appreciation is due to many persons for encouragement, counsel, patience, and other help during the preparation of this book: to Raymond Rigdon; to Broadman Press personnel; to my teaching colleagues at Southwestern Baptist Theological Seminary. Special gratitude goes to my faithful and efficient secretary, Suzanne Woosley Gray, who typed the manuscript.

Finally, my dear family—Jean, my wife; Al, our son; and Evelyn, our daughter—deserve my eternal gratitude for their patience and, most of all, for their love which helped sustain me during this time of labor. And beyond them, I have had a sense of a great cloud of witnesses comprised of many, who here shall remain unnamed, who have touched my life and helped to form my concepts, many of which are here reflected. For all of these I give thanks to God.

CHARLES A. TIDWELL
Fort Worth, Texas

To the churches
in whose fellowship it has been my joy
to belong and to serve

Emmanuel Baptist Church, Montgomery, Alabama

Seventh and James Baptist Church, Waco, Texas

Bruceville Baptist Church, Bruceville, Texas

Clayton Street Baptist Church, Montgomery, Alabama

Gentilly Baptist Church, New Orleans, Louisiana

Durant Chapel Baptist Church, Bay Minette, Alabama

First Baptist Church, Newnan, Georgia

First Baptist Church, Canton, Mississippi

Daniel Memorial Baptist Church, Jackson, Mississippi

Clinton Baptist Church, Clinton, Mississippi

Brook Hollow Baptist Church, Nashville, Tennessee

Columbia Baptist Church, Falls Church, Virginia

Faith Baptist Church, Kaiserslautern, West Germany

University Baptist Church, Fort Worth, Texas

and many others
whose fellowship I did not join
but who allowed me to render some ministry
and to be blessed by them

Contents

Part I
Necessity

Prologue

To say that the educational ministry of a church is necessary is to imply that the educational ministry belongs to the very nature or essence of a church. Indeed, the educational ministry is so necessary that its removal would jeopardize the church itself.

How can we justify referring to the educational ministry as being essential to a church? The remainder of this book is based on this premise. A beginning perspective is important at this point. No more than a beginning is possible for there are many volumes on each dimension here introduced: *education, ministry, church.*

What is education? What is ministry? What is a church? These are old words. They represent basic ideas whose inherent characters might not have changed, but whose forms and methods have changed, and the descriptions of which have changed even more frequently. What do these words mean? What do *we* mean when we use them?

Education is the act or process of developing and cultivating mentally or morally. It is preparing one for a calling by systematic instruction. It is teaching, training, disciplining, or forming. It is the disciplining of mind or character. It is a science which deals with the principles and practices of teaching and learning. Some trace it to the Latin infinitive *educare,* to bring up (a child), to train, to nourish. Some relate it to the Latin infinitive *ducere,* to lead, which when accompanied by the prefix "e," out, means to lead out. There are elements of both origins in our use of the word. In the context of the educational ministry of a church, education is not mental *or* moral, but mental *and* moral; it is not mind *or* character, but mind *and* character. It is bringing up, training, nourishing, and leading out. It includes knowledge of facts—learning of a cognitive nature. It includes attitudes, how we *feel* about things—learning of an affective nature. Somewhere beyond the cognitive and the affective there is wisdom—that capacity to assess facts and feelings, and to respond

13

in the best way for the long term. The response of wisdom might appear unrelated to the facts or feelings apparent to others.

One can be considered educated only when measured by an accepted standard. Standards are finite, generally. The only standard which is not finite is the Infinite One: God himself. The inference we draw from this concept regarding education is that it is partial and incomplete, short of measuring up to God. In the context of the educational ministry of a church, one must see education as a lifelong enterprise, completed only when one attains "the measure of the stature of the fulness of Christ" (Eph. 4:13).

Education occurs by way of experiences, some direct and some indirect with regard to the involvement of the sensory systems. Some educational experiences can be accounted for only as revelations (as in Gal. 1:12 and Matt. 16:17). Education that is Christian might occur in any of these ways. Typically, education occurs through what one sees, hears, touches, smells, and/or tastes. Such experiences might be either planned or unplanned (even accidental!). In speaking of an educational ministry of a church, we usually have in mind the experiences we intend or plan to occur. These intended or planned experiences we call *the curriculum*. In truth, a great deal of education occurs through experiences which are not intended or planned to be primarily educational. It is that education which occurs as we live, strive, and love together. A church would do well to learn to make the most of the laboratory of life to bring about more desirable educational experiences.

Ministry is the act of doing things needful or helpful. From a Christian perspective, ministry has a connotation of service rendered, labor or duty performed for the benefit of another. In biblical times the services rendered were often associated with labor or duty done by a person of servant or even slave status. Jesus did numerous acts of service of a lowly nature, as though he were a servant. Christian ministry, however, is not limited to that which is menial. There are things to be done that are needful or helpful which are not lowly. There are some very demanding and complex tasks which some must perform. Ministry is ministry because of the helpfulness of that which is done, without regard for who does it, or for where the task ranks in terms of status. It comes out of love.

In the context of the educational ministry of a church, ministry is that which is done to advance the educational intentions of those who comprise a church. This leads us to look briefly at the meaning of church.

A *church* is a body of persons who have become children of God by receiving Jesus Christ, by believing in his name, and who have voluntarily joined themselves together to share the fellowship of his love, and to carry out his will in the world. Loving obedience to him as we live our lives together is a primary focus of a church.

Essential to the life of this body, a church, are the functions of worship, proclamation and witness, nurture and education, and ministry. These are the natural, proper, and characteristic actions of a church, vital to its life. To whatever extent a church fails to perform these characteristic actions, to that extent the vitality of a church is threatened. Conversely, a church which faithfully and obediently performs these functions is reflecting the life—his life—which is in the body.

We make no great distinction in this book between "religious education" and "Christian education." The religious education fostered by a Christian church certainly could benefit by presenting fairly the basic beliefs of other religions. None should fear to engage in a comparative study of religions. However, it is our view that a Christian church should advocate and promote education in the Christian faith, and that religious education in such a church should be understood to be Christian education.

Why a church must educate is the concern of Part I. Our objective is to help persons gain increased understanding of the necessity of the educational ministry of a church. We shall review the bibilical example and command that a church educate, survey the historical affirmation of the place and value of education in the church, consider the needs of persons for religious education, reflect upon the nature and mission of a church which require that it educate, and describe conditions and trends of our world which demand that a church educate.

1
Biblical Precedent

The Bible is the basic book for the educational ministry of a church. Biblical truth in all its rightful expressions in text and in life has been the content of religious education from the earliest days of the faith. This was so in the time of the ancient teacher Moses, the great lawgiver. It continued to be true through the centuries of the Old Testament era and the New Testament period.

It is important for the church leaders in education of any time to know something of the powerful precedent the Bible reveals regarding the necessity of teaching and learning. For all who accept the authority of the Bible as the guide for faith and practice, there can be no justifiable ambiguity as to whether or not education is a primary function of a church.

Christian educators must avoid the inclination to think of their ministry as educational rather than biblical and theological. As vital as good methodology is to an effective ministry of education, the best methodology cannot make up for shallowness or for inaccuracies in dealing with the truths of the gospel. They must know good methodology and good biblical theology, and find ways to bring these together effectively in the lives of learners.

Ministers who serve as pastors must not fall prey to the misconception that a pastor can fulfill the responsibilities of ministry without an emphasis on education—teaching and learning. Even those who have other ministers or laymen responsible for giving specialized leadership to the educational ministry of a church must not relinquish their responsibility of being pastor to the educational ministry. With or without others to help carry the load of leadership in education, the pastor must be the primary educator in a church. Fortunate is the pastor who can count on others to share the leadership; unwise and incomplete is the ministry of any pastor who forfeits this leadership responsibility.

James D. Smart, in *The Teaching Ministry of the Church,* aptly characterized the all-too-frequent plight and response of the pastor:

> Under heavy pressure, if any duty has to be dropped or left with scant attention, it is the educational one. When asked why they do not have classes for the training of teachers, ministers invariably answer that there is no time for them. They would not excuse themselves from preaching or . . . from any of the other essental functions of their ministry with a plea of "no time." Yet here they do so without any qualms, for to them the educational function is not essential to their ministry. Many theological seminaries in their curriculums mirror this defective conception of the ministry. They are organized for the training of a ministry that will be almost exclusively homiletic and pastoral and in which education is not expected to have much place.[1]

The sketch of the biblical precedent which we present here does not claim to be complete. It is our hope that by scanning education in the Old Testament and the New Testament it will be clear that the educational ministry of a church is essential.

Education in Old Testament Times

The Bible is its own strongest advocate of education in the faith and life of God's people. In the earliest section of the Bible, the Law, there is a steady repetition of the command of God that Israel teach the law. The law was considered to be God's voice to men. One passage, Deuteronomy 6:4-9, called the "Shema," "has embedded itself in Jewish consciousness more deeply, perhaps, than any Constitution or similar document has ever been woven into the mind of any Gentile people."[2]

> Hear, O Israel: The Lord our God is one Lord; and you shall love the Lord your God with all your heart, and with all your soul, and with all your might. And these words which I command you this day shall be upon your heart; and you shall teach them diligently to your children, and shall talk of them when you sit in your house, and when you walk by the way, and when you lie down, and when you rise. And you shall bind them as a sign upon your hand, and they shall be as frontlets between your eyes. And you shall write them on the doorposts of your house and on your gates (Deut. 6:4-9).

The *Law* and *history* were the main subject matter of Hebrew education. The *Law* was the foundation of the *written* Torah. Together with the *Prophets* (which included history books as well as the prophets) and with the *Hagiographa,* or Holy Writings (which included such books as Psalms, Proverbs, Job, and others), the written Torah was complete. In addition to the written Torah was the body of oral interpretations of the legal portions, especially of the Pentateuch, which was called the "Mishnah." The importance of Torah and of its teaching came to be equated with life (Prov. 14:13).

History, along with law, was essential in the teachings of Israel. It was considered so because it showed how God works among men. "The Hebrew was profoundly convinced of God's leading in the past. One of his gravest fears was that a generation might forget God's hand in the past, and thus become incapable of seeing that same hand in one's own day."[3] (See Deut. 4:9-10 and Ex. 10:2.) Historical events were told and retold, to the point that brief references in a discourse could enable a listener to recall whole sets of facts and events.

Education in the Old Testament developed along with the life experiences of the nation of Israel. It is helpful to examine the education of this era in the periods before and after the Babylonian Exile, which followed the destruction of Jerusalem in 586 BC.

The Pre-Exilic Period

Before the Exile, "Education took place in the midst of living. The family was the chief educational institution. The teachers of first importance were parents, prophets, priests, sages, and poets."[4] Education was not lifted out or segregated from the other major sectors of life. It was so intricately interwoven with life that to fail in teaching and learning was to fail in life itself.

1. *Parents had the major responsibility.* Parents, in the context of the family, were directed to be the principal teachers. "Fathers and mothers were enjoined in the most impressive manner to teach the history, the precepts, and the ordinances of the Law to their children."[5] This teaching in the life of the family was implemented in three ways: through informal participation by family members in the everyday activities and in the special events (such as feasts and fasts); through the parental control of children's conduct; and through oral tradition passed along in the family.[6]

The informal education began with the mother. The way she performed the household duties was instructive to the children. Her preparation of the sabbath meal, the lighting of the sabbath lamp, the setting apart of a portion of the dough from the bread of the household, prayers, and various domestic rites were part of the child's development.

Fathers were expected to assume the initiative for teaching their children. The faithful ones considered this responsibility to be an honor. A father taught his child a birthday text at a very early age. This text was associated with the child's name, such a verse beginning with, ending with, or containing the letters of his Hebrew name.

The father served as drill master for his children as they recited portions of Scripture. The ability to repeat accurately the law was considered as knowing the law. Much attention was given to memorizing and to reciting. To forget what had been memorized was looked upon as being as bad as not knowing in the first place.

The father worked patiently and earnestly to impart knowledge, and to keep before his children the purpose of the learning. His teaching focused on the repulsiveness of sin; on industry, honesty, sobriety, and obedience as virtues; and fear of the Lord as the beginning of wisdom. That the faithful father felt most seriously the responsibility for teaching his children, especially his sons, is illustrated by the fact that when a son reached the age of personal accountability under the law (*bar mitzvah*—son of the law), the father would stand in a public place, look into heaven, and beat his own breast and thank God that no longer was he himself responsible for the actions of the son. Until that time the father was responsible.

Not incidental in the family educational setting was the observance of the commands of the "Shema." The frequent telling by either parent of stories of patriarchs, prophets, poets, patriots, and national heroes contributed significantly to education in the home. Further, the regular observances of the rituals related to the feasts and fasts, often including dramatic enactments of events, served to stimulate learning not only for children in the family, but also for parents. The latter constituted an indirect way of educating adults, as parents retold and interpreted, doubtless with new insights of their own, the facts related to these occasions. Nowhere in the Bible has parental responsibility been rescinded regarding the teaching of children.

2. *Prophets also educated.* Prophets were significant as unique

educators in the time before the Exile. They proclaimed knowledge of the will of God drawn from events in daily affairs, and from inner experiences. Predominantly they were *forthtellers,* those who spoke forth for God; less frequently they were *foretellers* who predicted what was to come. Often they were esteemed as towering individuals who served as the voice of God to bring his revelation to men.

Prophets interpreted the meanings of events. They sounded ethical notes and declared spiritual insights which found meaning among the disinherited, the victims of injustice, the sincere official, or the simple man at his tasks.[7]

> It was especially their role to speak forth for God in times of degeneracy, or in times of national danger. Even more significant, the prophet could speak of unfulfilled possibilities in one man or in a race. He could stir popular thought, making it reach out beyond the limitations of the sacrificial system. He could teach richer conceptions of the nature of God. And he could expand the understanding of human duty until men saw it was never set forth in any mere letter of the law.[8]

The great Samuel, who served his nation as it became a kingdom, had established schools of prophets at his official posts in Ramah, Shiloh, Gilgal, and Mizpeh.

> In this way promising young men were brought together to live and study under the direction of a prophet or teacher. Presumably they studied the law of Moses, sacred music and poetry. Under able and experienced teachers they would learn much that would enable them to go back to their respective communites as the harbingers of better days. Undoubtedly these schools were largely responsible for the improved conditions that were to come in the political, moral and religious life of the people of Israel.[9]

Some might claim that the prophets belong to the exhortative train, focusing only on their public preaching to describe their place in the life of Israel. Such could scarcely be the case. According to James D. Smart:

> The prophet himself seems to have been both preacher and teacher. It is impossible to conceive of an Isaiah or a Jeremiah contenting himself with saying no more concerning God and his purpose with Israel than what could be expressed in those public utterances to the nation as a whole which are preserved in the collections of their prophecies. We have in their books only fragments of all that they had to say in their lifetime. From a prophet of such

stature as Nathan we have only a single dramatic incident, preserved because of its importance in the history of David. But here and there we find hints that groups of disciples gathered about the great prophets. Only once are they mentioned by Isaiah (ch. 8:16). Jeremiah had his disciple and scribe, Baruch, and may well have had others who were not satisfied to hear him only on public occasions. Second Isaiah, with his warm personal message of encouragement to faith, drew about him a circle of believers. They appeared at a number of points in his writings. He distinguished them sharply from the unbelievers (chs. 50:10,11; 57:1-3), and addressed them as "ye that tremble at his [God's] word" (ch. 66:5). In circles of disciples such as this, the prophets exercised a teaching function. We see it quite distinctly with John the Baptist, who preached to the crowds but taught his disciples. Thus, even in the prophet, alongside the work of preaching stands the work of teaching, both of them services required of the prophet by the word of God which he served.[10]

Prophets were teachers of adults. They taught and preached that God's purpose and reign extended beyond Israel, and that his love embraced even those who had never bowed before his altars.

3. **Priests played a vital role.** The priests reflected their understanding of the will of God through ritual, altar, and sacrifice. Their stance that those who were participating with them in the priest-led practices of worship were the people of God created some stimulating tensions between priest and prophet in the minds of Hebrew adults. Their contrasting ways set in motion conflicting thought processes which are seen as constructive in the educational life of the Hebrews. The tensions seemed to be felt by parents, even as they taught their children in the homes. As a father repeatedly reflected on truths of God as conveyed by prophet and by priest, he often had a learning experience himself which he would not have otherwise had. "From the angle of education one would say that the most daring imagination could hardly have devised so stimulating a way for causing adults to learn."[11]

The priest was responsible for instructing not only in the details of the Temple service, but also in the law itself. Deuteronomy 31:9-13 declares that Moses wrote the law, gave it to the priests the sons of Levi, and commanded that they read it to all Israel, to include men, women, children, and sojourners, so that they might hear the law and learn to fear the Lord. In effect, priests were the public teachers for Israel.

4. **Sages were wise teachers.** The sages were mostly unidenti-

fied figures who nonetheless had an impact upon Hebrew education. Their work began before the Exile, but climaxed in the post-
exilic period.[12] In the East where there was great emphasis given to
meditative thought, it was not unusual for a sage who had observed
life keenly to condense his wisdom into a pithy saying—a proverb
which summed up a view about some facet of life. Such sayings
were especially suited to people who were accustomed to much
learning by hearing, and they became part of the legacy of each
succeeding generation.

Eventually, much of this wisdom of the sages was written down
and became a rich body of material to guide people, especially the
young, in morals and conduct. That these truths were designed for
teaching and remembering is evident in that often they are presented in ways to make them easier to teach and to remember. For
example, many of the sayings are in a kind of free verse, in poetic
form, in which the second line of the two-line saying is either
antithetical to the first line, or progressive, or comparative. The
Book of Proverbs has illustrations of this poetic form.

5. *Poets contributed teaching literature.* The poets of Israel,
particularly the psalmists and the writers of certain proverbs, surely
instructed by way of their writings. The reading of the poetry,
sometimes by various groups, sometimes in unison and sometimes
antiphonally, must have been strikingly impressive. Many were
sung, others were chanted. "Among the Christians . . . no part of the
Old Testament has been taken more deeply into living than the
Psalms. If the singers of Israel have taught Christians so well, surely
they must also have left their mark upon their own people."[13] "No
other poems are so cherished and so continuously studied and
appreciated as the works of the singers of Israel. Many scholars hold
that the poetry of the Old Testament is the most significant
contribution of the Hebrew people to the literature of the world."[14]

6. *Religious festivals were vehicles for teaching.* Another
major feature of education was the religious festivals, the feasts and
the fasts. The feasts were basically celebrations of great events in the
nation's history. The feast of the Passover recalled the deliverance of
Israel from Egypt. The fasts were solemn days of commemoration
generally related to recalling defeat or loss, or some calamity. In
either case these feasts and fasts had an educational function. This

can be seen in connection with the institution of the Feast of the Passover:

> You shall observe this rite as an ordinance for you and for your sons for ever. And when you come to the land which the Lord will give you, as he has promised, you shall keep his service. And when your children say to you, "What do you mean by this service?" You shall say, "It is the sacrifice of the Lord's passover, for he passed over the houses of the people of Israel in Egypt, when he slew the Egyptians but spared our houses." And the people bowed their heads and worshipped (Ex. 12:24-27).

The Feast of Purim, the Feast of Tabernacles, the Feast of the New Year, and the Day of Atonement, were among the festival cycle. The public aspects of these festivals were occasions for the priests to instruct in an official capacity. Parts of the festivals were observed in the homes, where the parents were the teachers.

7. *Government support was part of the plan.* Government support of religious instruction was a clearly expected dimension of pre-exilic education. Any king God chose to give to Israel was to heed this admonition:

> And when he sits on the throne of his kingdom, he shall write for himself in a book a copy of this law, from that which is in charge of the Levitical priests; and it shall be with him, and he shall read in it all the days of his life, that he may learn to fear the Lord his God, by keeping all the words of this law and these statutes, and doing them (Deut. 17:18-19).

Good kings, such as Jehoshaphat (2 Chron. 17), Hezekiah (2 Chron. 30:22), and Josiah (2 Chron. 35:2-3) were faithful in their commitment to religious instruction. Sherrill credits Sanday with the idea that the publication of the document (believed to have been the main body of the Book of Deuteronomy) discovered and read to all the people under Josiah's reign is perhaps the greatest landmark in the history of Israel in that it marked her religion's beginning as a religion of a book![15]

The Post-Exilic Period

Then came the Exile in 586 BC. The Temple at Jerusalem was destroyed. The Hebrews who were not taken captive to Babylonia were scattered. The records focus mainly upon those who were taken to Babylonia. The captivity itself was a time of great learning and of change.

The minority who chose to return to Jerusalem and to rebuild the Temple had learned some valuable lessons and instituted some significant changes. They were thoroughly cured of idolatry. They began to use smaller houses for worship and instruction, since they no longer had a Temple. These centers became the synagogues, and also served as social centers. They collected much of their literature during the Exile. Religion became distinctly more spiritual and personal. The law of Moses took on such new significance for them that it is said that Judaism was born in this period. They became genuinely united in ideals and purpose. They came to a new understanding and appreciation of their destiny as a nation. They became a people with a mission.[16] It seems as though what relative prosperity and opportunity had failed to teach them in previous centuries, adversity taught them in about seventy years!

1. **Religious education received unprecedented emphasis.** The most important change to result from the Babylonian Exile was the new emphasis upon religious education.[17] Those who chose to return to Jerusalem and rebuild the Temple and restore their national identity were from the most religiously devout segment of the captives.

2. **Family responsibility remained foremost.** The complete education system following the Exile had three major dimensions: the home, the synagogue, and the school system (part of which related integrally to the synagogue). The Hebrews placed continuing emphasis upon the family as the foundational setting for religious instruction. Among the faithful this emphasis upon the family responsibility has not diminished through the succeeding centuries. When through oppression, calamity, and suffering the formal schools and the synagogues have had to be abandoned, the family has been the vital sustaining link which has accounted for the strengthening and the continuance of the faith.

3. **Schools emerged, especially synagogues.** The school system developed to include elementary and secondary education, and, eventually, academies for use in advanced studies by scholars and for the higher education of the rabbis. Most of the formal education was limited to the boys, though girls were instructed in the home and in the synagogue services through the worship and

ritual. At times there was also instruction for proselytes to Judaism as part of the systematic plan.

The synagogue became the main public institution in Judaism. The Temple had its place, but the synagogue became the center around which the corporate life of Judaism revolved. It had three major roles to serve in Jewish life: it was a worship center, a center for teaching and learning, and a social center.

The principal purpose of the synagogues was teaching and learning. This was so evident by the time of the "New Testament [that the words] 'synagogue' and 'teaching' are constantly used in the same breath, as if everyone understood that a synagogue was a place where teaching is carried on."[18] The teaching was centered in the Scriptures.

The worship in the synagogue changed the emphasis from sacrifice to teaching. Teaching was seen as an act of worship. Sherrill stated the impact of this fact:

> The synagogue represents, as it were, a marriage between worship and education, so close that thereafter genuinely *religious* education, whether in its Jewish or its Christian stream, cannot be entirely divorced from worship and still remain whole.[19]

He indicated that the influence of the synagogue worship service on Christian worship was strong, and that in early days of Christian worship, "preaching was teaching . . . until the costly mistake of separating the two was made in modern times, with extreme peril to both."[20]

4. *The rabbi was the synagogue teacher.* The rabbi became the most important leader in the school system in the synagogue. In some instances the rabbi was also a scribe. He taught the law, delivered addresses in the synagogue, and had custody of the Scriptures. *Rabbi* means "my teacher," or "my master." One rabbi was allowed to have up to twenty-five pupils. If the number grew to forty, an assistant was engaged. At fifty, a second rabbi was appointed.

The rabbi was generally held in highest esteem. Benson wrote:

> The honor shown to a teacher bordered on that given to God. To dispute with a rabbi, or to murmur against him, was as sinful as to murmur against God. The Jew gave preference to his teacher over his father; the one gave

him temporal life, the other eternal life. The highest and most honored profession to which a Jew could attain was to be a rabbi or teacher. Wealthy merchants with marriageable daughters were accustomed to visit the schools to discover some bright student whose tuition they would gladly defray that they might be honored in having a rabbi for a son-in-law."[21]

Children began attending the elementary school of the synagogue at age five, six, or seven. Apparently the age of first admission moved up from the earlier age of five as the new system was improved and refined. The Book of Leviticus—a book of law—was the first subject of instruction. There were sessions in the morning, in the afternoon, and sometimes at night to accustom a child to learn at any hour. Vacations were granted only on the afternoon preceding the sabbath or a holiday, and on the holiday itself.

On the sabbath the students could review lessons, but not learn anything new. The rabbi could look to see if a pupil were reading from the right location on the sabbath, during the review, but could not himself read the Scriptures during that time.

Pupils were to learn a minimum of one verse or short section of Scripture each day. It was to be committed to memory. Also, pupils were taught to ask questions of the rabbi, whose responses often came as counter questions or parables. This interlocutory method kept participation at a high level. The rabbi might pose a question to the students, hear their several answers, and then conclude by declaring which answer was most appropriate. Reflecting on this approach to teaching and learning, one can easily see the naturalness of the experience of Jesus and the teachers in the Temple when he was there at the age of twelve. The extraordinary aspects of this experience were the wise questions and answers he offered (Luke 2:46-47).

Education in New Testament Times

Many of the primary aspects of education which were in operation in the Old Testament continued to be in use in New Testament times. With the notable exception of John the Baptist, there is almost no notice of the work of prophets in the New Testament times. There is even less evidence of contemporary sages. Nevertheless, even their wisdom, as well as the great literature of the poets, along with the rest of the Scriptures which comprised the Old

Testament, served as the literary base for education in the New Testament.

The basic streams that made up the education of the Old Testament continued into the New Testament: the family, the system of schools, and the synagogue. Sketched here are some highlights which indicate the place of education—teaching and learning—in the life and ministry of Jesus, and of Paul.

Education in the Ministry of Jesus

Jesus demonstrated by every essential indicator that he was the master teacher. He had the most important concepts of life and eternity as his subject matter. He excluded no one from the concern of his teachings. And he was the master of the skills of teaching.

He sometimes preached, and when he did it was with great and unmatched power and skill. *He sometimes healed,* and the impact of these occasions uniquely underscored and magnified the power of God. *More rarely, he raised individuals from the dead,* but these extensions of physical life were not his main mission. *Almost always,* in the biblical record, *he taught.* Preaching, teaching, raising from the dead, and healing were important enough for him to take up his time doing them. While contemporary Christians do not have power to restore physical life to the physically dead, there are contemporary ministries of preaching, teaching, and healing which Christians share with him in the redemptive enterprise.

It serves nothing to exhalt one of the ministry methods of Jesus above others. He belongs to no function or method of the church, to the exclusion of any other. The preacher cannot identify his role with the role Jesus filled and fills as head of the church. Those in healing ministries (and here we refer to such ministries as Christian medical care) cannot assume authority over others because they identify with Jesus as a healer. Neither can those who teach set themselves over others, *even though the evidence of the biblical record shows Jesus preponderantly used the teaching approach in his ministry.*

As we point out some of the evidence that Jesus made extensive use of education in his ministry, the intent is to encourage others to see its great potential for extending the gospel. This potential has only begun to be acknowledged and utilized in the efforts of Christians to share the gospel of Christ with the world (that portion of society which does not order its life around Jesus and his way). Each dimension of Christian ministry has its rightful place as a way of functioning in the work of the church, and all are to be subordinated to Christ, the head of the body, and utilized harmoniously and with mutual respect in the redemptive enterprise.

1. *Jesus considered himself a teacher.* There are numerous times when Jesus identified himself as a teacher. Most of his recorded contacts were with individuals or small groups, whom he was teaching. Only occasionally did he address crowds of people, as in "The Sermon on the Mount." (Notice in Matt. 5:1 that even here "he sat down"; and in 5:2, "he opened his mouth and taught them"; and in 7:28-29, "the crowds were astonished at his teaching, for he taught them as one who had authority, and not as their scribes.") He forthrightly acknowledged himself to be a teacher in John 13:13, when he said to his disciples (his pupils), "You call me Teacher and Lord; and you are right, for so I am."

2. *Friends, followers, and foes considered Jesus a teacher.* Others regarded Jesus as a teacher. They addressed him as teacher, and he permitted it, even to the point of seeming to welcome the title. "Of the ninety times our Lord was addressed in the Gospel record, sixty times He was called rabbi or teacher. Only rarely did His disciples address their Lord by any other title."[22] His disciples called him teacher (as in Luke 11:1 and Mark 4:38). Nicodemus called him teacher in John 3. So did the rich young ruler in Matthew 19. Even the accusing scribes, Pharisees, and the Herodians addressed him as teacher (Matt. 22:24; Mark 9:17; 12:13-14,32; Luke 12:13; 19:39).

3. *Jesus taught masterfully.* Jesus was master of the art of teaching. This fact further attests to the emphasis he placed upon teaching. His knowledge of Scriptures, his ability to extend the teachings of Scriptures to their deeper and more significant meanings, his personality for teaching, his ability to relate to his learners, his appropriate use of a variety of teaching methods, his manner of teaching, his capacity to communicate, his living demonstration of the lofty spiritual and moral concepts he taught, his grasp of essential elements of teaching theory, his effectiveness in the lives of his disciples, all support the claim that he was the master teacher.

4. *Jesus commissioned followers to teach.* Jesus commissioned his disciples—then and now—to teach. The passage labeled

"The Great Commission" (Matt. 28:18-20), is a commission to make disciples—professed followers who receive instruction—of all nations, to baptize them, and to teach them to observe all he has commanded. He bracketed that commission with his assertion that he has all authority, and that he will be with his disciples always. That his followers of that time took his commission seriously can be seen in the developments which are recorded in Acts, especially in chapter 5:17-21,40-42; and 11:19-26. It surely is not incidental that following the year of teaching by Barnabas and Saul at Antioch the disciples were for the first time called Christians. The most effective disciples of all the ages since the New Testament period, including today, have been those who have continued faithfully to carry out this commission, which is at its heart an educational strategy for communicating the gospel.

Education in the Ministry of Paul

The other prime illustration of the place and importance of education in New Testament times is the apostle Paul. Paul stands second in greatness as a teacher only to Jesus, the Master Teacher. Of the followers of Jesus, he has been the most influential.

1. *Paul was educationally advantaged from birth.* Although Paul did not study directly with Jesus, he was uniquely suited to teach. He was born a Roman citizen, in Tarsus. The scholarly reputation of that city was such that, when Paul was arrested in Jerusalem and the tribune asked him if he knew Greek, he had only to respond, "I am a Jew, from Tarsus in Cilicia, a citizen of no mean city" (Acts 21:39). The soldier then knew he was dealing with a learned person.

2. *Paul had a superior education.* Paul declared that he was brought up "at the feet of Gamaliel, educated according to the strict manner of the law of our fathers" (Acts 22:3). Though he was a Roman citizen, he was a Jew—a nation noted for its strong emphasis upon education. Not only that, but he had studied at the feet of one of the greatest teachers of the day, Gamaliel. Perhaps Paul (then Saul) was the prize pupil of Gamaliel and was in line to succeed the great teacher until the time of Paul's conversion on the road to Damascus. He had received the best education Judaism could offer, and he had been one of its most promising scholars.

3. *Paul was perceived as a teacher.* Paul felt some need to

assert his claim and to advocate his right to apostleship, apparently because some were not easily convinced of the validity of his apostleship. But none contested his claim that he was a teacher. Even those who clamored for his arrest accused him of teaching (for example, Acts 21:28).

4. *Paul's teaching was effective.* Early in his ministry he taught effectively. This is clear from the account in Acts 11:19-26. The church at Jerusalem sent Barnabas to Antioch of Syria to inspect the unprecedented responses of Greeks to the gospel. Barnabas was pleased with the situation he found. He exhorted them to remain faithful to the Lord with steadfast purpose. Later he went to Tarsus, found Saul, and brought him to Antioch. "For a whole year they met with the church, and taught a large company of people; and in Antioch the disciples were the first time called Christians" (v. 26b). They established an educational ministry! Some would even say that Paul was the first minister of education! And the ministry was effective to the extent that they were called Christians, apparently by those outside the church and probably not as a label of commendation.

5. *Paul taught in the synagogues.* Paul was received in the educational institution, the synagogue, to teach in the early days of his missionary travels. He would enter a community, go to the synagogue, and attempt by teaching to show the Jewish people how Jesus was the fulfillment of their hopes, their prophesies, and their Scriptures. Acts 13:14-52 and 17:1-3,10-12 are among the passages which illustrate his approach. Later he changed his strategy and did not always go first to the synagogue to teach or to preach, since he began to concentrate on carrying the gospel to Gentiles.

6. *Paul taught wherever and whomever he could.* Paul taught in a variety of places, such as the marketplaces, by the riversides, in prisons, and in courthouses, as well as in homes. He taught Hebrews, Greeks, Romans, slaves, friends, enemies, strangers, and rulers. Preach he did; but he also introduced and explained the gospel through teaching.

7. *Paul used various methods to teach.* He taught by a variety of teaching methods. He used discourse and discussion (see Acts 13:14-52). Even in his writings he was teaching, to instruct, to correct, to persuade. His Letter to the Romans is a kind of

discussion like he might have carried on orally with the Romans had he been with them. "Every one of his epistles was a teaching document, intended for the instruction of his converts."[23]

8. *Paul admonished pastors to teach.* Paul explicitly required that anyone who aspired to the office of bishop (comparable to our pastors) "must be . . . an apt teacher" (1 Tim. 3:2). He wrote his pupil in ministry, Timothy, instructing him to follow the pattern of the sound words he had heard from Paul, and to guard the truth (2 Tim. 1:13-14). He wrote, "And what you have heard from me before many witnesses entrust to faithful men who will be able to teach others also" (2 Tim. 2:2). Again, he stated that "All scripture is inspired by God and profitable for teaching, for reproof, for correction, and for training in righteousness, that the man of God may be complete, equipped for every good work" (2 Tim. 3:16-17). "Preach the word, be urgent in season and out of season, convince, rebuke, and exhort, be unfailing in patience and in teaching" (2 Tim. 4:2).

9. *Paul taught faithfully throughout his ministry.* Paul was faithful in his practice of what he advocated. In his last reference to Paul's confinement in Rome Luke wrote: "And he lived there two whole years at his own expense, and welcomed all who came to him, preaching the kingdom of God and teaching about the Lord Jesus Christ quite openly and unhindered" (Acts 28:30-31). He believed in education. He advocated it for others. He modeled his convictions!

Conclusion

Education is an essential part of the ministry of a church. Those who lead in a church stand on solid biblical precedent when they attempt to maximize the possibilities of extending the gospel and developing persons through good religious education. Any who would slight or avoid responsibility for giving appropriate leadership to the educational ministry of a church are on shaky footing, to the point of being unbiblical.

One who would heed biblical precedent, and who would look to the ministries of Jesus or of Paul for guidance in ministry, must have in their own ministry a major place for education. A church whose members would likewise learn from these must do the same.

Concerns for Further Study

Consider these questions as you continue to reflect upon the meaning of the biblical precedent for education.

1. What are the implications for our time of the enormous biblical responsibility of parents for educating children: (1) to parents, (2) to a church, (3) to ministers, and (4) to others?

2. What could be done to help ministers and church leaders appropriately to maximize the potential of education in the work of a church?

3. What importance are you willing to give education in your ministry? How do you justify the importance you are willing to give?

Notes

1. James D. Smart, *The Teaching Ministry of the Church* (Philadelphia: The Westminster Press, 1954), p. 13.

2. Lewis Joseph Sherrill, *The Rise of Christian Education* (New York: The Macmillan Company, 1944), p. 21.

3. Ibid.

4. Ibid, p. 6.

5. Clarence H. Benson, *A Popular History of Christian Education* (Chicago: Moody Press, 1943), p. 16.

6. Sherrill, pp. 18-20.

7. Ibid, p. 13.

8. Ibid., p. 14.

9. H. I. Hester, *The Heart of Hebrew History* (Liberty, Missouri: The Quality Press, Inc., 1962), p. 169.

10. Smart, pp. 15, 16.

11. Sherrill, p. 16.

12. Howard P. Colson, "The Biblical Precedent," *The Ministry of Religious Education,* edited by John Sisemore (Nashville: Broadman Press, 1978), p. 16.

13. Sherrill, p. 17.

14. Hester, p. 301.

15. Sherrill, p. 33.

16. Hester, pp. 256 ff.

17. Benson, p. 24.

18. Sherrill, p. 45.

19. Ibid.

20. Ibid., p. 47.

21. Benson, p. 25.

22. Ibid., p. 31. For a more detailed explanation, see Sherrill, pp. 83-89.

23. Howard P. Colson and Raymond M. Rigdon, *Understanding Your Church's Curriculum,* revised edition (Nashville: Broadman Press, 1981), p. 17.

2
History

History is a systematic account of events. One who would relate most effectively to the present and the future must have some awareness, understanding, and appreciation of events that have gone before.

The history of religious education is like a rugged terrain with lofty peaks and dark valleys, and there is ordinary landscape here and there. Equating religious education with the Bible school, H. Clay Trumbull in his classic *Yale Lectures on the Sunday School* noted the parallel between the history of the "Christian Church" and that of the "Bible School," and the dependence of the former upon the latter.

> From the beginning, in short, all the way down the centuries, the history of the Christian Church shows that just in proportion as the church Bible School . . . has been accorded the place our Lord assigned to it in the original plan of his Church, has substantial progress been made in the extending of the membership, and in the upbuilding—the "edifying"—of the body of Christian believers in the knowledge of God's Word and in the practice of its precepts. And just in proportion as the Sunday-school agency, or its practical equivalent under some name or form, has been lacking, or has been ignored, has the Church failed of retaining and continuing the vital power of its membership.[1]

Such strong endorsement of the educational function encouraged historian Clarence H. Benson to state: "The progress and permanency of Christianity has been dependent upon a program of education."[2]

Claims like these, and those of many other observers of the history of religious education and of Christianity in general, support the assumption of this chapter that history affirms the value of education. We will describe the place of education among the very early Christians and then review the centuries until the present.

Early Christians and Education

Christianity moved gradually and somewhat mysteriously westward from those earliest days—from Jerusalem to Antioch to Athens, Corinth, and Alexandria; and later to Rome and Carthage. Across the centuries, the westward movement reached the western hemisphere. With this continuous westerly flow, education was an integral part of the Christian faith.

Teaching Continued as a Major Responsibility

In early Christian history, during the lifetimes of those who had been with the Lord and others who had been in their company, there was a continuation of education in much the same way as there had been during the earlier New Testament times. Colson and Rigdon described:

> In characterizing the Christian community as it functioned after the great ingathering at Pentecost, Luke wrote that "they were continually devoting themselves to the instruction given by the apostles, to the fellowship, to the breaking of bread, and to the prayers" (Acts 2:42, author's translation). By this process of sharing, the church assimilated the new converts to its own distinctive way of life and worked to bring them to maturity in Christian character and service.[3]

They affirmed that the church of the New Testament was a teaching-learning fellowship, and that teaching was its very lifeblood.[4]

Every pastor was expected to be "an apt teacher" (1 Tim. 3:2). In addition, there was a special order in the ministry whose primary task was to teach. (See Rom. 12:6-8; 1 Cor. 12:4-10, 27-31; Eph. 4:11; 1 Tim. 3:1-13; and Titus 1:7-9.) And there was still another significant feature about education as we review the earliest days: apparently *many* who were not identified as ministers were active as teachers and as preachers. Citing Acts 8:1,4, Colson commented that

> at the time of persecution that arose in connection with Stephen's martyrdom, the Christians "were all scattered . . . except the apostles" . . . and "those who were scattered went about preaching the word." If the average Christian in those days was a preacher, are we stretching the point to say that doubtless the average Christian was also a teacher?[5]

The involvement of the "average Christian" in teaching is a feature which has received recurring emphasis throughout the history of religious education since New Testament times.

There is evidence, also, that great importance continued to be placed on parental responsibility for teaching the children. In Ephesians 6:4, Paul declared, "Fathers, do not provoke your children to anger, but bring them up in the discipline and instruction of the Lord." Hence, Christians of the New Testament times followed essentially in the directions, if not all the forms, of their predecessors in teaching and learning regarding the faith.

Formally and informally these early Christians taught. For a time they tried to continue to relate through Judaism, with its synagogue schools, the feasts and fasts, and many other features. But the significant differences between the faith of Christians and that of Jews who remained unconverted to Christ eventuated in the separation of Christians from formal Judaism.

New Concerns Emerged

The gospel was too potent and too unique to stay confined to the "old wineskins." People of various strata of the social order responded to the gospel—poor, rich, slave, soldier, artisan, man, woman, Jew, Gentile, official, peasant, Greek, and Roman. There was an exhilarating sense of equality of believers before God and of unique power through the Spirit. This first flush of the awareness of the implications of the gospel brought with its wondrous excitement some inevitable concerns which this minority called Christians had to face and resolve.

These concerns stemming from the religious commitment of the Christians ranged across vast areas of consideration: ethical, moral, social, legal, civil, familial, administrative, and economic. How should a Christian live and deal appropriately with other Christians, cults, pagans, misguided believers, family, work, property, social rank, slaves, masters, divorce, remarriage, the Torah, the sabbath, the tithe, ritual, feasts, fasts, worship, government, their own governance, children, history, doctrine, eschatology, precept, to name some major concerns? Sherrill aptly focused on preaching and teaching as the approaches these early Christians used to inform themselves and to deal with the concerns they faced.

Education in the primitive church, as pictured in the New Testament and other earliest Christian writings, took its form from the issues created when men, liberated into Christian autonomy under God, began to launch out into a growing Christian society, with no precedent to guide them. Teaching is closely related to preaching, yet distinct from it. It is carried on in the Christian meetings and elsewhere, especially in families. The earliest Christian writings, those which we call the New Testament and others as well, are perhaps without exception directly related to primitive Christian education.[6]

1. *They educated through preaching.* The best preaching is always informing to the mind as well as warming to the heart. Early Christian preaching informed the mind as to the truths of the gospel, the proofs of the gospel's validity, and exhorted the heart and the mind to repent and believe.

The message was a clear statement of Christ's life, death, burial, resurrection, appearances, ascension, and his promised return. This was usually a brief statement at the beginning of the sermon, and comprised part one of the message. Part two, the proofs of the truth of the message, had two parts: the use of Scriptures to show that Jesus was the fulfillment of their prophecies, and the testimony of witnesses to the passion and the resurrection. This latter feature in time was replaced by the written accounts of the witnesses. Of the third part, the exhortation, Sherrill's description is noteworthy:

The sermon ended with two great imperatives: Repent! Believe! Repentance, as in the preaching of Jesus, was changing one's mind, turning away from sins and vain things. Its direction was toward God. The outward sign of the inward change was being baptized into Christ. And the faith called for was believing that the report of the witnesses was true, believing that Jesus was the Messiah, and entrusting the whole self to him, in the present and forever.[7]

While this preaching was intended to persuade and to exhort those convinced that they must respond to Christ in faith, it was based upon informing the hearers as to what the truth was, and why they should respond. It was a good blend of preaching and teaching.

2. *They educated through teaching.* In the early church teaching was an essential complement to evangelizing. From the time of the apostles, almost always those who preached also taught. It is also clear that there was the unique gift of teaching which was practiced in the church by its recipients, who were considered

divinely appointed. And, as we have seen earlier, ordinary Christians must have taught as they were scattered abroad.

Apparently there were at least five kinds of teaching in the educational efforts. *First* was the Christian interpretation of the Hebrew Scriptures, especially when the gospel was proclaimed to Jews. *Second* was the teaching about the central facts of the gospel, "our gospel" (2 Thess. 2:14), which was the core of a developing Christian tradition. Paul admonished the Thessalonians to "stand firm and hold to the traditions which were taught by us, either by word of mouth or by letter" (2 Thess. 2:15). A *third* kind of teaching seems to have related to the individual Christian's confession of personal faith. This simple, though varied, assertion was a public avowal, at times, of obedience and loyalty to Christ as king, to be ruled by his will, and to seek his mind upon the issues of life. It may have been uttered at the moment of one's baptism; at times it was a greeting, such as "Jesus is Lord," from one believer to another. A *fourth* way was the oral transmission of information about the life, and especially the sayings, of Jesus. Some of the New Testament books were written to help set forth accurate accounts of this information (Luke, for example). These oral teachings continued even after the New Testament was written. A *fifth* way of teaching was ethical instruction which dealt with the "Two Ways," one being "The Way of Life," and the other "The Way of Death." The *Didache,* a manual dated about the end of the first century, is an example of this teaching.[8]

One of the principal times for teaching in a professed believer's life was just prior to baptism. Instruction prior to baptism came to be such a focal time of teaching that distinctive educational jargon developed to identify the elements of the teaching situation. The pupil was a "catechumen." The content was called "catechesis" (later "catechism"). The method of teaching was a system of questions with prescribed answers, which came to be called the "catechetical" method. This vital instruction, originally devised for adult converts, was intended to discipline the convert's moral life, acquaint him with the Christian tradition, and create in him a profound devotion to the Christian faith and way of life.[9] At one point in the early centuries this period of instruction extended for as much as three years, though this length of time was probably not uniformly practiced. Later it was reduced to two years and eventually was shortened or eliminated altogether at least as a requirement for entry into the church. By the seventh century, in the churches of the West, this instruction almost disappeared and was replaced by brief liturgical acts.

3. *They educated in their meetings.* Early Christians convened for two and possibly three kinds of meetings, all of which would contribute to and be used for education. These meetings were held in a variety of places—homes, riversides, and eventually the catacombs of Rome.

One kind of meeting was the "meeting for the Word, the purpose of which was edification."[10] This meeting included prayer; psalms, hymns, and spiritual songs; occasional reading of apostolic letters; a period of teaching; prophecies; and, in the New Testament times, speaking with tongues—of which there appeared no more mention in the New Testament after Paul's instruction.

A second kind of meeting was for a common meal, followed by the observance of the Lord's Supper. The fellowship during the meal, and the time of instruction and examination which comprised the Lord's Supper were very meaningful to Christians.

Some think there was a third kind of meeting, held for the church to transact certain business. During New Testament times, 1 Corinthians 5:1 ff. and 2 Corinthians 2:5 ff. seem to infer as much, with the church meeting for discipline and forgiveness of certain members. Any who have ever observed a congregation in session for these kinds of purposes can attest to the educational potential in such meetings!

4. *They educated in the family.* Not as much is known about the details of the teaching in the home among early Christians as is known about such teaching in Judaism. But it is a reasonable assumption that these Christians considered instruction in the family setting to be vital. Some entire households received Christ. Other families were divided in their faith. Christians often met in private homes. It was not until the third century that independent buildings were erected by churches, or set apart for their use. Even then, they were frail. "During the persecution of Diocletian, the famous church of Nicodinea was leveled to the ground by the Praetorian guard in the course of a few hours."[11]

Jewish converts to Christianity probably continued to instruct in their homes much as they had done before their conversion. It is speculated that the use of Scriptures might have been increased in the homes of converts, while the use of ritual probably diminished rapidly among Jewish Christians. Sherrill asserted:

> It is reasonable to conclude that in the latter part of the first century children of Christian parents were being taught from our Old Testament and from parts or all of at least the first three Gospels. It is not clear whether this was in the household, or in Christian meetings. Perhaps both were intended.[12]

The instructions of Paul regarding the parental responsibilitiy to teach and guide their children can be supposed to have been obeyed not only by those who first received his letters, but also by those who followed thereafter.

5. *They educated through worship services.* By the second century the three meetings described earlier were combined into one meeting. It consisted of reading of Scriptures, instruction (including exhortation), and the Lord's Supper. In the fourth, fifth, and sixth centuries, Christian worship in the East and the West differed at many points. But they were alike in that the format had two major parts: the first, with the catechumens present, and the second for the faithful, with the catechumens dismissed. The first segment of worship was largely given over to instruction; and this instruction was largely for adults.[13] These catechumens were adults converts who were being prepared for church membership.

6. *They educated in catechetical schools.* Relatively few locations in these early centuries had the formal educational institution known as the "Catechetical School." The most notable ones were at Alexandria, Antioch, Edessa, and Nisibis. Of these, the school at Alexandria excelled. It was a school of higher education, traditions attributing its founding either to Mark or to Athenagoras. Its most famous teachers were Clement, who began teaching there about AD 190, and his pupil Origen, who was his successor. Origen took charge of the school when he was only eighteen years of age, and served it from AD 202 to 231. Later he taught at Caesarea until 254. In the fourth century Jerome was one of the pupils in the school of Alexandria.

Of all the teachers at Alexandria, Origen left the most voluminous legacy. He was a prolific writer, with rumors suggesting that he wrote six thousand books. He was considered great as a teacher because it was said that his teaching liberated the greatness in his pupils. No subject was considered out of the bounds of his legitimate interest in his classes. Such openness cost him posthumous condemnation at Rome, Alexandria, and Constantinople.[14]

By the end of the fifth century, most of the catechetical schools no longer functioned. By that time the world into which Christianity had intruded, and in which it eventually flourished, had changed radically for the worse.

Education Across the Centuries

Up to the time when the Roman emperor Constantine made his decision "that it would be better to conquer *in* the sign of the cross than to try to conquer the cross,"[15] the Christians had been a minority group. The state had tried to stamp out the church through various forms of prohibitions, campaigns, and persecutions. In spite of these oppressive acts which snuffed out the lives of thousands of Christian martyrs, the church continued to grow. Morally, they outlived the adherents of the pagan religions and the worshipers of emperors.

Full religious freedom as a right to every man, recognition of the church as a corporate body, and reparations were decreed by the edict of Milan in AD 313. Persecution of Christians ended, and the church became favored by the state. Then Theodosius I established Christianity as the religion of the Empire, and authorized the name of Catholic Christians in AD 380.[16]

The Period of Darkness

These developments establishing Christianity as the state religion brought on significant changes in the Christian movement, and education changed radically because of these. Christianity assumed nationalist forms. A Christian had to be loyal to the state and to its approved interpretation of the tradition. Infants were declared to be members of the church. The preparation of catechumens (mostly adult converts) for membership waned, and soon disappeared. Nothing substantial replaced the teaching about membership in the Christian body. The earlier perceptions of equality of all members before God, in which the church had gloried and had prospered, was replaced by the ascendancy of a spiritual hierarchy which soon fixed itself as a hierarchy of governance for the corporate body, the church.

Eventually there arose a "metropolitan bishop" in each major population center which resulted, after some time of tensions regarding who of *these* should be preeminent, in the predictable assumption by the bishop of Rome that he was the Pope. His determination of the mind of God in spiritual and moral concerns was to be taken as the voice of God himself. Although throughout these centuries various groups of Christians did not comply or conform to the development of a state church, it was the latter which substantially dominated the development of the Christian movement for centuries, and with it the educational activities.

The blend of church and state brought on dramatic reversals which impacted both life and learning.

> In the second and third centuries, death was the risk of being a Christian. But by the fourth century, and thereafter, until the conscience of men would bear it no longer, death was the possible price of *not* being a Christian. Therefore when a man taught the Christian faith he must keep an eye out, discreetly. And when a man heard any Christian teaching it was more natural to ask whether it conformed, than to ask whether it was true.[17]

The Empire known as Rome began to decline in power. Hordes of tribal groups pressed in upon the Empire, wreaking devastation so that even the city of Rome itself was sacked. The scattered remnants of governmental power were no match for the problems they faced. Paralysis spread into every aspect of life, resulting in broken trade, disorganized economic life, soaring prices, oppressive taxes, spreading poverty, vanishing personal security, neglected roads, closed schools, common ignorance and illiteracy, and declining literature, arts, and sciences.[18] The world which Christianity knew was plunged into centuries of darkness from which it emerged only after great agony.

Until the time of Martin Luther and the Reformation, the church turned more to liturgy than to education. Priestly acts and penitent responses according to prescribed and approved forms replaced for many the internal qualities of the Christian experience. The result was an externalizing of religion, the effect of which was not unlike the external understanding of religion which Christ had come to change. Jesus could have preached and taught again his great

"Sermon on the Mount," easily substituting the forms more recently developed for those he addressed in Matthew 5—7, as he contrasted evidences of approved righteousness with the way he came to proclaim.

Conditions for education were deplorable during these dark centuries. Here and there were pockets of people who struggled to preserve the legacy of learning and rational understanding of the faith. Some strong and often strange individuals isolated themselves from society for study and contemplation of the faith. These hermits drew about them others of similar interest, and their isolation developed into little colonies of hermits who ate, prayed, and worked together in monasteries or nunneries. Some copied the Scriptures and other writings, thereby preserving some basis for continuing limited training for clergy and a reservoir of materials for future reference when the lights of learning were rekindled.

Even so, many of the church leaders were illiterate and ignorant of the great truths of the faith. Many lacked foundational cognitive knowledge which might have served them in their search for these truths. Benson wrote:

> When Hooper was bishop of Gloucester, he found that out of 311 of his clergy, 168 were unable to repeat the Ten Commandments. Thirty-one did not know where to find them. Forty could not tell where the Lord's Prayer is to be found and thirty-one did not know the Author.[19]

The established church had become a custodian of the religious heritage and of general culture and was no match for the challenge. A few leaders had some access to formal education. Any scholar of conscience who excelled in a search for truth risked failing to conform and was discouraged. Those who proceeded in the face of the risk became the objects of persecution from the very institution, the church itself, which had been their base.

The plight of the masses of Christians can be described simply. They were largely ignorant and illiterate, subject to the institutional church which itself had but a flickering light aglow. Teaching was reduced to rudimentary forms and formulas which were crystallized and authoritative. Teaching

> was communicated through drama and sacraments, through architecture, through pictures of mosaic and stained glass, and through the confessional

where sacramental developments led believers to seek priestly guidance. Thus in the absence of formal schooling and literate culture, liturgy, drama, and architecture became more important educative instruments.[20]

The Dark Ages produced ignorance feeding upon ignorance. World governments were in repeating states of chaos, and the official church could claim to be in no better condition. Leaders and members leaned upon the authoritarian church and looked to it for grace to be given or withheld. When given, such grace came through "mysterious rites which no mind could understand, but in which they must trust."[21]

Christianity and its child, the teaching and learning of truth, had reached a point of darkness so that even little glimmers of light here and there stood out in contrast. Numerous antichurchly sects struggled to find and follow the way of Christ. Their stories in history have been documented in many volumes. Eventually they, as well as some searchers for truth within the established church, were to become the instruments of change for the better, again turning on the light of learning. Until these years of renaissance and reformation came, the cause of education, even in the authorized church, was grim.

> Instead of advocating education, the popes were busy hunting and murdering the Waldensian believers. John Huss and Jerome of Prague were martyred as by barbarians. The monasteries were filled with the timid, the lazy and the disappointed. The pulpit was largely given up to what was fanatical, ridiculous or political, and in many parts scarcely employed at all. The whole ecclesiastical system was used mainly either for money-getting or the gaining of secular power.[22]

The Reformers and Education

Truth will out. However slowly, men here and there began to break through the darkness of ignorance.

Copernicus propounded his theories of astronomy, describing that the earth rotates daily on its axis and that the planets revolve in orbits around the sun. The world actually was not flat, as had been supposed! Johann Gutenberg printed the first Bible to be produced with the use of movable type in Mainz, Germany, in 1456. Until that development the literature had been limited to what could be copied by hand.

The city of Constantinople fell in 1453 to the Muhammadan army, causing the few scholars of Greek to flee to northern and western Europe, taking with them the keys to the long-suppressed world of classical thought, literature, and art. Great and courageous linguists began to translate the Bible into the language of the people. Several were martyred for their work, and others were forced to spend their lives as fugitives from religious and civil authorities. John Wycliffe initiated the first complete Bible in English about 1384. He survived as a fugitive, only to have his body exhumed, burned, and scattered after his death!

Nations of Europe became interested in knowing more about the cultures of Rome and Greece. The ways of other peoples of the earth became of interest to Europeans. Their interests developed in the possibilities of interchange with other peoples for commerce and industry. Nationalism developed rapidly, accompanied by colonizing and empire building. New trade routes were sought by explorers. Columbus, on a voyage in search of a new route to the East, came upon the Western hemisphere.

The awakened interest in learning, labeled the Renaissance, prepared the way for the awakening of widespread interest in the Christian faith. The growing availability of Bibles in the language of the people set the stage for a growing interest in the contents of the Scriptures.

Eventually increasing numbers of scholars and persons of the general populace were convinced that the Bible should be taken as the sole authority for faith and life. Further, they held that justification comes by faith alone. Perhaps most disturbing to those in power, these troublesome people were convinced of the priesthood of all believers. They wanted to share these newly discovered truths with others, and to let them impact and reform the established church.

But, in a repetition of history's cycle reminiscent of the situation Jesus faced, the religious power structure accumulated over numerous centuries of focusing on the external evidences of religion, was not capable of receiving the volatile new wine of biblical truths which the reformers proffered. The old wineskin burst and what historians have termed a "Reformation" actually became a revolution.

Reformers were expelled from the church. Some left before they were expelled. In the spirit of Martin Luther, they could do no other.

They continued their search for truth and biblical faith, and they wanted others to study and to learn of it. Several were outstanding in their advocacy of teaching and learning.

1. **Erasmus advocated popular Bible study.** Erasmus was a Dutch scholar whose life spanned parts of the fifteenth and sixteenth centuries. He translated the New Testament from Greek. He edited editions and translations of classical authors and the Church Fathers. He declared that everyone should have opportunity to read the Bible for himself (even herself!). He wrote:

> I totally dissent from those who are unwilling that the sacred Scriptures translated in the vulgar tongue should be read by private individuals; as if Christ had taught such subtle doctrines that they can with difficulty be understood by a very few theologians; or as if the strength of the Christian's religion lay in man's ignorance of it. The histories of kings it were perhaps better to conceal. But Christ wishes His histories to be published as widely as possible. I would wish even all women to read the Gospels and the epistles of Paul. And I wish they were translated into all languages of all people. I wish that the husbandman may sing parts of them at his plow; that the weaver may warble them at his shuttle; that the traveler may, with their narratives, beguile the weariness of the way.[23]

2. **Martin Luther championed education.** The bold German whose name is associated most prominently with the Reformation, Martin Luther, was firm in his commitment to education. He preached and wrote often of the importance of teaching. He strongly admonished parents to teach their children. He challenged the government to support compulsory education. For the preachers he exalted teaching and exhorted them to do it without fail.

Parental responsibility to teach children was called "the big work of parents, and when they do not attend to it, there is a perversion of nature as when fire does not burn or water moisten."[24] He went so far as to say that people should not marry until they were competent to teach their children in religion, and bring them up as true Christians.[25]

He saw the education of the public as essential for the success of the church, and for the future of the state. He called upon the government to compel the people to send their children to school.[26] His concept was that the state should be the agent of education which advanced the teachings of the church.

He highly esteemed the work of teaching school, and decried the inclination of young preachers to avoid it. He was not sure which should be preferred, preaching or teaching.[27] He wrote:

> I would I knew one chosen for a preacher who had previously been a school teacher. But at the present time our young men want to become preachers at once and to avoid the labor of school keeping. Yet the schoolmaster is as important to a city as a pastor. We can do without mayors, princes and noblemen, but not without schools, for these must rule the world.[28]

3. *Philipp Melanchthon reformed education.* Philipp Melanchthon influenced the development of the University of Wittenberg, Germany, through forty-two years of working there. The University took on Protestant lines, and became a model for many new universities throughout Germany. He was to educational reform what Luther was to religious reform. At age sixteen he prepared a Greek grammar which served as the universal text for German schools. He later produced a popular Latin grammar, along with texts in rhetoric, ethics, and theology. He was considered the preceptor, the master teacher of Germany. Benson wrote of Melanchthon that

> at his death there was scarcely a city in the entire country that had not modified its schools according to his program of learning, or that did not number some pupil of his among its teachers.

He was clearly the outstanding leader of the Protestant revival in education.

4. *John Calvin urged the church to teach the young.* John Calvin in France and elsewhere was a staunch proponent of the use of the interlocutory teaching approach to instruct the young and ignorant. To assist in these times of instruction he prepared catechetical lesson guides in French and in Latin, and some consider these to be his greatest contribution to the cause of religious education. He also stressed the importance of careful parental instruction of children in the home.

Calvin encouraged that children be taught to sing the songs of the church to encourage their participation in congregational singing. He also insisted upon good training in "sound learning and doctrine . . . in manners, good morals, and common sense."[30] It was his belief that the work of the Reformation could not be conserved without a systematic program of reaching and teaching the young. Both the *Heidelberg Catechism* prepared by Ursinus and the *Westminster Catechism* of England were based on Calvin's system of catechetical helps.

5. *John Knox advanced Sunday education.* John Knox of Scotland called for a full Sunday of religious activity to be centered around worship and education. He wrote that Sunday should be straightly kept and attendance at worship should be carefully observed. Moreover, he instructed ministers that young children should be publicly examined in the afternoon in their catechism, in the audience of the people. The minister was instructed to be diligent to see that the people understood the questions and the answers and the doctrine with which they dealt. It was the minister, according to Knox's *Book of Discipline,* who was to instruct the children and youth of the parish in their first rudiments, with special emphasis on the catechism.

Knox also directed that religious instruction, "the principles of the Christian religion,"[31] be taught to children, servants, and family in every household. He charged the master of every household to either instruct or cause to be instructed those of his house.

6. *Ulrich Zwingli favored indoctrinating children.* Ulrich Zwingli of Switzerland believed that "when the truth entered the consciousness of the people evil practices would fall into decay."[32] He courageously led his people step by step in reform, with faithful dependence upon the Scriptures for authority. Zwingli's principal connection with education was the book he prepared for publication, *The Christian Education of Youth.*

The catechisms and related materials which the great reformers wrote or encouraged, used, and directed others to use comprise perhaps their greatest educational contributions. Luther's *Short Catechism* ranks close to the Bible as one of the most widely circulated and translated books ever published.

All in all, these great reformers and their followers were the instruments of renewed focus upon the value of education in the Christian faith. To them it was not an option but a basic necessity if the faith were to be truly received and followed. They were united in their commitment to the necessity of the Christian education of the children. They all advocated the responsibility of the home, the school, and the church in this endeavor.

Post-Reformation Education

The Reformation set in motion many developments which bear upon religious education history, and some of which are felt even in the present generation. Certain highlights will be indicated here.

1. *The Catholic Church countered with education.* Threatened by the virtual capture of entire nations by the sweeping tides of the Reformation, there arose in the established church a movement recorded as the Counter-Reformation. Prominent in this movement was the work led by the Society of Jesus, a brotherhood within Catholicism founded by Ignatius Loyola. While elements of the Catholic Church were engaged in efforts to stamp out those of opposite beliefs through a vast "search and destroy" plan called the Inquisition, the Jesuits moved ahead of the distracted Protestants in two significant fields: missions and education.

In the 1500s these missionary Jesuits entered and made substantive gains in North America, South America, the Orient, and other parts of the world. They established missions and started schools. Francis Xavier, a companion of Loyola's, sought to carry salvation to India and Japan, with hopes of moving into China. He died without entering China. "In the two and a half years that Xavier labored in Japan he founded more than two hundred churches and baptized 150,000 persons."[33] He focused especially on the teaching of little children. He is credited with saying, "Give me the children until they are seven years old and anyone may take them afterward." By the time Protestantism developed a missionary vision in the eighteenth century, the Catholic missionaries had preceded them to many parts of the world.

Most significant was the educational work of the Jesuits. They established free schools for children and offered quality education in religion and in secular subjects. Their scholars wrote the textbooks. Their teachers received quality training.

> Jesuit teachers thus were far superior to any of their contemporaries, and they not only commanded the Catholic universities, but also found their way into such schools as received State support. Not until the rise of the normal

school in the nineteenth century did either the State or the Church give such
careful attention to the preparation of teachers.[34]

The Jesuits, along with other efforts by the Catholic Church,
stemmed the tide of reform and fixed boundaries between Protestants and Catholics, especially in Europe, that have change little
since shortly after Luther broke with Rome. Both Catholic and
Protestant historians agree that it was the religious school system of
the Jesuits which played the major part in this arrest.

2. *Education in America reflected the Reformation.* Most of
the settlers of what is now the United States of America came from
the countries of Europe which had embraced Protestantism in some
form. Those who migrated from predominantly religious motives
were committed to the religious education of their children. "From
the landing of the Pilgrims in 1620 until the birth of the American
Republic in 1787, there was scarcely any difference in secular and
religious education."[35]

In colonial America the forms of education were molded by the
uniqueness of the settlers of any given area. Virginia, and some
other Southern colonies, was led in settlement by persons of the
English upper class. They provided private education for their own
children and apprenticeship education in the trades for the poor.
The middle colonies had mostly parochial schools related to the
various sponsoring faith groups, with clergymen usually serving as
their teachers. These schools often favored religious subject matter
to the neglect of other subjects. Out of the Puritan concepts of New
England, the democratic idea of state support for education for all
developed; and in colonial days there was no separation of religious
education from public education.

The most important volume in colonial education, the *New
England Primer,* came from the educators of New England. Next to
the Bible, it is regarded by many as the most important literary
molder of those who founded the republic. This eighty-eight page
book was in every school and in most homes. It was said that it
taught millions to read, and not one to sin. What did this powerful
little book contain?

The contents of the primer included the alphabet, vowels and consonants,
capitals and small letters, easy syllables for children, the Lord's Prayer, the

Apostles' Creed, the Shorter Catechism, an account of the martyrdom of John Rogers, and a dialogue between Christ, youth and the devil. Eighty-seven per cent of the wonderful book was made up of selections from the Bible.[36]

For many years the influence on education by religious forces continued. Gradually, and almost imperceptibly at first, the secularization of public education in America occurred. Religious, educational, and political debate continued to focus on the appropriate relationships which should prevail. One primary result of the secularization of public education seems clear: churches must generate, sponsor, and support the religious education they desire their constituents and others to experience.

The Modern Era

The extent and the effectiveness of religious education varied among the countries of Europe, as did the general education of the populace. It seems fair to conclude that neither the religious nor the general education of the masses reached any admirable level by the eighteenth century. The same was true in America, though it was in America that the most was to be made of religious education.

1. *The Sunday School movement set the pattern.* While churches in Europe and America were seeking ways to educate their constituents and others, the masses remained without instruction in religion or in much of anything else. Robert Raikes, of Gloucester, England, was a reformer and philanthropist, a layman who published a weekly newspaper. Through the complaint of a resident about the rowdy behavior of some children in a slum area, Raikes became concerned about the welfare of the children.

There were then no child labor laws to protect the children from having to work from sunup to sundown six days a week in the factories in England in the wake of the industrial revolution. Moreover, there was no provision for the education of the masses of children. On their only day off, Sunday, they often roamed the streets in packs. They were dirty, ignorant, and unchristian. Many were unwanted, except for their economic value as laborers.

Raikes believed that if these children could be taught to read, they might read the Bible for themselves, and learn the way of salvation. In 1780 he rented a meeting place, employed teachers, and started a school on Sunday for these children to receive secular instruction and knowledge of God and the Bible. Only the teachers had a copy of the Bible, the textbook.

Each child had to stand inspection at the door for admittance: a washed face and combed hair was the price of admission. In fact, at the end of each session, as they piled out the door, each received a coin for attending. Friends labeled his efforts, "Bobby Wild Goose and his ragged regiment." The churches thought his efforts were hopeless. Further, they thought such use of the sabbath to be a sacrilege. Many came to feel the Sunday School was in competition with the church. Sermons were preached against this "work of the devil." Raikes continued, and the idea grew.

A problem emerged which had to be solved to release the movement to the populace. The money to support the Sunday School was consumed in the modest wages for the teachers. There was no money for Bibles for pupils, or for other learning materials. After three years of success with the school, Raikes published an account of its work in November 1783. His article was reprinted widely, even beyond Great Britain. One result of the publicity was that ladies of fashion began to volunteer their services as teachers in Sunday School. Even the Queen sent for Raikes and had him tell her his story about the Sunday School.

Others helped in the early expansion of Sunday Schools. A layman, William Fox, a wealthy Baptist merchant of London, learned of Raikes's Sunday Schools. On September 7, 1785, he organized the Sunday School Society for the express purpose of organizing and supporting Sunday Schools. They furnished Bibles, Testaments, and spelling books for the schools and money for teachers. Paying the teachers continued to drain the financial resources until John Wesley aligned himself with the movement. He called for volunteer teachers to replace paid ones. More literature and the free services of teachers contributed significantly to the preservation and extension of the Sunday School movement. By the time of Raikes's death in 1811 there were Sunday Schools scattered over England with a combined attendance of 400,000 pupils.[37]

There was a parallel movement in America to begin Sunday Schools. In 1785 a Virginian, William Elliot, began a Sunday School in his plantation home on Sunday evening. He taught blacks and whites at separate times. In 1801 the school was moved to the Oak Grove Church building, a Methodist church in Accomac County, Virginia. It is considered to be the oldest Sunday School in America. Some consider the Sunday School established in the Broadway Baptist Church of Baltimore, Maryland, in 1804, to be the oldest and first denominational Sunday School in America, as well as the first Raikes-type school in this land.

2. *Southern Baptists experienced phenomenal educational growth.* The denomination of Baptists known as the Southern Baptist Convention has been viewed by many as the "miracle" group in America regarding the development of church ministries in religious education, especially the Sunday School.[38] Organized as a denomination in 1845, many of the churches of this denomination had Sunday School for women and children (and a few men) even earlier. They had able representation on the editorial board of the Uniform Lesson committee from its beginning in 1872. This committee is an interdenominational effort to bring some pattern to the selection of Scriptures for use in preparing Bible study materials for the Sunday Schools.

In 1891, after several earlier attempts had failed, this denomination established a publishing house for Sunday School materials. With the addition of materials for several other teaching and training ministry approaches and organizations, the Sunday School Board of the Southern Baptist Convention became the largest publisher of religious materials in the world.

Using the Sunday School as the principal agency for Bible teaching and learning, the Baptists also learned to use the Sunday School as the principal method for organized outreach to persons not engaged in active church life or study. Presently they are the largest denomination of Evangelicals in America, and more than 99 percent of their churches have a Sunday School. They consider the Sunday School to be the foundational organization in growing churches.

The "miracle" of the Southern Baptists does not end with Sunday School. Woman's Missionary Union, founded in 1888 by some women of the denomination with deep concern for missions, sponsors an age-graded organization in the churches for missions education, action, and support. In 1907 laymen in the denomination organized a Laymen's Missionary Movement. Known today as

Baptist Men or as the Brotherhood, this organization is similar to the Woman's Missionary Union in its design for ministry, with a unique focus on active involvement of men and boys in mission action and in personal ministry.

In 1918 the denomination in Convention session directed the Sunday School Board to foster the work of training Baptist young people in the church. A youth organization already existing in many churches since 1912, the Baptist Young People's Union, then came under the sponsorship of the Sunday School Board. This action for the first time, made that Board more than a board for Sunday School support. By 1931 this educational organization expanded to become an all-age plan. It has the responsibility for training church members, training church leaders, and for new church member orientation.

Other developments of an educational nature have emerged among the Southern Baptists. In organized church music ministries they have a vital and fast growing program of music for worship and a music education structure which serves their churches well. They sustain a network of institutions of higher learning. Presently, approximately one in ten persons in America who are attending a seminary preparing for leadership roles in Christian ministry are enrolled in one of six Southern Baptist seminaries.

There can be little reason to doubt that the emphasis on education has been a major contributor to the unusual growth of Southern Baptists.

Conclusion

It is important to the present and the future for one to reflect upon history in order to gain from its lessons and to avoid repeating its errors. When churches have remained free to teach and learn, to search the Scriptures and to let biblical truth direct their life and work, the faithful have multiplied and the course of history has been improved. Truly history affirms the value of education.

Concerns for Further Study

Consider these questions as you continue to reflect upon history's affirmation of the value of education.

1. What are some positive lessons you observe in history which might help strengthen churches in their educational ministries?

2. What are some of the "errors" of Christians in history which churches should avoid repeating in education?

3. What do you sense in current thought and events affecting churches which seem to parallel some of the historical experiences? Which of these suggest possible benefit? Which suggest possible harm?

Notes

1. H. Clay Trumbull, *Yale Lectures on the Sunday School* (New York: Charles Scribner's Sons, 1904), pp. 66-67.
2. Clarence H. Benson, *A Popular History of Christian Education* (Chicago: Moody Press, 1943), pp. 13-14.
3. Howard P. Colson and Raymond M. Rigdon, *Understanding Your Church's Curriculum,* revised edition (Nashville: Broadman Press, 1981), p. 17.
4. Ibid.
5. Howard P. Colson, "The Bible Precedent," *The Ministry of Religious Education,* edited by John Sisemore (Nashville: Broadman Press, 1978), pp. 22-23.
6. Lewis Joseph Sherrill, *The Rise of Christian Education* (New York: The Macmillan Company, 1944), p. 140.
7. Ibid., p. 142.
8. See Sherrill, pp. 142-53, for a fuller discussion of these five kinds of teaching.
9. Ibid., p. 186.
10. Ibid., p. 153.
11. Benson, p. 44.
12. Sherrill, p. 159.
13. See Sherrill, pp. 183-97, for a fuller discussion of education in early Christian worship services.
14. Ibid., pp. 201-207.
15. Ibid., p. 173.
16. Ibid.
17. Ibid., p. 174.
18. Ibid., p. 175.
19. Benson, p. 64.
20. William Bean Kennedy, "Christian Education Through History," *An Introduction to Christian Education,* edited by Marvin J. Taylor (Nashville: Abingdon Press, 1966), p. 23.
21. Sherrill, p. 207.
22. Benson, p. 64.
23. Ibid., p. 69.
24. Ibid., p. 78.
25. Ibid.
26. Ibid., p. 80.
27. Ibid.
28. Ibid., p. 81.
29. Ibid.
30. Ibid., p. 82.
31. Ibid., p. 83.
32. Ibid., pp. 83-84.
33. Ibid., p. 93.

34. Ibid., p. 95.
35. Ibid., p. 100.
36. Ibid., p. 109.
37. Ibid., p. 123.
38. Ibid., p. 236.

3
Needs of Persons

The wisdom and the way of God must come to bear upon the experience of persons. This is what the educational ministry of a church is about. The Bible is the authority and guide for the educational ministry, and the primary subject matter base for Christian learning and development. The subject matter, the Bible, must relate to the experiences and needs of persons. Hence, an effective educational ministry is not only Bible-centered; it must also be life-centered.

Ministers and others who lead a church's educational ministry must have a basic and growing knowledge of the main subject matter. Likewise, to give effective leadership in education, they must be aware of and responsive to the needs of persons. The needs of persons, especially from the standpoint of their needs for religious education, is the focus of this chapter.

Who Man Is

One of the great psalms of praise asks the question, "What is man that thou art mindful of him, and the son of man that thou dost care for him?" (Ps. 8:4). This has been one of the fundamental inquiries since man was created. It is a question which must be asked, answered, and asked again. From a theological point of view the truth of the answer remains the same. Our knowledge of mankind, however, constantly grows and develops.

A Theological Viewpoint

Man is a person. Man is created in the image of God. This image of God is reflected in man's personality, and the capacity and responsibility for being moral—for discerning what is right, and with God's help, doing right. It is reflected in man's capacity to rationally anticipate a future, to plan. What animals do by instinct, people may do by intent. This image of God is reflected in man's potential for eternity, and his capacity to respond to God with fellowship. Each one is of infinite worth and possesses the dignity of personhood.

Man is a thinking, feeling, willing being. By nature man is both body and soul. Man's will is free, and cannot be coerced unless he chooses so. Each person is competent under God to deal with God for himself. He must personally and voluntarily choose in matters of spiritual faith and moral choice.

Man is a sinner. His moral nature is corrupted by evil. He is inclined toward sin. He needs salvation from sin, but is helpless to save himself. Man is utterly dependent upon the grace of God. At heart man hungers for God. This hunger is reflected in man's search for forgiveness, for inner peace, for security, and for self-realization. He has the capacity to respond to God in faith and to be transformed through the redemptive power of God in Christ. By this transformation man becomes a child of God. All people are creatures of God, "But to all who received him, who believed in his name, he gave power to become children of God" (John 1:12).

Redeemed man partakes of the divine nature. This enables man to have immeasurable possibilities for growing and maturing in Christlikeness. He is indwelt by the presence of the Holy Spirit, whose judgment, power, instruction, guidance, and comfort are his to claim. He is not only a citizen of the kingdom of God, he is a lifelong disciple. He is a member of the family of God, a joint heir with Jesus himself.

An Educational Viewpoint

Persons have inherent capacity for growing and developing physically, intellectually, emotionally, and morally. They hunger to know. They search for a meaningful understanding of life. They seek to belong, to adjust to the world around them. They seek to meet their basic physiological needs. They strive for safety, security, recognition, and for power. They feel morally responsible. They yearn for God, and for assurance of life after death.

Persons are members of families, citizens of states, and are related to the total human society. Their capacities and needs can be fulfilled in ways that are pleasing to God. Many of these capacities and needs require a family relationship and the experience of community.

Those who would minister to persons through education need to understand certain factors about persons regarding teaching and learning. Learning is gaining in knowledge, understanding, skill, attitude, appreciation, feelings. Teaching is helping in learning. Here are some factors about persons in the educational context which are foundational in religious education.[1]

1. *The individual can learn.* God made man an intelligent being. Man can think and reason. Man can recall the past, observe and act thoughtfully in the present, and anticipate and plan for the future. Man can participate creatively in his own growth and development. He can choose purposes and goals, observe contrasts between these and his achievement, and plan change in relation to these contrasts, and choose to direct his energies toward achieving goals and fulfilling purposes. When positive change occurs, it is usually observable in the individual's growth and in the improvement of his environment or his relation to it. The individual can learn.

2. *Learning occurs through experiences.* The individual is aware of the world through senses—seeing, hearing, touching, smelling, tasting. He is also impacted by revelation. Upon experiencing some impact of one or more sensory stimuli, or of revelation, man can respond intellectually and emotionally. The experience might be planned or unplanned, and result in learning. Planned experiences might be chosen by the individual, by some other person or persons, or by some combination of these. The individual usually learns better by experiencing more than one kind of stimuli at the same time, such as seeing *and* hearing.

There are many kinds of experiences. Some are direct, real-life experiences. Some are direct, but they are made-up or play-like experiences. Some are indirect, using words or other symbols. Some are indirect, using representations of real things. Direct experiences use more senses than indirect experiences. They also take more time than indirect experiences. Indirect experiences can speed up learning.[2]

No *one* type of experience is always best. The learner's differences determine the kinds of experiences which are best for him. When the learner has had many real life experiences, it is easier for him to learn from indirect experiences. Generally, the older and more experienced the learner, the fewer direct experiences he must have.[3]

**Let's picture these experiences
as a "pyramid."**

This pyramid shows learning experiences arranged
according to how direct or indirect they are.
• The closer to the bottom of the pyramid, the more
direct the experience.
• The closer to the top of the pyramid, the more indirect the experience.
• The closer to the top of the pyramid, the fewer
senses are used.
• The closer to the bottom of the pyramid, the more
senses are used.[4]

Figure 1

(See Figure 1 for a graphic presentation of direct and indirect experiences.)

The educational ministry of a church should seek to help individuals have experiences which direct their growth toward accepted goals. Learning may be improved by helping the individual to participate in the choices of goals and the experiences for their attainment.

Knowledge is not usually the ultimate goal in religious education. More often, the ultimate learning goals should be in terms of advancing in Christlikeness in living and serving. However, experiences which result in more knowledge might be essential to provide "tools" with which to have other experiences on the way to some more ultimate goals. Plainly stated, *one rarely behaves or acts better than one knows to behave or act.* There is some correlation between knowledge and behavior; and whatever gap exists between these, especially in matters moral or spiritual, becomes the concern of an individual's conscience.

3. *Learning continues throughout life.* Learning begins at birth. During infancy and early childhood, learning develops in proportion to experiences the child has alone, with parents, other members of the family, and with persons outside the family. Learning also occurs at a high rate during childhood and adolescence. It continues throughout life, though the rate of learning might decrease in adulthood. The ability to learn and the rate of learning might be influenced at any age by the desire of the learner.

4. *Group experiences contribute significantly to the individual's learning processes.* Learning with others and from others is significant to the personal growth of the individual. Group experiences usually begin in family life. Parents are significant teachers in the young child's life. The general atmosphere of the home is educative. The family has a profound effect upon the child's learning; it has the child first and during his most impressionable years. The individual learns through group experiences in the community, both in the immediate neighborhood and in wider experiences in the institutions, organizations, and activities of community life which influence his thinking, choices, and goals.

The classroom should be a community of learning, whether at church or at school. Group experiences in the classroom can contribute to learning by the encouragement of creative activities;

the free expression of interest, ideas, and opinions; participation in group experiences related to life situations; and the sharing of information and experience.

5. **Teachers influence individual learners.** Teachers and other leaders exercise significant influence upon individual learners. This is especially true in the areas of spiritual and moral education. The life and example of the teacher are among the most effective and influential factors. As has often been said, in these areas more may be "caught" than "taught."

The teacher and members of the group become partners in the growth of one another. Freedom of expression is encouraged. Participation is anticipated and sought. The teacher seeks to know the members' problems and needs, to teach to meet these needs, and to guide members toward their maximum growth. Teachers seek to do this in an atmosphere of guided freedom. They must recognize and attempt to modify any lack of interest or concern, or any indication of idleness and inattention.

6. **Spiritual resources are necessary to maximum growth.** The individual has the capacity for and the opportunity for access to fellowship with God, and may avail himself of unlimited spiritual resources. He initially gains access to these spiritual resources by personal regeneration, becoming a new person in Christ, and experiencing fellowship with God. In this way Christian education not only includes but also goes beyond the limits of mere intellectual understanding and activity.

What Man Needs

A person's needs are what one *has* to have to make it in life, with meaning. Man has many needs. Classifications of needs abound. One way of classifying and labeling man's needs is: spiritual, physiological, safety, social, esteem, and growth.[5] Any educational leader in a church who really cares about persons must learn what he can about the basic needs of persons. This is fundamental to an effective educational ministry in a church. It is contradictory to profess to have concern for man's spiritual needs and not be sensitive to his other needs. The parable of the good Samaritan is as much a part of biblical truth as is the parable of the prodigal son (or the loving father).

For our purposes we shall attempt to describe people's needs in terms of their needs for Christian teaching and learning, and let our concern for their other basic needs be reflected in later suggestions as to how a church might provide such teaching and learning. The format for this review of people's needs with reference to the educational ministry of a church will be first to make an overarching concept statement of these needs, and then to show how the implications of this statement reflect the needs of persons in the major age groups in a church's educational ministry.

Needs for Christian Teaching and Learning

An overarching statement of a person's needs for Christian teaching and learning could be stated as follows:

> A person needs to become aware of God as revealed in Scripture and most fully in Jesus Christ, respond to him in a personal commitment of faith, strive to follow him in the full meaning of discipleship, relate effectively to his church and its mission in the world, live in conscious recognition of the guidance and power of the Holy Spirit, and grow toward Christian maturity.[6]

What are some of the dimensions of this statement that apply to the individual? What does the individual need, if this statement is to be a guide?

1. *The individual needs to experience Christian conversion.* Each person needs to have the genuine experience of the forgiving and saving grace of God through Jesus Christ. It is accurate to say that no one can learn enough to earn his salvation. But one must learn and acknowledge certain things before he can effectively avail himself of salvation. This elemental learning centers around his lostness and need for salvation, his inability to save himself, the availability of new life in Christ, and how one receives Christ for salvation.

2. *The individual needs vital membership in a New Testament church.* Each Christian needs to be vitally related as a member of a New Testament church. He needs to intelligently, actively, and devotedly participate in its fellowship as it functions in the world through worship, proclamation and witness, nurture and education, and ministry. Believers need to maintain relationship to the body, the church, just as parts of a human body must be functioning together in harmonious relationship if the body is to thrive and have unified purpose.

3. *The individual needs experiences of Christian worship.* Each person needs to experience encounter with God frequently and with some regularity. These encounters with God should deepen his faith and strengthen his commitment to serve God. Worship is always an individual experience, although it might occur in the company of others. Worship is essential for a believer's expanding experience as a Christian.

4. *The individual needs growing knowledge and conviction.* Each person needs to continue to grow throughout all of life in Christian knowledge, understanding, and conviction. A person should always be maturing as a Christian. The growth in knowledge one "holds" should result in the growth of right convictions which "hold" one, and which lead one to live a more Christlike life.

5. *The individual needs developing attitudes and appreciations.* Each person needs to continue to develop in such Christian attitudes and appreciations that will enable him to have a Christian approach to all of life. One's knowledge, understanding, and convictions contribute to this development, as does the general behavior of fellow members, individually and in church life.

6. *The individual needs growth in Christian living.* Each person needs to develop habits and skills which promote spiritual growth and the application of Christian standards of conduct in every area of life. Christian living is the arena of education which registers the fruit of all the other areas of growth and development.

7. *The individual needs to engage in Christian service.* Each person needs to discover and exercise his gifts for the good of the church and for extending the faith to others. A gift is a gift, not an accomplishment for one to brandish in some attempt to establish superiority over others. Persons need to discipline their gifts, to improve any skills which will strengthen their gifts, and use their gifts in Christian service.

Needs of Persons in Major Age Groups

It is important to observe the needs of persons from the standpoint of the individual's human growth and development. While all persons may share the same categories of needs for Christian teaching and learning, the ways of meeting these needs and the immediate outcomes of the educational efforts vary according to the readiness of the individual. This readiness can be fairly closely ascertained by the age of the individual. For example, few if any would attempt to evoke from a child in the nursery a profession of Christian conversion. However, basic foundations which are established for an individual of nursery age have the potential for fulfillment when he is consciously ready to receive Christ of his own volition.

These needs will be described according to one of the frequently used patterns of age grouping: *preschool* (birth through three years, *nursery*; and ages four and five, *older preschool*); *children* (ages six through eight or grades one through three, *younger children*; and ages nine through eleven or grades four through six, *older children*); *youth* (ages twelve through seventeen or grades seven through high school); and *adult* (age eighteen or high school graduation through age twenty-nine, *young adult*; and ages thirty and up, *adult*).

1. Needs for Christian Conversion

Preschool.—In the nursery child's earliest experiences, he needs (1) to begin to associate God and Jesus with feelings of love and happiness; (2) to think of the Bible as a special book that tells about God and Jesus; and (3) to feel that the church is a place to go to learn more about God and Jesus.

As an *older preschooler,* the child needs (1) to feel that God loves him at all times; (2) to realize that there are some things that please God; to love God and want to please him; (3) to learn that the Bible is a special book that helps us know how to please God; and (4) to think of Jesus as his friend and helper.

Children.—The *younger child* needs (1) to feel love and reverence for God and to know that God loves him; (2) to have a real desire to do things that please God and to grow in his understanding of ways to please God; (3) to learn to love and trust Jesus as his friend and to have a growing awareness that Jesus is God's Son; (4) to grow in his understanding of what it means to forgive and to know that God wants to forgive him when he does wrong; (5) to develop a consciousness of his personal need for God's help in doing right things; and (6) to feel free to approach Christian adults for understanding guidance.

The *older child* needs (1) to understand that all people do wrong and that all wrongdoing is displeasing to God; (2) to face the fact that the wrong things which he does are sins against God; (3) to realize that Christ's death for our sins makes possible forgiveness and new life for every person who repents of sin and trusts Jesus Christ; (4) to understand that a person becomes a Christian by trusting Jesus as Savior—not by being baptized and joining the church or simply trying to be good; (5) to realize that he needs God's forgiveness for his own sins; (6) to turn from sin to simple trust in Christ as his personal Savior and Lord when the Holy Spirit has made him ready for such response and commitment.

Youth.—The *youth* needs (1) to recognize his failure and inability to live up to God's standard of righteousness and his consequent need of a Savior; (2) to turn from sin and commit himself to Jesus Christ, trusting him to give complete and continuous salvation; (3) to gain, after conversion, a growing sense of assurance as to the reality of that experience and its implications in terms of the lordship of Jesus.

Adult.—The *young adult* needs (1) to become aware of the nature and prevalence of sin and to recognize God's judgment upon it; (2) to realize his own sin and consequent need of the salvation which God has provided in Christ; (3) to turn from sin and commit himself to Jesus Christ, the Son of God, who gives complete salvation to all who trust him; (4) to gain, after conversion, a growing sense of assurance as to the reality of that experience and its implications in terms of the lordship of Jesus.

The *adult* needs (1) to become aware of God's judgment concerning sin and of his mercy; (2) to realize his own failure and inability to measure up to God's standard of righteousness and his consequent need of the salvation which God has provided in Christ; (3) to recognize the all-sufficiency of Jesus Christ, working through the Holy Spirit, to give complete salvation to all who trust him; (4) to turn from sin and commit himself wholeheartedly to Jesus Christ as his personal Lord and Savior; (5) to gain, after conversion, a growing sense of assurance as to the reality of that experience and its implications in terms of the lordship of Jesus.

2. Needs for Church Membership

Preschool.—The child in the *nursery* needs (1) to have happy experiences with friendly people at church; (2) to feel that the church is a special place where all members of the family may go to learn more about God and Jesus.

The *older preschooler* needs (1) to think of his church as a place where he has happy experiences; (2) to grow in his ability to participate in church worship services with his family; (3) to feel that he is a part of the church life.

Children.—The *younger child* needs (1) to like to attend church and to participate in the worship services with his family; (2) to grow in his understanding of the fact that members of the church are a special group of Jesus' friends who have had the experiences of conversion and baptism; (3) to begin to understand that joining the church is a serious matter, always to be preceded by conversion, and that it involves responsibilities as well as privileges.

The *older child* needs (1) to form the habit of regular church attendance and of participating with understanding and joy in church services and activities; (2) to understand that a New Testament church is composed of persons who have already become Christians and who have been baptized in obedience to Christ; (3) to understand that a person joins the church *only* after he has trusted Jesus as his Savior, with a conviction that he is a Christian and should be baptized in obedience to Christ.

Youth.—The *youth* needs (1) to unite with a church by baptism upon public profession of faith in Christ as Savior and Lord (if he has not already done so); (2) to grow in understanding and appreciation of the nature, mission, practices, and leadership of his church; (3) to grow in loyalty to his church and to endeavor to render faithful service to Christ and fellowmen through the church; (4) to develop the habit of attending services regularly and of participating in the fellowship and program of the church with understanding and appreciation; (5) to give regularly and proportionately for the support of his church and its worldwide program; (6) to transfer his church membership promptly when he changes his place of residence.

Adult.—The *young adult* needs (1) to unite with a church by baptism upon a personal profession of faith in Christ (if he has not already done so); (2) to grow in understanding and appreciation of the meaning, purpose, faith, and practices of his church; (3) to grow in loyalty to his church and the world program of Christ; (4) to participate wholeheartedly in Christian service in and through the channels of his church; (5) to transfer his church membership promptly when he changes his place of residence.

The *adult* needs (1) to unite with a church by baptism upon a personal profession of faith in the Lord Jesus Christ (if he has not already done so); (2) to grow in understanding and appreciation of the meaning, purpose, faith, and practices of his church; (3) to participate in and actively cultivate the fellowship in his church; (4) to participate wholeheartedly in constructive Christian service in and through the channels of his church; (5) to grow in loyalty to his church and the world program of Christ; (6) to have his membership in a church in the community where he resides.

3. Needs for Christian Worship

Preschool.—The *nursery* child needs (1) to feel that he can talk to God at any time; (2) to want to say thank you to God; (3) to grow in his enjoyment of beauty, music, and meaningful Bible stories.

The *older preschooler* needs (1) to know that he can talk to God at any time and anywhere; (2) to have satisfying experiences in talking to God; (3) to grow in his ability to participate in worship with children of his own age; (4) to develop a growing appreciation of beautiful surroundings, music, Bible passages that are read aloud, prayer, the offering, and the preacher's message.

Children.—The *younger child* needs (1) to feel and demonstrate loving respect for God; (2) to talk to God spontaneously and naturally at any time he feels a sense of wonder, worship, or need; (3) to have meaningful experiences in private worship and in worship with members of his own age group; (4) to participate regularly in public worship and to find satisfaction in doing so.

The *older child* needs (1) to understand that worship is an experience of reverent communion with God and that a person may engage in worship alone, with his family, with his friends, and with groups at church; (2) to cultivate the practice of regular private worship, including daily Bible reading and prayer; (3) to do his part to maintain and to participate in family worship; (4) to attend regularly the worship services of his church and to participate meaningfully and reverently in praying, singing, Bible reading, and listening.

Youth.—The *youth* needs (1) to understand further the meaning of worship and to desire to engage in worship; (2) to grow in appreciation of all elements that make worship meaningful, both in worship services and in personal devotions; (3) to grow in ability to participate meaningfully in worship experiences with members of his own age group and with the church congregation; (4) to practice daily individual worship, including devotional reading of the Bible and prayer for self and others; (5) to encourage participation in family worship experiences.

Adult.—The *young adult* and the *adult* need (1) to develop a deepening understanding of the meaning and values of worship; (2) to develop a growing appreciation of all the elements that make for meaningful worship, whether in private or in the group; (3) to develop and maintain the practice of daily individual worship, including the devotional reading of the Bible, meditation, and prayer; (4) to develop the habit of regular attendance at the worship services of his church and the ability to participate with understanding and appreciation; (5) to encourage, provide, and participate in experiences of family worship.

4. *Needs for Christian Knowledge and Convictions*

A person has many needs for Christian knowledge and convictions. He needs to know and have convictions about a number of things with respect to the Bible, the great realities of the Christian faith, the Christian movement, and his church and denomination.

Preschool.—The *nursery* child needs:

A. With respect to the Bible—(1) to grow in awareness that what the Bible says is more important than what other books have to say; (2) to gain some acquaintance with meaningful Bible stories and verses.

B. With respect to the great realities of the Christian faith—(1) to begin to think of God as the one who made him; (2) to begin to think of God as the one who helps him to have good things; (3) to begin to think of God as the one who cares for him; (4) to begin to think of Jesus as the one who loves him.

C. With respect to his church—(1) to begin to think of his church as a place where people love Jesus and help others; (2) to begin to be aware that there are many churches.

The *older preschooler* needs:

A. With respect to the Bible—(1) to begin to understand that God helped men know what to write in the Bible; (2) to become familiar with some of the surroundings and customs of the people the Bible tells about; (3) to enjoy hearing Bible stories and verses in his understanding of Bible truths and learn to relate them to his own experiences; (4) to grow in the realization that the Bible is God's way of telling us how to live happily with others; (5) to know that the Bible was meant for all people.

B. With respect to the great realities of the Christian faith—(1) to know that God made the world and everything in it; (2) to know that Jesus can do things that no one else can do because he is God's Son.

C. and D. With respect to his church, denomination, and the larger Christian movement—(1) to know that there have been churches for a long, long time; (2) to know that his church is one of many churches all over the world; (3) to know ways his church and other churches help people to know about Jesus; (4) to know that the money brought to church is used to help others know about Jesus.

Children.—The *younger child* needs:

A. With respect to the Bible—(1) to develop love and appreciation for the Bible as a unique book and to feel that it is true and deserves respect and obedience; (2) to develop an elementary understanding of its structure, how it came to be written, and how it has been preserved; (3) to become acquainted with customs, geography, and other facts concerning Bible backgrounds; (4) to enjoy hearing, reading, and learning Bible stories and truths; (5) to grow in his understanding of ways the Bible can help him in everyday life; (6) to commit to memory many Bible verses.

B. With respect to the great realities of the Christian faith—(1) to have a growing understanding of what the Bible teaches about God, about Jesus, and about right and wrong; (2) to realize that the friends of Jesus should believe and do what the Bible teaches.

C. With respect to the Christian movement—(1) to realize that the church he attends is one of many such groups of Jesus' friends in many parts of the world; (2) to recognize that people of other Christian groups also help in Jesus' work.

D. With respect to his church and denomination—(1) to know why we have churches and some of the things churches do; (2) to find answers to his questions about church ordinances and church membership.

The *older child* needs:

A. With respect to the Bible—(1) to recognize that the Bible is an inspired message from God and that its teachings are to be accepted and followed in all that we believe and do; (2) to develop an increasing understanding of the origin, structure, and transmission of the Bible; (3) to learn about the customs and geography of Bible lands in order to understand better many of the teachings of the Bible; (4) to develop a growing knowledge of basic stories and truths; (5) to gain from individual and group Bible study increasing guidance and motivation for daily living; (6) to grow in skill in the use of the Bible; (7) to memorize appropriate Bible passages.

B. With respect to the great realities of the Christian faith—(1) to recognize increasingly that God is real and that a vital relationship with him through faith in Christ is the most important factor in one's life; (2) to begin to understand that the Christian faith includes many doctrines which are important for one's belief and conduct; (3) to gain increasing knowledge of basic Christian doctrines.

C. With respect to the Christian movement—(1) to grow familiar with the lives and work of some of the early leaders in the growth of the Christian movement; (2) to become acquainted with the names and work of some of the great leaders of one's denomination; (3) to gain some acquaintance with the history and beliefs of other Christian groups; (4) to learn some ways in which our beliefs are like those of other groups and some ways in which they are different.

D. With respect to his church and denomination—(1) to grow in understanding and appreciation of beliefs and practices of his denomination; (2) to grow in knowledge of his denomination's life and work and to develop increasing loyalty to his denomination.

Youth.—The youth needs:

A. With respect to the Bible—(1) to accept the Bible as a way by which God speaks to him and as the final authority in all matters of faith and conduct; (2) to understand something of the origin of the Bible and of God's use of people in writing, preserving, and translating it; (3) to grow in understanding of the contents of the Bible and of the customs, geography, and history out of which the Bible came; (4) to acquire a growing comprehension of how Bible truths apply to personal daily living and to community and world problems; (5) to commit choice passages to memory.

B. With respect to the great realities of the Christian faith—(1) to grow in his concept of the reality and nature of God as a personal, loving Father; (2) to grow in his understanding of God and man, sin and salvation, and the Christian's life and work; (3) to develop a growing conviction about the truth and finality of the Christian faith.

C. With respect to the Christian movement—(1) to learn some of the outstanding facts of Christian history; (2) to become acquainted with some of the outstanding facts about other Christian groups and our common heritage with them; (3) to become aware of present-day trends and issues in the Christian movement and to realize that they hold meaning for his own life as well as for the cause of Christ.

D. With respect to his church and denomination—(1) to grow in understanding distinctive features of his denomination's doctrine and polity and to develop growing convictions as to their soundness; (2) to add to his knowledge of the history, organization, programs, problems, and needs of his denomination and to develop an increasing sense of responsibility for the work of his denomination.

Adult.—The *young adult* needs:

A. With respect to the Bible—(1) to recognize the Bible as a unique revelation from God and to accept its authority as supreme in matters of faith and conduct; (2) to gain fuller understanding of the origins of the Bible, the history of its preservation, and the significance of the many translations and versions; (3) to achieve an increasing knowledge of the content of the Bible and a growing understanding of the customs, geography, and history out of which the Bible came; (4) to acquire a growing comprehension of how Bible truths apply to personal daily living, to family life, and to community and world problems; (5) to commit choice passages to memory.

B. With respect to the great realities of the Christian faith—(1) to grow in understanding of the nature, attributes, and disposition of God; (2) to grow in understanding of the nature of persons, of sin and salvation, and of the varied elements of Christian experience; (3) to grow in understanding of the Christian concepts of personal righteousness and social responsibility; (4) to develop a growing conviction about the truth and finality of the Christian faith.

C. With respect to the Christian movement—(1) to know something of the general outline of Christian history; (2) to learn some of the outstanding facts about other Christian groups and our common heritage; (3) to grow in understanding of present-day trends and issues in the Christian movement and to develop ability to evaluate their significance for his own life, his own church, and the cause of Christ throughout the world.

D. With respect to his church and denomination—(1) to understand something of the history of his denomination; (2) to understand the distinctive features of the doctrine and polity of his denomination; (3) to grow in his understanding of the program, missionary outreach, problems, and needs of his church and denomination; (4) to develop worthy convictions about the doctrines and mission and of his denomination and about his personal responsibility to his denomination.

The *adult* needs:

A. With respect to the Bible—(1) to recognize the Bible as a unique revelation and message from God and to accept it as authoritative in all matters of faith and conduct; (2) to understand the origin of the Bible and its history, preservation, and translation; (3) to understand the customs, geography, and historical backgrounds out of which the Bible came; (4) to gain an orderly and increasingly comprehensive grasp of the content of the Bible; (5) to acquire a growing comprehension of how Bible truths apply to personal daily living, family life, and community and world problems; (6) to commit choice passages to memory.

B. With respect to the great realities of the Christian faith—(1) to grow in understanding of the nature, attributes, and disposition of God; (2) to grow in understanding of the nature of man, of sin and salvation, and of the varied elements of Christian experience; (3) to grow in understanding of the Christian concepts of personal righteousness and social responsibility; (4) to develop a growing conviction about the truth and finality of the Christian faith.

C. With respect to the Christian movement—(1) to learn some of the outstanding facts of Christian history; (2) to learn some of the outstanding facts about other Christian groups and our common heritage with them; (3) to understand significant present-day trends in the Christian movement and to evaluate their meaning for his own life and the cause of Christ.

D. With respect to his church and denomination—(1) to learn some of the outstanding facts about the history of his own denomination; (2) to understand the distinctive features of the doctrine and polity of his denomination and to have solid convictions as to their soundness; (3) to know the organization, program, missionary outreach, problems, and needs of his denomination and to understand his personal relationship to the whole of the denomination enterprise.

5. *Needs for Christian Attitudes and Appreciations*

The individual needs to develop Christian attitudes and appreciations regarding God, the meaning of existence, self, others, the Bible and divine institutions, and the present world.

Preschool.—The *nursery* child needs:

A. and B. Regarding God and the meaning of existence—(1) to begin to associate feelings of happiness with God; (2) to want to thank God for good things; (3) to begin to be aware of the difference between fantasy and reality.

C. Regarding self—(1) to begin to realize that he is a person; (2) to feel loved and wanted; (3) to begin to realize that there are certain things he can and cannot do.

D. Regarding others—(1) to begin to be aware of the feelings of others; (2) to begin to adjust to the needs and interests of others; (3) to experience some feelings of wanting to help others; (4) to begin to be aware of what others do to help him.

E. Regarding the Bible and divine institutions—(1) to enjoy the Bible as a special book; (2) to enjoy church as a special place; (3) to enjoy Sunday as an especially happy day; (4) to begin to feel that God wants families to be happy.

F. Regarding the present world—(1) to begin to feel that the world God made is good; (2) to begin to be aware of life and death processes of plants and animals.

The *older preschooler* needs:

A. and B. Regarding God and the meaning of existence—(1) to experience a deepening reverence for God's power and greatness; to accept the fact that God made the world; to have a growing appreciation of ways God cares for the things in it; (2) to love God and to want to do the things that please him; (3) to trust God as the one who loves and cares for all people; to feel that God is near and that one can talk to God any time, anywhere; to want to talk to God; (4) to feel thankful for the many ways God helps him; (5) to grow in awareness of the difference between fantasy and reality.

C. Regarding self—(1) to feel secure in God's world, because he is an important part of God's plan; (2) to begin to realize that God made him and gave him the ability to think; to make choices and decisions, and to be creative; to begin to realize that people are more important than anything God made; (3) to realize that God wants him to have a strong, healthy body and to use it in ways pleasing to God; (4) to realize that God can help him in ways that no one else can; (5) to want to do things in ways pleasing to Jesus and to want to grow in the ways in which Jesus grew.

D. Regarding others—(1) to realize that it is a part of God's plan for people to be friendly and to help one another; (2) to grow in his appreciation of others and what they do for him; (3) to develop in his ability to share, to work, and to play happily with others; (4) to accept the fact that God made and loves all people and to have kind attitudes toward them; (5) to want others to know about Jesus.

E. Regarding the Bible and divine institutions—(1) to develop a growing love for the Bible and a growing appreciation for ways it can help him in everyday life; (2) to grow in his understanding of the importance of his church; (3) to think of Sunday as a special day of worship and activities pleasing to God; (4) to think of happy homes as a part of God's plan; (5) to grow in his appreciation of people in authority and in his willingness to cooperate with them.

F. Regarding the present world—(1) to feel that the world God made is good and that nature, work, and the ability to do many things are gifts of God; (2) to want to help others in making his (the child's) world a better place.

Children.—The *younger child* needs:

A and B. Regarding God and the meaning of existence—(1) to experience deepening reverence and respect for God and his work in the world; (2) to trust God as the one who created, loves, and makes provision for the needs of all people and other creatures; (3) to feel assured that God listens when people pray to him and answers in the way that is best; (4) to feel sorry when he disappoints God but to know that God loves him and wants to forgive him; (5) to feel a sense of gratitude to God for all of his good gifts; (6) to feel that Jesus loves and helps him, to love and trust Jesus as his friend, and to desire to please him.

C. Regarding self—(1) to develop wholesome appreciation of his own value as an individual whom God loves and who can make important contributions to the group at home, at school, at church, and at play; (2) to think of his body as something good and something to be cared for and used in ways pleasing to God; (3) to grow in ability to evaluate himself and to recognize his responsibilities; (4) to grow in understanding of the values of cooperative work and in ability to be a good member of the group; (5) to recognize all his talents and abilities as gifts from God and to want to develop and use them in worthwhile ways.

D. Regarding others—(1) to feel kindly toward all people everywhere, regardless of their differences; (2) to respect the feelings, the rights, and the property of others; (3) to grow in his willingness to share his work, play, and possessions with others; (4) to recognize that others make real contributions to his life and to want to make some friendly return; (5) to want to help others to know about Jesus.

E. Regarding the Bible and divine institutions—(1) to grow in his love for the Bible and his desire to use it in his everyday living; (2) to love and show respect for the church building as a special place of worship; (3) to begin to appreciate the elements of public worship; (4) to think of Sunday as a special day to be spent in worship and other activities which honor God; (5) to recognize the home as part of God's loving plan for people and to develop an attitude of love, respect, and consideration for all in his home; (6) to continue to grow in his appreciation for authority and in his willingness to cooperate with persons in authority.

F. Regarding the present world—(1) to feel secure in the knowledge that God's plan for the world provides for each person's needs; (2) to begin to realize that although he sees others doing wrong and is often tempted himself, Jesus can help him to choose the right way; (3) to realize that work is part of God's plan for everyone and to want to do what he can to help.

The *older child* needs:

A. Regarding God—(1) to reverence God and to want to know and to obey his commandments; (2) to love and trust God as the all-wise and all-good Heavenly Father, who loved us and gave his Son to be the Savior of the world; (3) to feel secure in God's care and grateful for his goodness.

B. Regarding the meaning of existence—(1) to think of the beauties and wonders of the world and of science as expressions of God's greatness and goodness; (2) to feel secure in the world because God made it and controls it and cares what happens to people; (3) to believe that God has a purpose for his life and to want to use his life for God's glory and for the good of others.

C. Regarding self—(1) to realize that because God made him, his mind, body, and life are important; (2) to realize that he needs God's forgiveness, love, and help; (3) to understand that his mind and body are gifts from God to be cared for and developed; (4) to want to use his mind and body in Jesus' service.

D. Regarding others—(1) to begin to appreciate the worth of all people, regardless of their race or other differences; (2) to feel responsible for the way he treats people of all groups, races, and nationalities; (3) to grow in his ability to love other people and to treat others as Jesus would have him treat them; (4) to feel responsible for telling others about Jesus.

E. Regarding the Bible and divine institutions—(1) to develop a growing love for the Bible and a deeper desire to govern his everyday actions by its teaching; (2) to grow in love for and loyalty to the church; (3) to develop increasing respect and appreciation for baptism and the Lord's Supper; (4) to respect Sunday as the Lord's Day and to enjoy doing on Sunday things that honor Jesus; (5) to appreciate his home as part of God's plan of caring for him and to desire to do his part to make his home happy; (6) to feel that rules and laws are a necessary part of God's plan for living and to want to obey the laws of his home, school, and community.

F. Regarding the present world—(1) to feel secure in the knowledge that God made and cares for the world and gave men the ability to discover and use the secrets of nature; (2) to feel that though there is sin and wrongdoing in the world, he can have the strength through Christ to choose the right way; (3) to want to do his part to make his home, school, and neighborhood better.

Youth.—The *youth* needs:

A. Regarding God—(1) to love and trust the Heavenly Father, Jesus Christ as Lord and Savior, and the Holy Spirit as ever-present counselor and source of power; (2) to reverence God, respect his commands, and seek to know and do his will; (3) to develop a sense of gratitude to God for all his goodness.

B. Regarding the meaning of existence—(1) to regard all existence as the expression of God's creative power, wisdom, and goodness; (2) to feel secure in the knowledge that this is God's world and that God's purposes are being worked out in it; (3) to realize that a person created in the image of God is of infinite worth, has marvelous possibilities, and possesses spiritual needs which only God can supply.

C. Regarding self—(1) to recognize his body, mind, and total personality as gifts from God to be cared for, developed, and used for God's glory and the good of others; (2) to have as his personal ideal the attainment of a mature Christian personality; (3) to evaluate his talents as he considers his future vocation; (4) to realize that he stands in constant need of God's forgiveness and help.

D. Regarding others—(1) to acquire a sense of kinship with every person in the world and to cultivate an attitude of unselfish devotion to the welfare of people of all cultures, races, and social levels; (2) to cultivate the desire to apply Christian principles in relationships within the family, at church, at school, and in the community; (3) to feel a concern for the salvation of others and to accept the obligation to help give the gospel to the world; (4) to develop wholesome attitudes toward persons of the opposite sex in his peer group.

E. Regarding the Bible and divine institutions—(1)(2) to develop a growing love for the Bible and appreciation of the purpose for which Christ founded the church and an increasing concern for its life and work; (3) to develop an increasing love and appreciation for his home and feel a growing obligation to contribute to the happiness and well-being of his family; (4) to develop increasing loyalty to the ideal of personal purity, looking toward marriage and family life; (5) to regard Sunday as the Lord's Day to be used to honor the risen Christ; (6) to respect the ordinances of baptism and the Lord's Supper as means of honoring Christ; (7) to respect civil government and to feel the obligations of good citizenship as set forth in principle in the New Testament.

F. Regarding the present world—(1) to feel that the world as God made it is good and that all the resources of nature and the necessity to work are gifts of God designed for the enrichment of life; (2) to recognize the many manifestations of evil in the world and to resolve to live a life dedicated to God, to resist the appeal of evil in one's life, and to be a positive force for morality and justice; (3) to feel a deepening sense of responsibility for the improvement of moral and social conditions in his community.

Adult.—The *young adult* and *adult* need:

A. Regarding God—(1) to reverence God, respect his commandments, and seek to know and do his will as the supreme good; (2) to love and trust the Heavenly Father, Jesus Christ as Lord and Savior, and the Holy Spirit as ever-present counselor and source of power; (3) to develop a sense of gratitude to God for all his goodness.

B. Regarding the meaning of existence—(1) to regard all existence as the expression of God's creative power, wisdom, and goodness; (2) to see himself in relation to all existence in such a way as to feel secure in the purpose and sovereignty of God; (3) to regard life as a trust from God to be used for his glory and the good of others; (4) to believe with confidence that the Bible and the Holy Spirit are his guides in making the best use of this life; (5) to believe that the main purposes of God for mankind are redemption and development in righteousness.

C. Regarding self—(1) to realize that as a person created in the image of God he is of infinite worth and has marvelous possibilities; (2) to realize that he stands in continuing need of forgiveness and strength from God; (3) to recognize that he possesses spiritual needs and capacities which only God can supply; (4) to acknowledge that his body is a divine trust to be cared for, to be protected from abuse, to be disciplined in habit, to be employed in honest labor, unselfish service, and healthful recreation; (5) to dedicate all of his God-given abilities to the pursuit and achievement of worthy aims and to test their worthiness by the teachings of Jesus; (6) to have as his personal ideal the attainment of a mature, well-balanced Christian personality.

D. Regarding others—(1) to cultivate an attitude of Christian love, the willingness to practice forgiveness, and the determination to apply Christian principles in all of his relationships; (2) to accept responsibility for the influence of his life upon all people whom his life touches; (3) to feel and manifest wholesome attitudes toward persons of the opposite sex; (4) to cultivate a sense of belonging to the human race as a whole; (5) to develop an attitude of Christian concern for the welfare of people of all cultures, social levels, and races; (6) to feel a concern for the salvation of all men everywhere and to accept the obligation to share the gospel and blessings of the Christian faith; (7) to feel a responsibility to pass on to future generations the good in his social heritage enriched by his own contribution to it.

E. Regarding the Bible and divine institutions—(1) to develop a growing love for the Bible and an appreciation of the relevance of Bible teaching to daily life; (2) to respect the divine nature and purpose of the church and to give it a place of sacred preeminence over all institutions of human origin; (3) to respect the ordinances of baptism and the Lord's Supper and to seek through the right observance of them to honor Christ; (4) to regard the Lord's Day as the Christian sabbath to be used to the honor of the risen Christ; (5) to accept the standards set by Christ and the New Testament for marriage and family life; (6) to respect the institution of civil government as being divinely appointed and to accept the responsibilities of good citizenship.

F. Regarding the present world—(1) to feel that the world as God made it is good and that all the resources of nature and the necessity to work are gifts of God designed for the enrichment of life; (2) to recognize that evil is a dominant force in the world order and that while the Christian must live in this world, he is not to share its spirit nor indulge in its sins but is to resist evil and be a positive force for morality and justice; (3) to develop a deepening consciousness of responsibility for the social order of which he is a part and a courageous purpose to work for its improvement.

6. *Needs for Christian Living*

Preschool.—The *nursery* child needs (1) to begin to associate some simple Bible truths with his daily living; (2) to begin to recognize the rights and feelings of others.

The *older preschooler* needs (1) to begin to accept the Bible as a guide for his conduct in everyday life; (2) to grow in his understanding of prayer and in his ability to pray; (3) to want to do things in ways pleasing to Jesus; (4) to grow in his ability to make right choices; (5) to develop in his ability to help make his home happy; (6) to have an increasing love for all people which will be expressed in friendliness and cooperation.

Children.—The *younger child* needs (1) to grow in ability to relate Bible truths to daily problems and needs; (2) to continue growing in his understanding of prayer and in his ability to pray; (3) to make sincere efforts to be more like Jesus; (4) to develop growing skill in self-control, self-direction, worthy self-expression, and ability to make right choices; (5) to develop habits of friendliness, helpfulness, cooperation, kindness, and courtesy toward all with whom he comes in contact, in work and in play.

The *older child* needs (1) to depend on Jesus each day to help him choose the right way; (2) to learn how to use his own Bible and to gain from it direction for daily living; (3) to make progress in developing Christian character which will express itself in all areas of his experience; (4) to gain strength for Christian living through private and group prayer; (5) to try to grow as Jesus grew—in mind, body, and in relationships with God and with other people; (6) to do his part to make his home happy by obeying his parents and accepting cheerfully his share in the work at home.

Youth.—The *youth* needs (1) to grow in consciousness of the living Christ as the Lord of his life; (2) to accept with confidence the Bible and the Holy Spirit as guides in making the best use of his life; (3) to grow in understanding of why and how to pray; (4) to seek to pattern all personal conduct in accordance with the teachings, spirit, and example of Jesus; (5) to strive to be Christlike in attitudes toward and relationships with parents and other members of his family; (6) to continue to make progress in developing Christian character which will express itself in all his relationships.

Adult.—The *young adult* and the *adult* need (1) to live daily in vital fellowship with Jesus Christ, seeking always to bring the whole life under the direction of the Holy Spirit; (2) to engage regularly in serious Bible study and to use the Bible as a guide for life; (3) to learn the spirit, art, and values of prayer and to practice prayer in daily experience; (4) to pattern all personal conduct in accordance with the teachings, spirit, and example of Jesus Christ; (5) to do all possible to make his family life Christian; (6) to refuse to enter into relations and participate in activities which compromise or violate New Testament principles; (7) to seek to apply Christian principles and standards of conduct to all social relationships.

7. Needs for Christian Service

Preschool.—The *nursery* child needs (1) to begin to help at home and at church; (2) to begin to learn to play happily with others.

The *older preschooler* needs (1) to tell others about Jesus; (2) to be a helper at home and at church; (3) to be happy as he gives his money to help others know about Jesus; (4) to do helpful things for others; (5) to begin to accept his limited abilities and to help as best he can; (6) to receive satisfaction from doing things with others; (7) to participate in group activities that make others happy.

Children.—The *younger child* needs (1) to tell others about Jesus; (2) to participate and cooperate in all the church activities in which he may have a part; (3) to enjoy giving his money and other possessions which he can share; (4) to begin to discover his talents and to have opportunities to develop and use them in worthy self-expression; (5) to accept his limitations and to use his abilities to achieve; (6) to participate in group activities that make others happy.

The *older child* needs (1) to show his love for Jesus by telling his family and friends about him and inviting them to church; (2) to serve in his church through the organizations, through attendance at regular church services, and through giving his money for the work of the church; (3) to try day by day at home, at school, and wherever he goes to treat others with kindness and fairness as Jesus would; (4) to begin to develop a sense of citizenship responsibility by participating in group and community service projects which contribute to fair play, justice, law enforcement, general health, relief of distress, and other worthy causes.

Youth.—The *youth* needs (1) to dedicate his talents to God and to develop skills in Christian service; (2) to seek God's will for his life and to begin to prepare for a vocation in keeping with that will; (3) to witness faithfully to his Christian faith and to seek to win others to Jesus Christ; (4) to appreciate and take advantage of the training and service opportunities offered in his church program; (5) to learn to work unselfishly on a team by filling well the places of service in his church suited to his ability and stage of development; (6) to be a good steward of his money as an expression of his gratitude to God and as a means of supporting his church in its world missions program; (7) to show compassion for persons in need; (8) to participate in group and community service projects which contribute to social welfare; (9) to accept the ideal of self-giving service as the true goal of life.

Adult.—The *young adult* needs (1) to seek and use opportunities to invest his talents and skills in Christian service; (2) to witness consistently to the truth and power of the Christian faith and to seek to win others to Jesus Christ; (3) to work faithfully for the building up of his church and to serve sacrificially in and through his church; (4) to give of his money for worthy motives and according to biblical teaching for the support of his church and its work; (5) to show compassion for persons in need and do deeds of helpfulness in his daily life; (6) to find God's will for his life, to prepare adequately for the vocation to which he is called, and to enter that vocation with a sense of dedication to Christian service; (7) to serve effectively as a member of a team and to serve without desire for self-glory; (8) to dedicate his total personality and resources to world missions as the means of carrying forward the redemptive undertaking of Jesus Christ; (9) to join with others in cooperative action for the improvement of social conditions, the creation of a more Christian society, and the realization of God's purpose for mankind.

The *adult* needs (1) to witness consistently to the truth and power of the Christian faith and to seek to win others to Jesus Christ; (2) to work faithfully for the building up of his church and to serve sacrificially in and through the church; (3) to give of his money from worthy motives and according to biblical teaching for the support of his church and its work; (4) to show compassion for persons in need and do deeds of helpfulness in his life; (5) to find God's will for his life and to fulfill that will in his vocation; (6) to engage in those phases of Christian service which are best suited to his individual capacities, environment, occupation, and social group; (7) to serve effectively as a member of a team and to serve without desire for self-glory; (8) to take a worthy part as a Christian in community service projects; (9) to dedicate his total personality and resources to world missions as the means of carrying forward the redemptive undertaking of Jesus Christ; (10) to join with others in cooperative action for the improvement of social conditions, the creation of a more Christian society, and the realization of God's purpose for mankind.

Conclusions

An effective educational ministry must be based upon the needs of persons as well as upon the Bible. Ministers and other church leaders need to know and to be sensitive to the needs of persons. They need a clear understanding of persons from a theological point of view. They also need to understand persons from an educational viewpoint.

People's needs are many, and can be classified in numerous ways. It is important for an educational leader to know everything possible about people's basic needs and to reflect a sensitivity to these needs. The needs of persons and the educational objectives of a church should be closely correlated.

Concerns for Further Study

Consider these questions as you reflect upon the needs of persons and their importance to the educational ministry of a church.

1. What do you think of the idea that an effective educational ministry must not only be Bible-centered, but also life-centered?

2. What is the place of sensory experience in religious education? Of revelation?

3. What benefits might a minister realize from a careful study of the religious education needs of persons that takes into account human growth and development?

Notes

1. The author drew heavily in the remainder of this chapter upon ideas and materials found in *The Curriculum Guide,* edited by Clifton J. Allen and W. L. Howse (Nashville: Convention Press, 1963), pp. 6-35.

2. LeRoy Ford, *A Primer for Teachers and Leaders* (Nashville: Broadman Press, 1963), pp. 138-39.

3. Ibid., p. 139.

4. Ibid., pp. 32-33.

5. For a discussion of these needs of persons see *A Church on Mission,* Reginald M. McDonough, compiler (Nashville: Convention Press, 1980), chapter 2.

6. Adapted from the educational objective as stated by designers of Southern Baptist curriculum materials, quoted by Howard P. Colson and Raymond M. Rigdon, *Understanding Your Church's Curriculum,* revised edition (Nashville: Broadman Press, 1981), p. 46.

4
Nature and Mission of the Church

The church has been given a unique place in the plan of God. Its place is at the center of God's redemptive purpose in Christ. In Ephesians 3:8-12 Paul declared that he was made a minister "to preach . . . the unsearchable riches of Christ . . . to make all men see what is the plan of the mystery . . . that through the church the manifold wisdom of God might now be made known." It is our intent here to focus attention upon the nature of the church, its mission, and the implications of the nature and mission of a church for education.

The Nature of a Church

To consider the nature of something is to discern its essential character, to identify the distinguishing quality or qualities. What is the essential character of a church? What are the distinguishing qualities?

Some Biblical Portraits

The Bible has many references to the church. Some of these refer to the concept of church, and others refer to actual churches. None gives us a complete and definitive statement. As Daniel Aleshire wrote:

> Why, on such an important issue as the mission and nature of the church, does Scripture not provide a clear statement? As in many other issues of profound significance (i.e., the nature of redemption, the quality of the disciples' life), no one image is adequate to capture the scope and meaning of all the concept implies. Frequently, we discover that the Scripture provides multiple images of some reality; and, like the blending of sounds in a symphony, the true vision emerges from the strength of the several parts.[1]

1. *Some biblical phrases on church.* Taken together, the

biblical portraits do provide a rich study of the nature of the church.

- People of God, "the Israel of God" (Gal. 6:16), "Abraham's offspring" (Gal. 3:29), "a chosen race, a royal priesthood, a holy nation, God's own people" (1 Pet. 2:9).
- "The church of God" (1 Cor. 1:2; 10:32; 11:22; 15:9; 2 Cor. 1:1; Gal. 1:13; 1 Tim. 3:5), "the churches of God" (1 Cor. 11:16; 1 Thess. 2:14; 2 Thess. 1:4).
- God's flock (Matt. 26:31; Luke 12:32; John 10:16; 21:15, 17).
- A new humanity (Eph. 2:14-20), "a new creation" (Gal. 6:15).
- Bride of Christ (2 Cor. 11:2-3; Eph. 5:25-32; Rev. 19:7-9; 21:9).
- "The pillar and bulwark of the truth" (1 Tim. 3:15).
- "God's field" (1 Cor. 3:9).
- "God's building" (1 Cor. 3:9).
- "The body of Christ" (Rom. 12:4-5; 1 Cor. 12:12-27; Eph. 1:22-23; 2:14-16; 3:3-13; 4:1-16; 5:30; Col. 1:18, 24; 2:16-19; 3:15).
- A family (Mark 3:33-35).
- Branch of the vine (John 15:1-8).
- A fellowship, a *"koinonia"* (1 John 1:3).
- "Children of God" (John 1:11-12).

What an array of ideas! *The church is people,* new persons, newly created by God. They belong to him. These biblical portraits indicate that a church is something very special. One should be cautious, however, in taking these exalted ideas of the nature of a church to mean that any church is perfect or that it always acts as Christ would act if he were present in the flesh. Anyone who has been around a church (the people, not the building) would be aware of imperfections. The favored standing of the church with God should not be taken to mean that some are chosen to be God's favorites, but should be understood to mean that some are given a special responsibility to share God's Word and way with the world.[2]

2. *A word study of "church."* The English word *church* translates the Greek word *ekklesia,* which means "the called out ones," or "assembly." It was used prior to the New Testament to designate the assembly of citizens of a self-governing Greek city. "In this sense an *ekklesia* was a local assembly operating through

democratic processes under the laws of the Empire."[3] It was also used in the Greek translation of the Old Testament, the Septuagint, to translate the Hebrew word *qahal,* "referring to the nation of Israel assembled before God and under his direct theocratic rule (Deut. 31:30, congregation; Judg. 21:8, assembly)."[4]

Sometimes the word *church* is used to refer to organized Christianity or to a group of churches, such as a denomination. Hobbs asserted that such use never occurs in the New Testament. "It denotes either a local body of baptized believers or includes all the redeemed through all the ages. The greater emphasis . . . in the New Testament, is on the local church."[5]

The Southern Baptist Convention in session in 1963 adopted a statement called "The Baptist Faith and Message." Although not intended as a creedal statement, "The Baptist Faith and Message" has come to be a very influential document. It includes a descriptive statement about the church:

> A New Testament church of the Lord Jesus Christ is a local body of baptized believers who are associated by covenant in the faith and fellowship of the gospel, observing the two ordinances of Christ, committed to His teachings, exercising the gifts, rights, and privileges invested in them by His Word, and seeking to extend the gospel to the ends of the earth.
>
> This church is an autonomous body, operating through democratic processes under the Lordship of Jesus Christ. In such a congregation members are equally responsible. Its Scriptural officers are pastors and deacons.
>
> The New Testament speaks also of the church as the body of Christ which includes all of the redeemed of all the ages.
>
> Matt. 16:15-19; 18:15-20; Acts 2:41-42, 47; 5:11-14; 6:3-6; 13:1-3; 14:23, 27; 15:1-30; 16:5; 20:28; Rom. 1:7; 1 Cor. 1:2; 3:16; 5:4-5; 7:17; 9:13-14; 12; Eph. 1:22-23; 2:19-22; 3:8-11, 21; 5:22-32; Phil. 1:1; Col. 1:18; 1 Tim. 3:1-15; 4:14; 1 Peter 5:1-4; Rev. 2—3; 21:2-3.[6]

The church is not interpreted to be the entire kingdom of God, and membership in a church should not be equated with salvation. In the broad sense the kingdom of God is the reign of God in his creation. "The local church is an earthy colony of that kingdom."[7] Writing about salvation, church membership, and the two biblical ideas of church, Hobbs stated:

> Thus while salvation is synonymous with membership in the church general, it is not true with regard to local church membership. Nor is membership in

the local church synonymous with salvation. "Fellowship," not "membership," is the New Testament word for Christian relations in the local church.[8]

Based upon a study of the Bible, one can develop his own
understanding of the nature of a church is to be. In keeping with the
priesthood of all believers, this is both the privilege and responsibility of the individual believer. The individual has primary responsibility for what one believes and for how one's beliefs impact others. If
the beliefs of one individual cause problems for the church, then the
members must determine how they will accommodate the situation.
All should seek to know and to obey the mind of Christ.

An Interpretive Model

It is important to study the church as an idea. It is also helpful to
look briefly at the nature of the church from an individual's
viewpoint.

1. *A call to discipleship.* Christ calls individuals to discipleship.
Many persons might respond to his call in the same time and place,
but each is called individually. This was true when Jesus called those
first ones to himself. This call is recorded in Mark 1:17: "And Jesus
said to them, 'Follow me and I will make you become fishers of
men.'" He was calling a pair of brothers, fishermen Peter and
Andrew.

What did Jesus have in mind when he called these individuals to
discipleship? What did he mean when he invited people to "Follow
me"?

It would seem that he meant for those who would follow him to
come and be in company with him. Since he invited several
persons, it would seem, too, that he intended that those who should
follow him would also keep company with one another. Yet there
must have been much more. He was not gathering about him a
group of individuals just with the idea of having some introverted
fellowship with him and with one another.

"Follow me" suggests much more than fellowship. It was a call to
a discipleship which is more than companionship. It was a call to
learn of him, to be his pupil. It was a call to his discipline for life. It
was a call to live life his way in relation to the Father and to others. It
was not a call to a standard of living in some material sense, but to a
standard for life. The new relationship begins with reconciliation

with God and is to be expressed in relationships with others. The Bible has much to say about both of these dimensions. They are core content for religious education.

One significant dimension of what the call to disciple meant and still means is the latter part of the spoken call: "I will make you become fishers of men." The call to discipleship integrally means a call to live his way *and* to join him in the redemptive enterprise. So committed was Jesus to our joining him in the redemptive enterprise that he gave this task to his disciples, with the promise of the indwelling Spirit to guide and to empower them. He also declared:

> Truly, truly, I say to you, he who believes in me will also do the works that I do; and greater works than these will he do, because I go to the Father (John 14:12).

Surely disciples could not do works greater in *kind* than those done by the Master. Whatever else he might have meant, surely he meant that his disciples are to be faithful in doing the things which would be a blessing to others, the highest blessing being reconciliation to the Father through Christ. Learning and doing this is also the work of religious education—teaching and the rightful exercise of other gifts.

What does the call to discipleship have to do with the nature of the church? *The call to discipleship is the nature of the church, when that call is lived out in its intended way.* An individual disciple is one part of that body, the church. Discipleship involves joining the company of others who are also disciples and working together with Christ to bring persons to God.

2. *Built upon the Rock.* A church is more than a collection of persons. It is a "building." It is not a building made of stones. It is a building made of people who are disciples of Jesus Christ.

Jesus came with his disciples into the district of Caesarea Philippi. He asked them who men were saying that he, "the Son of man," is. They mentioned John the Baptist, Elijah, Jeremiah, or one of the prophets.

> He said to them, "But who do you say that I am?" Simon Peter replied, "You are the Christ, the Son of the living God." And Jesus answered him, "Blessed are you, Simon Bar-Jona! For flesh and blood has not revealed this to you, but my Father who is in heaven. And I tell you, you are Peter

[Petros], and on this rock [petra] I will build my church, and the powers of
death shall not prevail against it. I will give you the keys of the kingdom of
heaven, and whatever you bind on earth shall be bound in heaven, and
whatever you loose on earth shall be loosed in heaven" (Matt. 16:15-19).

Hobbs wrote, "A *petra* was a large ledge rock such as a
foundation rock. A *petros* was a small stone broken off the large
stone and partaking of its nature."[9] He continued, "In the Old
Testament where 'rock' is used symbolically, it always refers to
deity."[10] So, what should one make of this complex passage and of
its meaning for the individual and the church? Consider this
treatment:

> Certainly the foundation of the church is Christ, not Peter or any other
> mere man (1 Cor. 3:11). . . . The writer sees "rock" as referring to Christ.
> Peter was a *petros,* a small stone partaking of Christ's nature. The church is
> built upon Christ, the building stones being all who, like Peter, confess him
> as "the Christ, the Son of the Living God." (See 1 Pet. 2:5.)[11]

Individuals who respond to his call to discipleship and confess
him as Lord, follow him and live his way in relation to God and
man, and share with him in the redemptive enterprise are his
church. Each individual is a piece of the rock, the foundation stone
of which the church is built. Each has equal opportunity of access to
the Father. Each has a share of the privileges. Each has a part of the
responsibility. Each has a voice and, when needed, a vote. Not all
have equal influence, though all have equal opportunity to earn
influence in the body. Such influence usually comes to those who
are faithful with the responsibilities or opportunities they have.

He has supplied certain ones with gifts which are to be used for
the good of the body as the church goes about the work of the
kingdom. The *gifts* are for functional services which are *to enable*
those in the fellowship, *to equip* them for the work of ministry.
There are varieties of gifts, but the same Spirit, same Lord, same
God. No part of the body, no member, whatever his gift may be, is
to disdain another, or to set himself over another as though he were
of a higher order.

3. *A living organism.* The individual believer has new life. He is
indwelt by the Spirit from the time of his new birth. He is a "new

person" in Christ, part of a new humanity. This new life is different from the old life. The believer is to live as Jesus lived in relation to the Father and to others. Banding together voluntarily under the lordship of Christ, individual believers comprise a church.

There is a sense in which the believers who are banded together to form a church have life in a corporate relationship. They become an entity of life. They take on qualities of an organism. In this instance, an organism is any highly complex thing or structure with parts so integrated that their relation to one another is governed by their relation to the whole. This seems to be the concept of church Paul advocated in 1 Corinthians 12:14 ff. and Ephesians 4:11 ff.

Just as Christ is the source of new life in the individual through the Holy Spirit, he is also the source of life and strength of the body of believers—the fellowship we call a church. He is to direct the life of the organism. He is to supply its power, its strength.

The Mission of a Church

The noun "mission" means first "a sending forth." It implies that there is some *charge* for which those are sent forth are responsible. There is *purpose* to be fulfilled. There is an *errand* to be performed. There is a *commission* to be carried out. All of these elements grow out of the nature of the church. A church does what it does because it is what it is. What is its mission?

Make Known the Manifold Wisdom of God

It is the mission of a church to make known the manifold wisdom of God (Eph. 3:10). The individual who comes to know the manifold wisdom of God, the "plan of the mystery" (v. 9), can respond in faith, receive Christ, and become a child of God. The people who have already received Christ are to make known the wisdom of God. This wisdom is the gospel, the good news.

Christ gave his church the responsibility of unbinding the gospel, letting it loose in the earth. But with this responsibility comes also the possibility that a church might *not* unbind the gospel, and by this very default will bind it. Not all children obey the Father. Consider this comment about Matthew 16:19:

The keys of the kingdom are the gospel which Jesus deposited in his church. If the church binds it on earth by not proclaiming it, heaven has already decreed that there is no other way whereby men may be saved and enter into the kingdom of heaven. But if the church looses the gospel on earth by proclaiming it, heaven has already decreed that men will hear it, some will believe it, and those who do will be saved or enter into the kingdom of heaven. It is a privilege and a tremendous responsibility![12]

It is essential to the nature of a church that its members be faithful in proclaiming the gospel. It is the only hope of salvation for mankind. As Peter declared, "There is salvation in no one else, for there is no other name under heaven given among men by which we must be saved" (Acts 4:12).

A Fellowship on Mission

A church is a fellowship on mission. It is a fellowship of disciples making known to all the gospel of Jesus Christ. Its mission is not to be a fellowship. That is its nature. It is a fellowship.

Designers of Southern Baptist curriculum materials and program designs have done extensive work over recent decades in proposing accurate and practical answers to questions regarding the essential functions of a church on mission. They presently are working with this statement of a church's mission as their premise:

The mission of a church, composed of baptized believers who share a personal commitment to Jesus Christ as Savior and Lord, is to be a redemptive body in Christ, through the power of the Holy Spirit, growing toward Christian maturity through worship, proclamation and witness, nurture and education, and ministry to the whole world that God's purpose may be achieved.[13]

Reflecting upon these words, Colson and Rigdon feel that this statement is broad enough to include all of the educational activities provided for in a church's curriculum plan and all of the performance activities provided for in its program plan. They wrote: "The objective states the ultimate purpose for the church's total program and for each segment of it whether it operates in the community or throughout the world in cooperative efforts with other churches."[14]

Using this statement of a church's mission, we shall focus on the functional aspects as a valid expression of what a church does as it carries out its mission. A function is a basic activity natural to, characteristic of, and essential to the life of an organism. What are the functions of a church? They are four.

1. **Worship.** Worship is a basic activity of a church. It is an individual "encountering God in experiences that deepen a Christian's faith and strengthen his service."[15] It is a natural expression of one's relationship to God. No one should be surprised to find a believer worshiping. It is an act and an attitude which characterizes believers. It is essential to the life of the church. Without worship, frequently and regularly, the organism cannot long perform its other functions. Worship supports proclamation, protective nurture, maturing education, and ministry to others that is more than mere humanism.

A word of caution might be important at this point. Corporate worship, with believers gathering together and experiencing encounter with God as a body of his children, is imperative (Heb. 10:25). It is a beginning point and a melding point for a church with regard to its development into a genuine fellowship. Moreover, those who comprise a church must also experience worship individually, apart from the corporate occasions. These times of one-to-one encounter sustain the individual's identity as an individual disciple and contribute strength to his relationship to the others when they come together for worship or for other purposes. The caution is this: neither corporate worship, individual worship, nor both kinds together comprise the totality of one's responsibility to God nor to his church. A body of believers whose members only worship cannot be a complete church. Conversely, to whatever extent the members neglect worship, to that extent they limit the total ministry of their church.

2. **Proclaim and witness.** Proclaiming and witnessing comprise another basic function of a church. It is natural that disciples of Jesus Christ should tell others what they themselves have seen and heard, what they have experienced with Christ. It is characteristic of one who has had a vital experience to want to share the word with others in order that they might also experience such joy and relatedness. It is essential that the faithful proclaim and witness, both for what it does for those who proclaim and for those who hear. It is life-extending for the body.

A word of caution, too, seems in order regarding proclaiming and witnessing. Verbal proclaiming and verbal witnessing, both oral and written, are vital. One who has encountered Christ and experienced salvation has something to tell! But no amount of telling, even about a magnificent conversion experience, can adequately compensate for a careless life-style which seems to belie the care of Christ for persons which a believer's life should reflect. One who runs roughshod over others as though they were less than persons for whom Christ lived, died, and rose to live again cannot proclaim or witness with credibility. Also, not all of the verbal proclaiming and witnessing has to fall into one set pattern. Not every disciple feels free to be as bold or as confrontational as do some others. Certainly these less bold ones should not be shamed or ridiculed by fellow disciples. All need to develop some ways of verbally proclaiming or witnessing, but in ways which are natural to their own personalities. In any case, the witness of one's life and behavior might be the most effective word spoken.

A church must proclaim and witness. To whatever extent it does, a church can expect increased vitality and new life—indeed new lives—to be added to the body. To whatever extent a church neglects to proclaim and witness, to that extent it can expect to suffer loss of vitality and the absence of new life.

3. **Nurture and educate.** It is a basic function of a church to nurture and educate. It is natural for a church to "nourish, modify, and develop individuals within a fellowship."[16] This is one expression of concern for persons and their needs. It is natural for a church to provide for maturing and growing persons in knowledge, wisdom, moral righteousness, and performance. None should be surprised to find a church engaged in activities to help persons in these ways. Rather, it should characterize a church to be found faithfully working at nurture and education.

Again a caution seems in order. A church must engage its members in regular and frequent nurturing and educating experiences. But there is no amount of nurture or education which can substitute for the conscious submission of one's will to the lordship of Christ for salvation. Nor can nurture and education supplant worship, proclamation and witness, or ministry.

It is imperative that a church nurture and educate. The God of all truth intends for his truth to be made known for the good of his creation. Nurture and education are ways this can be done.

4. *Minister.* To minister is a basic activity of a church. To minister is to do things needful or helpful—to aid persons both in and out of its fellowship. Distinctively Christian ministering such as a church renders is that which is done in the name of Christ, through his power, in his Spirit, and for his glory. Just as those who comprise a church are emulating Christ when they worship, proclaim, and educate, so they emulate him when they minister to those in need. And, while any church might hope that those to whom they minister would accept their highest expression of loving concern—the gospel of Christ for their salvation—such acceptance is not a condition for the help to be given. Individually and collectively, the church actively ministers to the spiritual, mental, and physical needs of persons.

Ministry is largely made up of voluntary acts, those which a church consciously chooses to do to help persons because the people of the church love God, and they love and care for others as they care for themselves.

Now comes another word of caution. Some sincere persons might mistake the channel of ministry as the way to earn salvation. This is regrettable, because Christian ministering comes from one who is first a Christian. Salvation is something given, not earned. Just as one cannot be educated into the kingdom, neither can one work one's way in by helping people. But there is a serious error at the other end of this spectrum. There are many who declare themselves Christians, who will freely proclaim and witness and who will study and learn, but never minister beyond the verbal. These Christians need encouragement toward a fuller participation in the life of the church.

A church on mission is a fellowship on mission. One can tell when this is the case because a church will be observed doing with some regularity and balance of emphasis those characteristic, essential activities which are the functions of an organism we call a church: worship, proclaim and witness, nurture and educate, and minister.

How Education Relates

Each dimension of activity of a church on mission is vital to one another and to the total church. While worship might be seen as the essential beginning, it is not and cannot be the end. While proclaiming and witnessing are natural outgrowths of worship, one cannot stop there. And while ministering to persons is an essential expression of the validity of the proclamation and witness and the worship, it is not of itself adequate. Aleshire was accurate when he wrote that "the distinctive task of education is its undergirding of all the other tasks."[17]

This is not to say that one function of the body is superior to all others or to any other. Each is the most essential function for that which it performs. Education contributes to each of the other functions in indispensable ways.

For worship to be most meaningful, the worshiper must know something of what worship is. Who is the worthy object of worship? What worship is pleasing to God? How may people most effectively engage in worship? Why should one worship? What are some hindrances to worship, and how may they be overcome? What are some conditions upon which worship depends? What worship is not fitting? What are some of the values to the person who worships? How are others helped to experience worship? These, and numerous other questions, must be answered if worship experiences are to fill the vital central role in the life of a church which they must. Many of the answers must come through education.

Proclaiming and witnessing need to be strengthened by education. One does not have to be a scholar to be a witness, but a witness can be a better witness if he has developed and prepared himself. Peter wrote, "Always be prepared to make a defense to any one who calls you to account for the hope that is in you, yet do it with gentleness and reverence" (1 Pet. 3:15). Witness training is one of the most critical needs in any church. The basic facts of the gospel need to be known accurately by one who would witness aright. How a person receives Christ for salvation is essential subject matter for a witness. How best to present the witness is crucial. Education can help a witness develop into the quality witness he is capable of becoming.

Ministering to persons in the name of Christ needs to be enriched and made better by education. Learning such things as how to discover persons in need is important. Learning certain skills and knowledge about how to minister and to be received in order to minister are vital. Learning how to relate the resources of other ministering persons and groups to help meet the needs of persons is necessary in many instances. Education and training in ministry require teaching and learning.

The function of education itself requires the function of education. What goals and eventual outcomes should be the goals and outcomes of education? What should be the content of education? What should be the method? What are the needs of persons which call for education? What supporting materials, supplies, equipment, furnishings, and other helpful items are needed, and how can they be provided? Who should teach? What training do teachers need? What should be the limits of the educational efforts? These and many other questions call for education about the education function itself in a church. It is accurate to say, as Aleshire wrote of education in a church, "It informs and undergirds all the purposes of the church."[18] This is how education relates to the nature and mission of a church.

Conclusion

A church is uniquely placed in the center of God's redemptive purpose in Christ. It is important to know the essential character of a church. The Bible presents some word portraits of a church which, taken together, provide rich insights into its nature. Essentially, a church is a group of the people of God on mission. It is important to describe a church further in order to understand it fully, but this is its core concept.

It is useful to begin with an individual disciple and to think one's way to the church. Individuals are called to follow Jesus and to join him in the redemptive enterprise. Together with other persons who have responded to this call to discipleship, they become parts of God's "building," with Christ being the Rock upon which a church is built. Dynamically, these followers meld together into a kind of living organism, with qualities of life as a unit. They live out their common life expressing the reality and the validity of their corporate life by functioning together to worship, to proclaim and witness, to nurture and educate, and to minister. Each of the functions is the most important function for its purposes. They are intricately interrelated. Education informs and supports all the other functions, as well as itself.

The nature and mission of a church do, indeed, require education.

Concerns for Further Study

Consider these questions as you continue to reflect upon the nature and mission of a church, and upon their requirement of education.

1. What are some of the reasons you would suggest about the importance of one's understanding something of the nature and mission of a church?

2. How would you propose to help members of a church fellowship learn more about the nature and mission of a church?

3. What are some ways you might go about educating persons in a church regarding the functions of (1) worship, (2) proclaiming and witnessing, (3) nurturing and educating, and (4) ministering?

Notes

1. Daniel Aleshire, "Christian Education and Theology," *Christian Education Handbook,* Bruce P. Powers editor/compiler (Nashville: Broadman Press, 1981), p. 27.

2. Ibid.

3. Herschel H. Hobbs, *The Baptist Faith and Message* (Nashville: Convention Press, 1971), p. 75.

4. Ibid.

5. Ibid.

6. Ibid., p. 74.

7. Ibid., p. 79.

8. Ibid., p. 80.

9. Ibid., p. 76.

10. Ibid.

11. Ibid.

12. Ibid., p. 78.

13. Howard P. Colson and Raymond M. Rigdon, *Understanding Your Church's Curriculum,* revised edition (Nashville: Broadman Press, 1981), p. 45.

14. Ibid.

15. Reginald M. McDonough, compiler, *A Church on Mission* (Nashville: Convention Press, 1980), p. 17.

16. Ibid., p. 18.

17. Aleshire, p. 33.

18. Ibid.

5
World Conditions and Trends

Sensitive persons in almost any era could honestly say, "These are the times that try men's souls." There are forces at work in the world which, if not checked, seem destined not only to try men's souls but to doom them. Humanly speaking, the outlook for mankind seems grim. One writer said it this way: "I looked into the future, and it won't work!" Any prophet of doom can find ample evidence to support his prophecy. The glass is half *empty,* and leaking fast.

There are other forces at work than those which portend disaster. Conditions in some sectors are promising. Trends in some fields are hopeful. There are signs of progress in some areas of man's struggle for life with meaning. With the poet Emerson it can be said, "This time, like all times, is a very good one if we but know what to do with it." The glass is half *full,* and filling.

What are some of the conditions and trends which can be so ambivalently construed? What about the church in such a world? More specifically, what about religious education? It is to these questions that we turn our attention in this chapter.

World Conditions and Trends

It seems almost trite to say that we live in a world of change. Yet it is not trite, because there has been no previous time in the history of a changing world when the change has come at such a rapid pace. The threshold of man's ability to tolerate change has been eroded to the point of near disaster. Individuals are made to feel inadequate and hopeless in the face of such a pace of change. This "changepace" seems to be an inevitable producer of anxiety and frustration, even of despair. The changes are coming at such a fast pace and in such volume that many can no longer cope. How many changes will *this* generation experience? A glimpse at some of the major areas in which such changes are occurring will illustrate the problem.

Extensive and complex changes in technology astound even the most sophisticated at times. The changes in *transportation* in this century have been staggering to the imagination. Superjets move large numbers of people over distances in a few hours which would have required months of arduous travel several years ago. On the other hand, most of the world's millions have never set foot on an airplane—a fact which is still true even in sophisticated America. Moving sidewalks start, stop, and move accurately in response to a computer programmed pattern. Transportation tubes move large numbers of people quickly, encapsuled in carriers under the ground. Even reusable space shuttles are either present realities or near-future facts.

Communication developments are making the science fiction of a past generation the common experience of many. Edward R. Lindaman wrote: "We blink our eyes with the sudden realization that, thanks to science, all the filters have been removed from between us and everything that happens anywhere in the world."[1] The events of the moment are available to the people of the earth with sight, sound, and living color. Moreover, the technology presently exists to make possible individual two-way verbal communication almost anywhere in the world with equipment approximately the size of a wristwatch, via communications satellites. The developments in the present and potentially in the near future in communications almost defy description. Along with these capabilities for communication, we also need to work on understanding one another.

Medicine has experienced changes. Major organ transplants are still news, but they are no longer uncommon. Preventive medicine seems to be making great progress. Research to find the secrets of prevention and/or cure of dread diseases has virtually eliminated some diseases from the earth, and promises considerable hope for others. Life expectancy continues to be extended, with large credit due to remarkable advances in medicine and medical care.

Agriculture has undergone a methodological revolution in America, some of the benefits of which have been shared with underdeveloped countries. Fewer and fewer persons now supply more and more people with farm products. Farms generally are larger than before, and many who formerly lived and worked there have migrated to urban areas. Still, it is estimated that from 40 to 60 percent of the people of the world suffer from malnutrition or from outright hunger.

Space exploration reflects some of the highest achievements of technological advance. The *Voyager 2* spacecraft in August 1981 flew near planet Saturn exactly 2.7 seconds early for its four-year appointment, having traveled nearly a billion miles. After sending back to earth numerous photographs of the hitherto unseen sights of Saturn, and after having a mysterious operational problem corrected by remote control, it flashed on for a rendezvous with the planet Uranus five years and nearly two billion miles away!

Computer science has played a part in all of these areas of change and in numerous others. It has been a major instrument of a new "Renaissance" in modern history. In addition to its impact upon areas already mentioned, it is changing many of the fields of business and commerce. Computerized shopping for everything from banking needs to food and clothing are no longer doubted as near-future realities. The move seems well underway to equip many households in America with their very own set to be used for everything from controlling heating, cooling, and lights to providing accounting services, education, news, and entertainment.

Erratic changes in economics keep the people of the world in a stir. *Rampant inflation,* in some countries as much as 200 to 300 percent per year, devastates monetary systems and personal lives and plans. In the United States, whose stable currency has long been the standard of international trade, it required almost $2.90 in 1981 to pay for the goods and services that $1.00 would purchase in 1967. The price of the average new house during that same period escalated from three to four times, depending upon the region of the country. Overall per capita health care costs for all ages increased 123 percent from 1970-77, with persons under age sixty-five spending less than one third as much as those over sixty-five.

Inflation's economic counterpart (in classic economic theory), *unemployment,* threatens to topple governments, and does incite violence. In some areas and among some ethnic groups, the figure has approached 40 and 50 percent of the work force unemployed even in the United States, though the average for the nation never topped 9 percent during the decade of the seventies. To add to the confusion, some of the old "laws" of the economy have been breached. For example, an economy such as that of the United States could in the past expect unemployment to go down as inflation rose, and vice versa. Now there have been times when both rose, bringing attention to a new kind of problem labeled "stagflation." As if that isn't complicated enough, enter exorbitantly *high interest rates!*

Low growth of productivity as measured by the rate of growth in the Gross National Product has added fuel to the economic fires. *Obsolete plants and machinery* in some industries of America apparently have contributed to the loss of some markets to international competitors.

Wages for most in America have barely managed to keep pace with the growth of the Cost Price Index, only to have most if not all of the gain wiped out by unprecedented *tax increases.* Still, Americans have more left after taxes than do most other major industrialized countries. And the average American family has a share of the Gross National Product equal to more than twenty times that of families in the countries of the world outside of Europe and Scandinavia.

Concern for *dwindling natural resources* has mounted on a worldwide scale. *Energy sources* which come from fossil fuels virtually have been put on the "endangered species" list. Even *water* and *air,* previously considered free, abundant, and uncontaminated, are among the natural resources whose usable supply is a concern.

Generally, those things most basic to sustaining life, such as food, shelter (including fuel), clothing, medical care, and transportation, have escalated faster in costs than have some of the luxuries. All in all, the conditions in economics have been disturbingly erratic. It appears they will continue to be cause for grave concern in the long term.

Social changes are occurring at a faster-than-ever pace. *Explosion* is the word most often used to refer to the *growth of the populations* of the earth. Some expect the world population to double within twenty-five years! Ralph W. Neighbour, Jr., wrote:

> It required the entire history of man to give birth to the first billion people, by 1830. It took only 100 years to add the second billion. The third billion came

in thirty years. In fourteen more years, we added the fourth billion. By 2000 A.D., we will add three billion more! Demographers are conservatively forecasting 7.2 billion by the end of the century.[2]

The implications of such growth in population for every other area of concern—such as technology, economics, politics, education, and religion—are truly mind boggling.

A dimension of the population explosion is the phenomenon of *urbanization*. According to Neighbour, 5 percent of the earth's people lived in cities in 1800. Now the figure has passed 51 percent, on its way to a predicted 73 percent by AD 2000. From one hundred seventy-two cities of a million people in 1975, there are to be three hundred by the end of this century, with two hundred of these in Third World countries.[3] Providing means of subsistence for such areas of humanity challenges all of man's means.

Hunger is a stark reality for up to two thirds of the world's people. In spite of the fact that an estimated 60 percent of the wheat grown in the United States and one third of all farm produce are sold overseas, the extent of hunger continues to grow.

In the United States the *population is growing older*. Planners should anticipate this trend. Comparable numbers of the young are not entering the work force, thus creating havoc in tax-based support systems for the needy aged.

Antisocial behavior, including crime, alcohol abuse, drug abuse, tobacco use, sexual immorality, and family dissolution, continue to take heavy tolls in society. Security of persons from violent crimes is diminishing. *Acts of violence* formerly reserved for darkness are now common in broad daylight. *Alcohol abuse* is epidemic on a worldwide scale, not only destroying lives directly, but consuming criminal amounts of foodstuff used in its manufacture while a world totters near starvation. *Drug abuse* continues to victimize a growing number of people. In the United States the use of marijuana by males age twelve to seventeen almost tripled from 1971-77, reaching nearly 20 percent of that group. Females were not far behind.

Government in the United States with one hand supports the production of harmful products such as *tobacco* while with another hand it warns of its potential for death. The same government has laws which make it more advantageous financially for some to live together without benefit of matrimony. Adultery is a social problem because the results of such behavior are borne by many persons other than those who have given assent to such a style of life.

Family structures are shifting. Almost half of the work force in the United States is female, although women receive less than two thirds the pay of men for their labor. Single parent families have nearly doubled in a decade, approaching nine million households in 1981. The *rate of divorce* as compared with the rate of marriage in the United States has approached one for one. While many are doubtless the victims of very difficult circumstances, many others enter and depart the state of marriage with a casualness which is something of a social and moral felony. The debilitating effects of this latter group upon family stability is indeed against the best interests of society. These trends, along with numerous others of a social-moral-religious nature (such as the millions of persons who cohabit), leave social problems for all.

Political instability and turmoil afflict many nations of the world. The *assassination of political leaders* has become almost routine news. *Violent terrorist acts* strike frighteningly close to presumed bastions of security. *Hostage-taking* in many places occurs with alarming frequency.

There is a *new confusion of politics and religion.* Some preachers have moved into politics to try to influence the system directly. Many politicians sound more like preachers or missionaries. And then there are *the mullahs of Iran.* Sectarian strife rends the garment of the "faithful" in country after country, with terrorist acts, firing squads, and outright war the bitter fruits. Quite often it is Christian against Christian, or Muslim against Muslim.

The *military-industrial complex* in 1980 required more than *one million dollars per minute,* worldwide, for armaments and other military spending, according to the Stockholm International Peace Research Institute. There have been *one hundred thirty wars since World War II* (fifty in the period 1970-80) mostly in Third World countries. *Overt and covert intrusions of nation upon nation* keep the world in dread that some situation will get out of hand and bring on a worldwide conflagration that will destroy all parties. Acronyms for *strategies and weapons of war have become prominent* in the language of the superpowers of the earth: ICBM (intercontinental ballistic missile), MIRVs (multiple independently targetable reentry vehicles), LOW (launch on warning), and MAD (mutual assured destruction). So dreadful have become the *possibilities of holocaust* by the use of such tools of annihilation that free world governments have trouble with their own people in the search for places to station the weapons, in view of the fact that their locations would assure neighboring citizens of being programmed for death in the event of an exchange of weapons between superpowers.

Education, generally, has not kept pace with needs in the world at large, nor in the United States in particular. Expenditures for education have not kept up with inflation, even in the United States. Even here the inflated number of dollars spent for education represents a diminishing portion of the Gross National Product. The figure for 1979-80 was around 7 percent, down from a high of nearly 8 percent in 1975-76. In addition, there continues to be concern for what these dollars are actually buying. Learning and development of skills for living generally are not at a level to satisfy what it takes to conserve and improve the quality of life many feel is eluding our grasp. Sincere public educators are grappling with the problems, while many others are turning to alternative systems for schooling. *Private schools,* mostly church sponsored, are said to be multiplying in America at a current rate of *three new ones per day.* There is a paradox in higher education: there are more than eleven hundred *ethics courses in business schools* of American colleges and universities, while many *ethics teachers are focusing on the procedural realms.* The decade of the eighties portends to be pivotal in the patterns for educating a public in dire need of knowing all they can in order to cope with the fast-changing ways of life in these times.

Religious Conditions and Trends

Religious conditions and trends cannot be disassociated entirely from the conditions and trends in the areas previously scanned. For instance, the *entry of so-called conservative religionists into the political realm* at the same time *so-called liberal religionists are exiting* that realm is a somewhat curious phenomenon of the times in America.

On a worldwide scale, just under 40 percent of the world's population have no religious affiliation whatsoever as of 1981. Christianity claims 23.3 percent, with 36.8 percent claimed by world religions. The percentage claimed by Christianity is dwindling. *We seem to be losing the pace race.* Commenting on the situation, Neighbour wrote:

> To keep pace with this expanding population, the Christian community will have to add 62,500,000 converts a year from now to the end of the century! The alternative to such evangelism is frightening. At our present snail pace of evangelism, some missiologists forecast a world Christian community of less than 1 percent of the total population by the end of the century.[4]

In the United States the *trends of church membership and attendance are generally down,* with the *Southern Baptists as one of the few major exceptions.* In the period 1975-78 church membership in *three of the five largest denominations registered net losses.* Those losing were the Episcopal Church, the Lutheran Church in America, and the United Methodist Church, while the gainers were the Roman Catholic Church and the Southern Baptist Convention. In those same denominations, *only the Southern Baptists reflected a net gain in Sunday School enrollment,* and that was less than a 1 percent gain.[5] During a time of growing population, the percent of adults in the United States attending church in a typical week dropped from just under fifty million in 1958 to around forty-two million in 1978.[6]

Completing the "nickels and noses" indicators of religious involvement, the 1981 *World Almanac* reported that *religion and welfare together accounted for 1.3 percent of personal consumption expenditures for the United States in 1979.* Many denominations actually received fewer dollars than in previous years, and that during several years of double-digit monetary inflation. In the largest state convention within the Southern Baptist Convention, the Baptist General Convention of Texas, *the per capita giving of members represented a smaller portion of the individuals' total buying power than during the lowest years of the Great Depression,* even though many more dollars were given.

Research on trends in religion in America is more plentiful than ever before. Following is a summary of ten key trends in the religious and spiritual lives of Americans, as indicated by numerous national surveys conducted in 1979 by the Gallup Organization, Inc., the Gallup Poll, the Gallup Youth Survey, and the Princeton Religion Research Center:

(1) An intensive spiritual search and a desire for individual spiritual growth.

(2) A proliferation of religious groups to answer these spiritual needs—a clear warning to established churches that are sometimes not prepared to deal with religious experience.

(3) A blurring of boundaries between various faiths and denominations.

(4) The influence of charismatics and Pentecostals which is being felt across denominational lines.

(5) A growing interest in interfaith dialogue.

(6) A decline in the growth of most of the largest Protestant denominations and the growth and revitalization of the evangelical churches, notably the Southern Baptist Convention. (a) Not only has there been a decline in church membership for many churches, but attendance among certain denominations is on the decline. (b) Furthermore, the percentage of persons who have had religious training has declined sharply over the last quarter century. (c) In addition, the proportion of persons who say they have no religious preference has increased from 2 percent in 1966 to 8 percent in the latest surveys—a fourfold increase.

(7) An increase in secularity: Persons today believe religion cannot answer all or most of today's problems.

(8) An increase in religiosity, described by Martin Marty as "a diffusion of religion into the larger culture."

(9) At the same time, basic beliefs remain intact. Even those who are not church members are surprisingly orthodox in their Christian beliefs.

(10) While basic beliefs remain intact, a growing gap is noted between believing and belonging to a church. In many cases churches seem unprepared to answer spiritual needs.[7]

An Approach to the Future

There is no turning back. Golden ages in the past tense are but illusions. Some who yearn for such either didn't "read" the past accurately, or they have bad memories. While no one can know all about the future with certainty, each person has a measure of that godlike capacity to anticipate a future and to think somewhat rationally about it. There is consensus, according to Lindaman, *about the way a futurist approaches the future.* First, we make explicit the assumptions we hold about the future. This better equips us to connect the present with the future tense. An essential second step is to examine one's life and the world in general in terms of apparent trends and probable outcomes. Third, a futurist looks beyond the trends and probably outcomes to imagine other possibilities, from which choices are made which determine our directions.[8] It is this kind of approach which the leaders of a church's educational ministry must make in response to world conditions and trends.

A special planning committee of the Southern Baptist Convention has taken a similar approach to the future in the 1980s and has identified sixteen challenges and opportunities that press upon the churches. These should be of interest not only to Southern Baptists, but to those of other denominations. Following are the sixteen areas.

The number one problem faced by churches in the present and the near future centers around *family life*—dealing with problems of deteriorating marriages and changing families.

Second is the concern for *mission involvement*—a rising interest in missions and Bold Mission Thrust. Baptists are seeking to present the gospel to every person on earth by the year 2000.

Third is *leadership development*—preparing and involving lay persons in discipleship and leadership. It is imperative that the work force be multiplied, taught, and trained.

The fourth concern is *Bible learning*—taking advantage of the widespread interest in Bible study. This is an essential focal area if there is to be any great advance in reaching a world for Christ. Widespread interest and participation in Bible study have preceded almost every major advance of Christianity in history.

Fifth is the area of *church fellowship*—preparing a caring fellowship that recognizes and develops the need for personal relations between persons drawn to each other in Christ. It is the vital base from which evangelism and Christian discipline must spring.

Aggressive evangelism is the sixth challenge and opportunity— witnessing to the unreached masses.

Seventh is *efficient communications*—using modern technological means to communicate the gospel. In a time when the communications revolution is sweeping the world, it is imperative that all media capabilities be utilized to "make known the manifold wisdom of God."

Eighth is the concern for *urban life*—reaching the great cities with the gospel of Christ. The masses of the populations of the earth will be in the urban centers, and they must receive the good news of forgiveness and salvation.

Human suffering is the ninth challenge and opportunity—motivating Christians to help meet the world problems of human hunger and human rights.

Tenth is *personal adjustment*—helping persons whose roles in life are changing to find personal fulfillment in their new circumstances. In view of the changepace and the often-resultant stress individuals experience, churches must respond by helping persons to adjust.

Eleventh is the challenge of *influencing community life*—ministering to the spiritual and moral needs of the community. The almost unbridled sense of individual rights over those of the community poses a threat to the entire value system. Churches must help attain the essential and fragile balance between the individual and the society in the area of norms and values.

Christian morality—influencing society with Christian moral values—is the twelfth area. The Christian esteem for persons, along with other values, has been the foundation of Western civilization. People are more than animals and need to behave on a higher plane than animals. Churches must help to identify and clarify moral values and use appropriate means to influence society in right directions.

Positive leadership—meeting the waves of social, economic, and political crises that threaten the stability of society—is the thirteenth challenge and opportunity area. Churches must encourage Christians and others to give calm and resolute leadership when all about them seems to be in disarray.

Problem-solving—reconciling the mammoth discontinuities and conflicts that exist in society on a worldwide scale—is the fourteenth area.

Fifteenth is the area of *cross-cultural expansion*—establishing new congregations in ethnic and cross-cultural communities. Churches must take a new look at their mission obligations in America in view of the growing pluralism of the nation.

Sixteenth is the area of *women power*—finding new and creative ways for women to serve, especially in the ministries of churches.

The implications of these areas of challenge and opportunity for churches are numerous. The life and character of a local church is likely to change greatly. The organization of time and people to implement the life and work of the churches must be carefully examined and probably adjusted. Churches must give more effective help to the homes as they upgrade the responses of the homes for the spiritual formation of family members. Churches must find ways to strengthen their efforts in a higher quality and volume of effort in evangelism.

The members of a fellowship must become more ably engaged in the full scope of the life and ministries of a church. There are not and could never be enough vocational ministers to do all the work of a church. It would not be right for them to do it all, even if it were possible. Being a follower of Jesus Christ and sharing with him and with others in the redemptive enterprise are the responsibility and privilege of every believer.[9]

Conclusion

It would seem clear that world conditions and trends demand education. It is important for leaders in a church to know something of the conditions and trends affecting the lives of people, both at home and around the world.

Religious education will play an essential role in any church which looks to the future to meet its challenges and opportunities. The people of God cannot do less than to depend upon God and give him their best effort. Jesus said, "We must work the works of him who sent me, while it is day; night comes, when no one can work" (John 9:4).

Concerns for Further Study

Consider these questions as you continue to reflect upon the idea that world conditions and trends demand education.

1. Think of the change that has had the most impact on your own life in the areas of (1) technology, (2) economics, (3) society, (4) politics, and (5) education. How have these changes affected your life?

2. What factor of change in the area of religion has influenced you the most?

3. How would you describe the appropriate response of the educational ministry of a church to the challenges and opportunities presented in the decade ahead by world conditions and trends?

Notes

1. Edward B. Lindaman, *Thinking in the Future Tense* (Nashville: Broadman Press, 1978), pp. 27-28.
2. Ralph W. Neighbour, Jr., compiler, *Future Church* (Nashville: Broadman Press, 1980), p. 9.
3. Ibid., p. 11.
4. Ibid., p. 10.
5. These statements of trends are based upon those denominations which provide annual membership reports. They came from the *Yearbook of American and Canadian Churches*.
6. This data is from *Religion in America 1979-80,* p. 28, produced by the Princeton Religion Research Center and the Gallup organization.
7. Source: "Emerging Trends," Vol. 2, No. 1 (January 1980), published by the Princeton Research Center, Hopewell, N.J., via "Research Digest," Vol. II, No. 7 (December 1980), published by the Research Division of the Home Mission Board of the Southern Baptist Convention.
8. Lindaman, pp. 44-45.
9. For an enlarged discussion of these challenges and opportunities, and their implications, see *A Church on Mission,* chapter 3, compiled by Reginald M. McDonough (Nashville: Convention Press, 1980).

Part II
Basic Components

Prologue

There are many things a church might do; there are some things a church *must* do. One of the imperatives a church must do is to educate. Biblical precedent commands it. History affirms its value. Persons need it. A church's nature and mission require it. World conditions and trends demand it.

There are also many things a church might do to educate; there are some things a church *must* do. There are certain basic components which seem imperative in almost all churches. There are essential parts which make up the educational ministry of a church.

We have stated the assumption that the Bible is the basic book for the educational ministry of a church. It seems that a church must begin and continue a ministry of Bible teaching and learning. For those who rely upon the authority of the Bible as the primary guide in matters of faith and practice, such a ministry is not optional. It is the foundational dimension of the educational ministry. While all the other dimensions of a church's educational ministry might also engage in some Bible teaching and learning, a program is needed in which Bible teaching and learning are the dominant features. That is the theme of chapter 6.

There is a vital dimension of education which focuses upon a rather specific kind of educating, that of training. Narrowly defined, it means teaching to make one fitted and proficient. A church needs to engage in such a program of training disciples. Chapter 7 sets forth basic components of this ministry of discipleship training.

A church must extend beyond itself if it is to fulfill its mission as a church. There are certain understandings and skills Christians need to develop regarding missions. A church must teach missions. Its members must engage in mission action and in personal witnessing. They must pray for and give financially to support missions. They need to become involved in personal ministry and in missions.

119

Chapter 8 describes a church ministry of missions education and action.

The Christian faith is a singing faith. Music is a basic part of Christian worship. Increasingly, it is also an effective educational method. Too often in churches the ministry of music is left to "musicians." But music, like other means of praise and of education, is too important to be left to the "pros." A church needs to provide its members with suitable musical experiences in congregational services. The members need opportunities to develop musical skills, attitudes, and understanding. They need leadership in witnessing and in ministering through music. This is the emphasis of chapter 9.

There are other ministries which are essential to a comprehensive plan of education in a church. Prominent among these ministries of enrichment and support are the work of the media services, recreation services, and administrative services. These service programs support a church in the achievement of its mission. They enrich the entire effort of a church by making its ministries more effective, more meaningful, and more educational. Vital to a church's educational ministry is its ministry to the distinctive needs of families, senior adults, and single adults. A church has a responsibility to minister to the needs of families at all stages of development. Chapter 10 contains a presentation of these areas of ministry.

The objective of Part II is to help persons to identify and to understand the importance of the basic components of the educational ministry of a church.

6
Ministry of Bible Teaching and Learning

The ministry of Bible teaching and learning is the first of the basic components of the educational ministry of a church. The Bible is the source of multitudes of truths which make up the essential subject matter of religious education. Many other subjects relate to a "complete" religious education, but the Bible is the core subject.

Few, if any, have ever mastered the contents of the Bible. Many have memorized great portions of it. Some have learned many of its truths. All fail at some point to live by its teachings. Yet it remains the chief guidebook, setting forth models for faith and life as children of God. A church must begin and continue a ministry of Bible teaching and learning. This chapter will indicate why and how such a ministry might be performed.

The Bible Is the Foundation

Education that is Christian must first be education in the Scriptures. The Bible is the unique and foundational text for the educational ministry of a church. James D. Smart wrote:

> God's chosen way of coming to us is through a Word, a word that sounded in the ears of the prophets and psalmists, in the fullness of time was incarnate in Jesus Christ, was heard and spoken by the apostles, and of which the record is preserved for us in the Scriptures. Through that record, the Word that was once heard and spoken sounds ever anew into the life of the world. The revelation of God in the Scriptures is unique; it is not one among many revelations of God which are to be set in line with each other and weighed and compared. God speaks to man through the Scriptures a word of judgment and mercy which, if it is not heard in this place, is not heard at all. Where else in all the ages of human experience is God made known as the Father Almighty, Creator of the heavens and the earth, as man's Lord and Redeemer, taking up our humanity into his divinity, and as God's own Spirit, claiming the inmost self of every man as his dwelling place. Close the Scriptures, and that God, who alone is the God of Christians, is unknown.

And where he is unknown, the life that he alone gives to men through faith in him is unknown.[1]

James Marion Frost, whose concern for Bible teaching and learning among Southern Baptists led to the founding of the Baptist Sunday School Board in 1891, had a strong sense of the priority of Bible teaching through the Sunday School. He said: "The work of the Sunday School is threefold: First, teach the Scriptures; second, teach the Scriptures; third, teach the Scriptures."[2]

Southern Baptists are among those who have maintained a high interest in the Bible. They affirmed in Convention sessions and in other ways:

> The Holy Bible was written by men divinely inspired and is the record of God's revelation of Himself to man. It is a perfect treasure of divine instruction. It has God for its author, salvation for its end, and truth, without any mixture of error, for its matter. It reveals the principles by which God judges us; and therefore is, and will remain to the end of the world, the true center of Christian union, and the supreme standard by which all human conduct, creeds, and religious opinions should be tried. The criterion by which the Bible is to be interpreted is Jesus Christ.[3]

The Bible continues to be of unmatched interest in a church's educational ministry.

Why should persons be so drawn to Bible teaching and learning? In their chapter on "The Bible in the Curriculum," Colson and Rigdon indicate several good reasons.[4] They declare the Bible to be (1) the record of God's self-revelation; (2) the repository of God's redemptive message for the world; (3) inspired by God; (4) providentially preserved; (5) God's gift to his church; (6) the only authoritative guide for Christian life and work; and (7) the indispensable book that brings persons to Christ. They continued by showing the strengths of the Bible as based upon its relevance to the needs of humanity, its authority based upon the fact that it came from God, and its power in individual lives and in society. They conclude with guidance about using the Bible with integrity, how to interpret the Bible, and how to use the Bible with children.

Before we move into the suggestions about structures and curriculum, it seems worthwhile to call attention to some principles of biblical interpretation (hermeneutics) which should be observed by those in a church who lead in the ministry of Bible teaching and learning. Again, we have drawn heavily from the form and order of expression presented by Colson and Rigdon.[5]

First, each individual has the right to come to the Bible for himself. He might benefit by the efforts of others, but under God he must do his own thinking.

Second, the student must attempt to discover what the text says, exactly. It is essential to understand what the passage meant to the people to whom it was first addressed, and then to interpret what God is saying through it to us now.

Third, consider whether the passage is to be taken literally or figuratively. To mistake either for the other might be misleading.

Fourth, try to determine whether the passage presents a permanent and universal truth or one which is only local and temporary. The dietary laws of the Mosaic code is an example of the temporary.

Fifth, when dealing with narrative portions, the interpreter must recognize that beyond the event lies the witness of believers to the meaning of the event. The Exodus was not just a migratory trip; it was an act of God which demonstrated his steadfast love and his redeeming grace.

Sixth, in long or short passages, look for the central message. Without this principle, one could study passages such as the parables and miss the main point.

Seventh, interpret Scripture by means of Scripture. Understand difficult or obscure passages when possible in the light of passages which are clear. In any case, a passage should be interpreted in the light of the Bible's message as a whole.

Eighth, examine the findings of the best biblical scholars, ancient and modern. This can keep a student from going too far afield from the consensus of Christian thought.

Ninth, recognize that Jesus Christ is the Lord of the Scriptures. An interpretation that disagrees with his teaching cannot be right.

The Bible is the foundation of a church's educational ministry. There are at least three ways a church's educational ministry should be examined by the Scriptures to determine the validity and the rightness of the plans. First, determine whether or not the Bible explicitly calls for or supports the matter under consideration. For example, it seems clear that the admonition to "make disciples of all nations, . . . teaching them to observe all that I have commanded you" (Matt. 28:19-20) presents a permanent and universal truth to be obeyed by the faithful.

Second, determine whether or not the Bible forbids the matter under consideration. If so, do not proceed to do it. For example, James 2 is clear in its teaching against showing partiality. Third, if the Bible seems not to speak either for or against a matter, determine if it is compatible with other biblical teachings. Many of the methods available to Christians today in the work of ministry were not known to those who were God's instruments in producing the Scriptures. If these ideas do not violate the spirit of the Scriptures and if they are useful, there should be no hesitancy to use them. There are many things which are neither advocated nor prohibited in the Bible, but which seem compatible with its spirit to use— church buildings, electricity, visual aids, air conditioning, lesson helps, and many other things.

The Bible is the foundation, not only in that it is the principal text, but also in that it is the standard by which all of a church's educational ministry should be appraised. Ignorance of the Bible is a bane to the church and to the world. Knowledge and practice of it are a blessing to all. Teaching and learning the Bible must be the first concern of a church's educational ministries. We shall look now at some structures for a church to use as it engages in a ministry of Bible teaching and learning.

Structures for Bible Teaching and Learning

There are many ways a church might plan for Bible teaching and learning. One of the ways that is most obvious is through increased use of the sermon for teaching the Bible and its doctrines. The authors of A Church on Mission forecast a trend in this direction for the church of the eighties.[6] Certainly preaching must be strongly infused with the Bible if it is to be most effective. Our purpose here, however, is to focus upon the intentional teaching and learning a church might engage in beyond the pulpit.

Use the Sunday School

The most important structure for many churches of many denominations for Bible teaching and learning is the Sunday School. This remains true even in the face of serious problems which some denominations have experienced in recent years with Sunday School. Between 1970 and 1980, overall enrollments in American Sunday Schools dropped nearly 25 percent. Denominations which in the past have had strong support for their Sunday Schools are among the hardest hit in terms of losses—Methodist, Presbyterian, and Episcopal. Some experts feel that the Sunday School is in a struggle for its very existence. This probably has always been true.

The Sunday Schools of America remain the largest single voluntary enterprise in the nation. Some denominations and some congregations within other denominations are not only holding their own in Sunday School but are improving and growing in participation and in effectiveness. It is estimated that up to 90 percent of the new church members in non-Catholic churches have come from the work of Sunday Schools. Among the Southern Baptists, whose Sunday Schools continue to grow, there is a historical ratio of one in three persons enrolled in Sunday School becoming a Christian and church member. The ratio of those who profess faith and join the church without coming via the Sunday School has been approximately one in two hundred and forty. Sunday School outreach is a major strategy of Southern Baptists and accounts for a large measure of their growth to become the largest non-Catholic denomination in America. They have learned some important concepts about growing churches through growing Sunday Schools. The concepts of growth also apply to other parts of a church's structures.

A church has many important activities which it must perform to carry out its functions and to accomplish its mission. If a church had no organizations within its body to carry out these tasks, the church would still need to find some way to do them, because the tasks belong to the nature of the church itself. Certain of the tasks of a church, as it performs its educational ministry, can best be implemented through the Sunday School.

1. *Tasks of the Sunday School.* The *first task* of a Sunday School is: *Reach people for Bible study.* This means that the Sunday School begins by getting as many people as possible engaged in Bible study. It often is easier to get persons to take part in a Bible study group fostered by a Sunday School than it is to get them into the church for worship. There are many non-Christians,

many unchurched Christians (nonresident or completely inactive), many church members themselves, and many children of these who are not being reached for Bible study on any regular basis. It is the first business of those who work in the Sunday School to reach out to these.

It is the responsibility of the teacher, more than anyone else, to provide pupils to teach in Sunday School. Teachers, if people are to be reached as they must, have to accept responsibility to "drum up their own classes," along with help from others. (In chapter 15 we shall describe ways that organizations in a church might be organized for growth.) Persons must be reached in order to be taught; and a Sunday School, properly designed to include persons of all ages and conditions, is in the best position to accomplish the church's task of reaching people for Bible study.

The *second task* of a Sunday School is: *Teach the Bible.* Here the emphasis is to engage people in the study of the biblical revelation in Scriptures and in the application of its meaning for all of life. The Bible is the text. Other lesson materials might be used with profit in learning and in teaching, but it is the Bible and its truths which must be taught.

This teaching is with the hope and purpose that those who have not yet received Christ will, as appropriate in their own readiness under the leadership of the Holy Spirit, receive him for the forgiveness of sin and salvation. Too, the hope and purpose for those who are already Christians is that they will follow the leadership of the Holy Spirit and respond to God with maturing faith, love, and obedience. Believers and nonbelievers are taught together in their classes. Most of the Bible teaching and learning sponsored by Sunday School takes place in church buildings on Sunday morning. (We shall mention later other approaches which have come into use in recent years.)

The *third task* of a Sunday School is: *Witness to persons about Christ and lead them into church membership.* This means that members of a Sunday School who are Christians will join with those who are leaders in sharing the faith with other members and potential members who have not yet received Christ. They will try to lead them to receive Christ and to join the fellowship of a church. Faithful performance of this task is one of several evidences of effectiveness in teaching. At the same time this task is being performed, others are to be brought into the study of the Bible who are in need of Christ and the church.

The *fourth task* of a Sunday School is: *Minister to Sunday School members and nonmembers.* Sunday School leaders and members are in a unique position to help one another and others in the church and community. This is not only a vital service itself, but gives essential validity to the real learning that is taking place in the Bible study. It is putting into practice the teachings of the Bible. The authors of *A Church on Mission* wrote:

> It means every Sunday School member should be encouraged to meet the needs of other persons in the spirit of Christ. This may take the form of personal service, concrete acts of caring expressed in material support, encouraging words, affirmation, or simply taking the time to listen. This task is at the heart of a loving, caring fellowship.[7]

In many churches, the close relationships that develop in the relatively small Sunday School groupings provide the natural setting for the kinds of mutual support and help which often might not be known about or met in the larger body, the church. A Sunday School class or department often is a church's "front line" of pastoral service in situations of need among members and non-members.

The *fifth task* of a Sunday School is: *Lead members to worship.* Worship is the foundational function of a church. The Sunday School should regularly interpret the biblical teachings on worship and provide materials for use in personal worship. In many churches the Sunday School is the best organization through which to distribute materials to motivate individuals and families to worship and to guide them in doing it. Too, the Sunday School usually meets in conjunction with the morning worship services of a church. This gives leaders and members in the Sunday School good opportunities to encourage participation in the church worship service. In addition, there should be regular occasions in Sunday School, and in outside activities which it might sponsor, to provide opportunities for worship experiences. No other organization is in as good a position to implement this important task as is the Sunday School. Worship is another of the normal results of good Bible teaching and learning.

The *sixth task* of a Sunday School is: *Interpret and undergird the work of the church and the denomination.* This means that the Sunday School should be available to present the goals, plans, and activities of the church and the denomination, and to explain their significance. It also means that the Sunday School cooperatively supports the work of the other church ministries and those of the denomination. Each basic church organization should share this task. They are not organizations apart. They are organizations which are a part of a church which is part of a denomination. Harry Piland, national leader of Sunday School work among Southern Baptists, wrote:

> The Sunday School has more members than any other program organization. It has more leaders and prospects than any other. It has the organization and structure through which to do its work and much of the work of the church. Therefore, it is logical that it should interpret, support, and undergird all of the work of the church and the denomination.[8]

However, none of the church organizations should be so regularly or so completely co-opted for interpreting or promoting the work of groups other than itself that its own work is neglected. The information or support which might be presented or called for in an organization should be essential, compatible with the interpreting organization, and in keeping with the age, maturity, and need of the recipients. For example, a church budget subscription plan would not be appropriate for presentation to nursery children in the Sunday School.

2. *Special projects of Bible teaching and learning.* There are several short-term projects which are usually extensions of a Sunday School and which can render valuable service in Bible teaching and learning. Some of these projects, by virtue of the nature of the opportunities they present, are engaged in tasks not only of the Sunday School but also of other ministry organizations of the church. Some of these special projects perform other tasks like these: (1) develop musical skills, attitudes, and understandings; (2) witness and minister through music; (3) equip church members in discipleship; (4) teach Christian theology and doctrine, Christian ethics, Christian history, and church polity and organization; and (5) teach missions and engage in missions.[9]

The major projects which relate to this facet of the Bible teaching and learning program are a *church Vacation Bible School,* which is usually designed along lines of the Sunday School; a *mission Vacation Bible School,* usually designed for persons who do not attend a Sunday School; and *Backyard Bible Clubs,* "mini" Bible schools usually designed for children ages six through eleven, and conducted in yards, carports, patios, or open areas in a community. Other projects and Bible teaching and learning opportunities will be identified later in this chapter.

3. ***Organization for Sunday School.*** It is important for the effective operation of a Sunday School that it be appropriately organized. There is no suitable alternative to good organization if the Sunday School is to perform its tasks. It is impossible to function at near maximum potential in the present or to anticipate reasonable growth without proper organization.

Even the smallest Sunday School needs to be organized to function and to grow. Larger Sunday Schools need more organization than smaller ones. The work load simply must be distributed through organization. Responsibility must be placed where it belongs. Confusion must be avoided. Unnecessary duplication of work must be minimized or eliminated. An effective Sunday School is an organized Sunday School in which the organization is *used* to accomplish the tasks of the Sunday School.

Sunday School members, prospective members, and leaders need to be organized. With reference to members and prospective members, it is the members who are organized; the prospective members are "allowed for" in the design of the organization. Otherwise, growth that includes prospective members is not likely to occur. Leaders also need to be organized so they can work together more effectively in planning, conducting, and evaluating the Sunday School.

Figure 2[10] describes "The Grouping-Grading Plan." This plan for organizing and grouping persons for Bible teaching and learning in a Sunday School is based upon age grading. There are other principles upon which to grade persons for Sunday School purposes, but none serves as well in almost all instances as does the principle of organizing by age. By using the age basis, teaching can be geared more easily to meet pupil needs. Further, age grading helps to place responsibility for outreach where it belongs—with leaders and members of the group where the prospective member would belong upon being enrolled. Neither compatibility, intelligence,

THE GROUPING-GRADING PLAN

DIVISION TITLES

		Divisional Grouping Patterns		
	I.	**II.****	**III.****	**IV.****
PRESCHOOL DIVISION	Birth-1 1* 2 3* 4 5*	B-1 1 2 3 4 5	B-1 1 2 3 4 5	B-1 1 2 3 4 5
CHILDREN'S DIVISION	6 (Grade 1) 7 (Grade 2)* 8 (Grade 3)* 9 (Grade 4)* 10 (Grade 5) 11 (Grade 6)*	6 7* 8 9 10* 11	6 7 8 9 10 11	6 7 8 9 10 11
YOUTH DIVISION	12 (Grade 7) 13 (Grade 8)* 14 (Grade 9) 15 (Grade 10) 16 (Grade 11)* 17 (Grade 12)	12 13* 14 15 16* 17	12 13 14 15 16 17	12 13 14 15 16 17
ADULT DIVISION	18 (high school graduation) and up	18 (or high school graduation) Young Adult 29 30 Adult 59 (or retirement) 60 (or retirement) Senior Adult	18 (or high school graduation) Young Adult 1 2 29 30 Adult 1 2 59 (or retirement) 60 (or retirement) Senior Adult 1 2	18 (or high school graduation) 1 2 3 4 Young Adult 29 30 Adult 1 2 3 4 59 (or retirement) 60 (or retirement) 1 2 3 4 Senior Adult

*These ages will serve as the "focus group" for planning and offering curriculum materials to the churches for use with the pattern they select.

**Additional adult organization units should be added on the basis of possibilities in terms of classifications: college students, single or married persons, age.

Figure 2

achievement, nor even common interest not related to the life stage of the learners comes close to being as advantageous as the principle for organizing a Sunday School.

Notice in Figure 2 the brackets which designate the groupings. Consider the situation of a *small Sunday School*. Reading column I (vertically), it is suggested that there be at least four groupings: in the Preschool Division there is a *department* (preferably not called a *class*) for children ages birth through five years; in the Children's Division there is a *department* for children ages six through eleven (or school grades one through six); in the Youth Division there is a *class* for youth ages twelve through seventeen (or school grades seven through twelve); and in the Adult Division there is a *class* for persons age eighteen (or high school graduation) and up.

Continue to think of a *small Sunday School* while reading the chart in Figure 2 from left to right within each age division. Observe the changes in location of the brackets which designate the groupings from left to right. These brackets suggest the most appropriate subdivisions within an age division as the need arises to create more groups. Obviously it is advantageous to reduce the age span of groupings in any age division as soon as the number of members and prospective members warrant new groups (departments or classes). In order to determine more specifically when the need for new units (departments or classes) exists—along with such matters as suggested maximum enrollments of classes and departments, recommended teacher-pupil ratios, consideration of prospective members, and other considerations—study carefully Figure 3, "Organization Planning Chart."

The chart in Figure 3 also suggests separate groupings of males and females, beginning with age ten (or grade five), or at the latest with age twelve (grade seven) and continuing through the Adult Division. In recent years some churches have grouped some of their adult classes as "coed classes." Some of these classes have had good experiences in numerical and fellowship growth. However, for more individualized teaching to meet specific needs, for more effective outreach, and for supplying more class members to join the work force and serve in other groups as teachers, it is usually more effective to follow the plan of separate classes instead of coed classes. Leaders in a church should study their own needs in the

ORGANIZATION PLANNING CHART

Division	Classification Age (Grade)		Enrollment M	Enrollment F	Prospects M	Prospects F	Total Possibilities M	Total Possibilities F	Suggested Maximum Enrollment (Dept)	Departments Needed	Suggested Maximum Enrollment (Class)	Classes Needed	Suggested Worker/Member Ratio	Approximate No. of Workers Needed
	1		2		3		4		5	6	7	8	9	10
PRESCHOOL	Birth-1	Cradle Roll							50		x	x	1/6	
		Baby							12		x	x	1/4	
		Creeper							12		x	x	1/4	
		Toddler							15		x	x	1/4	
	2								20		x	x	1/4	
	3								20		x	x	1/4	
	4								25		x	x	1/5	
	5								25		x	x	1/5	
CHILDREN	Special Education								20		x	x	1/4	
	6 (Grade 1)								30		x	x	1/7	
	7 (Grade 2)								30		x	x	1/7	
	8 (Grade 3)								30		x	x	1/7	
	9 (Grade 4)								30		x	x	1/7	
	10 (Grade 5)								30		x	x	1/7	
	11 (Grade 6)								30		x	x	1/7	
YOUTH	12 (Grade 7)								50		10		x	
	13 (Grade 8)								50		10		x	
	14 (Grade 9)								50		10		x	
	15 (Grade 10)								60		15		x	
	16 (Grade 11)								60		15		x	
	17 (Grade 12)								60		15		x	
ADULT	18-29 (College)								125		25		x	
	18-29 (Single)								125		25		x	
	18-29 (Married)								125		25		x	
	30-39 (Single)								125		25		x	
	30-39 (Married)								125		25		x	
	40-49								125		25		x	
	50-59								125		25		x	
	60-69								125		25		x	
	70-up								125		25		x	
	Sunday Workers								125		25		x	
	Adults Away								75		8	x	x	
	Homebound								75		6	x	x	
Fellowship Bible Classes									x	x	x		x	
New Sunday Schools									x		x		x	
General Officers			x	x	x	x	x	x	x	x	x	x	x	
Totals									x		x		x	

Figure 3

light of the best experiences of others and design the most effective organization for their situation.[11]

A special word might help those in small Sunday Schools: each department in the Preschool and Children's divisions should have at least two workers. Normally one teacher per class can meet the needs in the Youth and Adult divisions.

It is critically important that a school of any size maintain a reasonably small teacher-pupil ratio. At the beginning of a new Sunday School class and annually at the beginning of a new church year, it is important to allow room for growth in each class or department, rather than to begin with a unit which already has reached its suggested maximum size according to the chart in Figure 3. To allow for reaching as many prospective members as possible, leave 20 to 40 percent room for growth in each unit. For example, in an adult class in which the suggested maximum enrollment is twenty-five, begin with an enrollment of fifteen to twenty, not twenty-five or more. The number of prospective members and the attendance pattern of present members are other factors to consider when determining at what size to begin a unit. But it is important to remember that unless growth is allowed for in the organization design, it is not likely to occur.

Leaders in a Sunday School need to be organized. In a small Sunday School all teachers and other leaders might need to meet in one group on a regular basis to plan and to evaluate the work of the total effort. A weekly workers' meeting is recommended as the best pattern. At least a monthly meeting, which in many churches is called the Sunday School council, should bring together all the workers of the small Sunday School. Should there be several who work together in one department, those workers need to meet frequently to plan and evaluate their work. Again, the weekly meeting pattern is far more productive than any other pattern. (More attention is given the work of the Sunday School council in chapter 13 of this book.)

In larger Sunday Schools a weekly workers' meeting is recommended also. However, the format for the meeting should allow both for general meeting time for all workers and for separate departmental meetings. In large schools the Sunday School council in its monthly meetings probably should include only heads of departments and divisions, along with general leaders of the Sunday School.[12]

Earlier we alluded to allowing room for growth in Sunday School units at the beginning of a new church year. Normally it is healthy for a Sunday School to capitalize upon the new church year to restructure the organization along recommended lines. This has been found to be the most advantageous time to begin new classes and departments (though they might be started at other times as well). With age as the basis of grading, this is the best time to "promote" those who should move to another age group.

Annual promotion on the age basis has many advantages. Harry Piland, in *Basic Sunday School Work,* listed ten values of annual promotion on the age basis. He said it (1) provides for normal advancement through the natural stages of life; (2) encourages a person to adapt to changing conditions; (3) provides (for the individual) guidance and influence of a larger number of consecrated teachers; (4) creates new places of service for many class members; (5) brings fresh interest in prospects by assigning them to new workers; (6) removes the vacuum in which cliques often develop; (7) brings new friends, new relationships; (8) brings new life; (9) means a "new beginning"; (10) makes possible new growth.[13]

Encourage and Guide Other Bible Teaching and Learning

A church might consider a number of possibilities for enabling individuals and groups to participate in Bible teaching and learning beyond the Sunday School and the special projects directly related to Sunday School. We shall identify several approaches to illustrate the many which might be available to a given church or individual.

1. *Seasonal study of Bible books.* There is considerable interest among church members, both those in Sunday School and others, as well as the unchurched, in opportunities to study books of the Bible in concentrated time frames. For instance, the annual January Bible Study conducted among Southern Baptist congregations for more than twenty years has become the largest project of its kind in that denomination. Materials are available for Bible study for all ages—a book of the Bible for adult and youth divisions, and age-graded units or books for children and preschoolers. Some conduct this study in a single week, beginning on Sunday and continuing

through Wednesday evening. Others schedule the sessions as appropriate to their needs, such as a series of Wednesday evenings. Quite often a church's pastor uses this occasion to teach the adults of the congregation. There has been a warm reception of the plan.

2. *Bible conferences.* The study of Bible books or themes in Bible conferences by persons of a single congregation or by groups of congregations is a viable supplementary Bible study activity. These conferences might be conducted in a church or some other convenient location.

3. *Bible study by correspondence.* Many individuals are participating with great interest in Bible study by correspondence. Several denominations have plans for guided correspondence Bible study. In this plan the individual learner follows a Bible study guide and progresses at his own pace. Upon completion of a unit of study, the individual might complete a furnished review form and return it by mail to the persons guiding the study. The correspondent receives a response to the review form and material for the next unit of study. At any given time there are hundreds of thousands of persons engaged in this process worldwide. Southern Baptists in recent years have entered this area of Bible study on a massive scale, under the direction of their Sunday School Board's Home Bible Study plan. An accompanying system of advancement encourages the student to move through an impressive series of levels of Bible study over a period of several years of correspondence work.[14]

Numerous courses in Bible study, as well as in many other subject fields, are available through such sources as the Independent Study Institute of the Seminary Extension Department. This Institute is part of the Seminary External Education Division of the Southern Baptist Convention. A student may enroll for either college-level home study or for the noncredit "Basic Series" of Bible study. In the noncredit series there are two certificates students can earn, each reflecting completion of ten courses of study from a variety of subjects including Bible. There are available four diplomas in college-level series, each requiring completion of sixteen courses.

4. *Study at extension centers.* Each year thousands of pastors and other church workers continue their education in Bible study and other ministry areas in various extension centers. These centers include vast numbers of church members who are not in vocational ministry, as well as many persons who are. A student may enroll for

a single course, or he may pursue a long-range study plan. For instance, the Seminary External Education Division of the Southern Baptist Convention presently operates in more than four hundred such Seminary Extension centers located throughout the United States and in several foreign countries. Normally a group of churches establishes and conducts these centers.[15]

5. *Bible study fellowships.* Numerous Bible study groups are conducted in homes of church members, with encouragement, guidance, and support of churches. These groups usually meet during the week rather than on Sunday. Some meet at places other than homes. They are especially helpful in engaging non-Christians in Bible study in a setting to which many respond openly. In the informal and friendly atmosphere of a home Bible fellowship, many persons receive Christ, and move into the fellowship of a church.

6. *Weekday Bible study.* A church might sponsor an ongoing weekday age-graded Bible study which extends through the public school terms. In some public school systems these courses have been conducted at a church during released time from school. More often they now are conducted after school hours at church.

7. *Other church-sponsored Bible study courses.* Many churches sponsor either class studies or individual studies (or both) with the use of special study materials, requirements, and recognition. A class or an individual alone might study a Bible survey series. Such courses might be scheduled in relation to the seasonal study of Bible books. Individuals can engage in such Bible study at their own pace.[16]

8. *Study in new Sunday Schools.* Many churches offer Bible study on Sunday (using Sunday School study materials) in locations where there is no other organized Bible study. Some of these study groups are in areas where the possibilities for further growth (such as their becoming a church) are limited if not impossible. A nursing home is an example. In some instances, however, the location might be conducive to later development into a congregation. In these places, the Bible teaching and learning provide a suitable foundation on which to begin a new congregation.

Creative leaders in churches small or large will seek and find ways to involve as many persons as possible in Bible teaching and learning. The near future will offer even more options. Advances in cable television and communication by satellite have great potential. Almost the entire nation could be serviced with software (program materials) for religious education. Leaders must be aware of these and other options for Bible teaching and learning.

Curriculum for Bible Teaching and Learning

There is no doubt that the Bible should be the basic curriculum material in a church's educational ministry. There is no better text than the Bible. But the Bible is admittedly a very difficult book even for adults. There is an evident need for curriculum materials which support and improve Bible teaching and learning.

Occasionally a pastor might decide to lead a congregation to "just use the Bible" in Sunday School and in other Bible teaching and learning efforts. The pastor then usually supplies the teachers with Bible teaching outlines, interpretations, and other teaching suggestions so that they can "just use the Bible." Often these teachers fail to observe that they are in fact using materials in addition to the Bible—those materials supplied to them by the pastor. Further, such materials usually reflect the limitations of the gifts of only one person, the pastor, instead of reflecting the gifts of many persons who are dedicated to and skilled in providing materials of remarkably high quality. Generally a church would be well advised to select curriculum materials from a reliable publisher, and free their pastor (and others) from the responsibility of producing curriculum materials. Then the pastor can perform those important pastoral duties which inevitably would be neglected if his time is consumed in curriculum production.

In no instance should curriculum materials displace the Bible. Some curriculum planners doubt the wisdom of even printing the Bible study passages in the periodical study materials ("the quarterly") or other study guides, because of their concern that persons might neglect to use their own Bibles in their study. Others perceive the deletion of the printed Bible passages in study guides as an attempt to minimize the use of the Scriptures. This dilemma remains unsolved. In any event, it is the intent of those who publish curriculum materials to augment and improve Bible teaching and learning. Harry Piland stated this fact clearly.

Curriculum materials can never be considered a substitute for a study of the Bible. Bible study materials are prepared to provide for each age group a systematic plan of study to provide tools for learning for both teachers and pupils. They are designed to help persons understand, appreciate, and apply the Bible in their daily lives.[17]

Many denominations provide curriculum materials for the congregations in their constituency. Some provide multiple lines or series of materials, which makes it necessary for local congregation leaders to try to choose what is best for their constituents. Secure catalogs from the publisher or publishers from whom materials might be desired. It is almost always best for congregations to look very carefully first to see if they can use the materials supplied by their own denomination. Select the curriculum series that best meets the wants and needs of those who will use the materials. Usually it is best to use the same series for all within one age division. Plan to stay with one series long enough to achieve maximum value from it rather than switching back and forth from one series to another. This kind of consideration will assist the Sunday School council in giving appropriate leadership in selecting curriculum materials for Bible teaching and learning.

Conclusion

Teaching and learning the Bible is the first of the basic components of the educational ministry of a church. The Bible is foundational. There are some organizational designs which promise more success than others. The Sunday School offers tremendous opportunities for effective Bible teaching and learning if it is well organized and operated. Essential to an effective Sunday School is an understanding of its tasks. The curriculum is vitally important in Bible teaching and learning. The Bible is the text. Church leaders, such as the Sunday School council, should very carefully select other materials which will best meet the wants and needs of those who will use them.

Concerns for Further Study

Consider these questions as you continue to reflect upon the ministry of Bible teaching and learning.

1. What has been your observation/experience regarding the attractiveness of the Bible as a subject for study among (1) church members and (2) nonmembers?

2. What do you think about the concept of a church using its Sunday School to carry out the tasks suggested in this chapter? Consider each task in light of this question.

3. What do you think you might recommend to your own congregation growing out of your study of the suggestions in this chapter about (1) structures and (2) curriculum for Bible teaching and learning?

Notes

1. James D. Smart, *The Teaching Ministry of the Church* (Philadelphia: The Westminster Press, 1954), pp. 117-18.

2. Harry Piland, *Basic Sunday School Work* (Nashville: Convention Press, 1980), p. 155.

3. Herschel H. Hobbs, *The Baptist Faith and Message* (Nashville: Convention Press, 1971), p. 75.

4. Howard P. Colson and Raymond M. Rigdon, *Understanding Your Church's Curriculum,* revised edition (Nashville: Broadman Press, 1981), pp. 104 ff.

5. Ibid., pp. 110-12.

6. Reginald M. McDonough, compiler, *A Church on Mission* (Nashville: Convention Press, 1980), p. 46.

7. Ibid., p. 90.

8. Piland, pp. 29-30.

9. McDonough, p. 92.

10. Piland, p. 37.

11. See the "Possibilities for Church Organization" chart for total church organization possibilities for five sizes of membership in Bruce P. Powers, editor/compiler, *Christian Education Handbook* (Nashville: Broadman Press, 1981), pp. 130-31.

12. For detailed help regarding the weekly workers' meeting and the Sunday School council, see Piland and Powers.

13. Piland, p. 51.

14. For further information about Home Bible Study, contact Home Bible Study, Nashville, Tennessee 37234.

15. For further information about the plans of the Seminary External Education Division, contact this office at 460 James Robertson Parkway, Nashville, Tennessee 37219.

16. The Church Study Course will be discussed more fully in chapter 15.

17. Piland, p. 156.

7
Ministry of Discipleship Training

A church's ministry of discipleship training is a unique part of its overall educational ministry. It is unique in that it involves a specialized approach to education. It is also unique in that it might be the most neglected area of educational ministry in the churches.

Early Christians seem to have taken quite seriously the responsibility of leading and directing the growth of one another in what it means to follow Jesus, to live his way in relation to the Father and to others, and to join with him and with others in the redemptive enterprise. Perhaps as the churches and the Roman Empire sank into the Dark Ages, this focus on specialized instruction also lessened, except in isolated instances.

The leaders of the Reformation strongly advocated and practiced discipleship training, and the outcome of their emphasis upon training is evident in the unprecedented and hitherto unmatched surge in vital Christianity. Unfortunately, much of this vigor seems to have waned among churches in recent decades. There are indicators in the eighties that another reformation surge of concern among Christians for effective discipleship training is emerging. A church which continues to neglect its needs for discipleship training limits its present vitality as a part of the body of Christ and threatens its very existence in the future. Conversely, a church which develops and continues faithfully a ministry of discipleship training enlivens and enriches its present fellowship and helps to assure its own extension into the future.

Training New Church Members, Church Members, and Church Leaders

A person becomes a member of a church upon that church's acceptance of the person's affirmation that he has received Christ for forgiveness of sin and for salvation. This profession of faith is often spoken of as being born again, using the language Christ used in conversation with Nicodemus. The newly born Christian then is baptized into the fellowship of a church. He is a new member. He is also a "babe in Christ." Most churches also have ways of receiving new members who already are Christians.

A church's training ministry should provide immediate care and follow-up for new Christians, and, for different reasons, for other new church members who come from other churches. New Christians need to understand their conversion experience and their commitment to Christ. They need help in using the Bible as their guide and the source of authority for their new lives. They need to begin a personal plan of growth in what it means to be a disciple of Jesus Christ, including daily disciplines of study, devotion, and prayer. They need encouragement and guidance in sharing with others their relationship to Christ. At this time, they probably know more non-Christian people than they will ever know well for the rest of their lives. They need to be received with warmth and care into their new family, the church. In the case of young converts, their parents also need guidance in understanding the experience of children and in nurturing their development.

New Christians need to know more about the meaning of church membership. They need to know that their change in commitment should be reflected in changes in the way they live. They need to develop an appreciation for the fact that being in the family of God is different from being a part of the world at large. They need to learn of their own church, its covenant, its beliefs, its history, its governance, its ministries, its organizations, and its leaders. They need to be prepared educationally to become involved (at the level of their readiness) in the church's life and work. They need guidance in discovering and developing their gifts, and in finding ways to exercise them for their good, for the good of the church, and for others.

New members who have joined after having been members of another congregation need an opportunity to affirm among their new church family their own commitment to Christ and to his church. They might need some of the same instruction as that needed by new Christians, depending upon how they have progressed in their growth as disciples. They at least need and deserve information about their new church which will help them to be assimilated effectively into its life and work.

Church membership either means something or it doesn't mean anything. Too often when one joins a church it seems to mean very little. Weldon Crossland, a great writer in Methodism, was painfully accurate when he observed that it is easier to join a church than it is to get on a bus. And he made this statement prior to the time one had to have correct change in order to get on a bus!

The education given at the entrance point to church membership could help raise the quality of the meaning of church membership. On mission fields there is often a waiting period following one's profession of faith so that the convert might be instructed and prepared for church membership. The rationale for this is that persons are often crossing such great cultural and social barriers to become Christians that time is needed for them to be instructed and prepared for participation as members of the church. Otherwise, they might actually become a detriment to themselves and to the church by defaulting upon their commitment and reflecting negatively upon the Christian faith. In what culture of this world is this *not* true? Surely, there can be no rational acceptance of the idea that there is such a thing as a Christian country in which such care would not be necessary. Remember, too, that in early Christianity the converts were trained for periods which ranged from one year to three years before they were even permitted into the full service of worship. We do not advocate such rigidity; but surely a few weeks of careful help and guidance in the areas we have mentioned would be warranted for the new Christian or new member by transfer, and for the eventual good of a church. A church should determine what its expectations are in terms of what it will offer to new members and what new members are to do to satisfy the church's expectations.

Church members who are not new members need training in discipleship on a continuing basis. They need guidance through training in continuing to grow in their own spiritual development. They need to continue to grow in personal skills essential to following Christ, living Christ's way in relation to the Father and to others, and sharing in the redemptive enterprise. They need to develop in their abilities to perform personal ministries to others.

Church members need to develop and to continue developing their personal understandings of theology. They need to know and to appreciate the great teachings of the faith, the doctrines as understood by their denomination. They need to continue to study what the Scriptures teach about what is right and wrong in the issues and circumstances of life today—Christian ethics. They need to know of the great ways, and those not so great, in which the people of God have come to the present—Christian history. They need to learn and to continue to examine their own church's polity—its theory and form of government—and their church's organization. A church member never outgrows the need to continue to train and grow as a disciple. This is a lifelong need for every individual. A church must help its members meet their needs.

A church should offer training for its members who are leaders. Leaders need help at times in discovering their gifts for leadership. They need the added knowledge that will enrich their leadership potential. They need specific skills which will make them as effective as they can become.

The leaders must continue to lead the way by their own growth as disciples and effective servants of the church lest those they lead either overtake them or stumble and fall on the nongrowth of their leaders. Leaders must lead, and usually from in front of followers. A church should provide continually the kinds of leader training which will assure that its leaders have ample opportunity to grow and develop as disciples and as leaders of other disciples.

Structures for Discipleship Training

It is helpful in a church to have an organization whose assignment is to lead in implementing a church's training tasks. Some churches are not large enough to sustain a separate organization for training in discipleship. In such churches the approach might be to designate one person, or a small committee of persons, to do what they can to advance the church's training activities. In any event, there are certain tasks which a church must find ways to fulfill.

The *first task* of a church's ministry of discipleship training is: *Equip church members for discipleship and personal ministry.* The focus of this task is on new church members, church members who are no longer new members, and church leaders. All three groups should have opportunities to grow and to participate effectively in the functions of a church: worship, proclaim and witness, minister, and nurture and educate.

The *second task* is: *Teach Christian theology, denominational doctrine, Christian ethics, Christian history, and church polity and organization.* These are essential content areas which, if not systematically taught in a ministry of discipleship training, might not be taught at all in any other educational organization. Other educational ministry organizations in a church have unique ways of basing their programs upon the Bible and other content areas, but none systematically addresses the subjects of this task of training. Hence, it is imperative that these subjects be part of the ministry of discipleship training. They are areas of vital importance to all church members.

The *third task* of a ministry of discipleship training is: *Equip church leaders for service.* It is our belief that a church has available to it the leaders and other resources needed to accomplish whatever God wants the church to accomplish. The church must take some initiative to identify its needs for leaders, help members to discover their gifts for leadership, and provide the necessary kinds of training for leadership.

This task suggests that potential leaders must be equipped for possible leadership before they are enlisted to serve in specific places of responsibility in a church's ministries. Such training should be offered not only to adults, but to older youth also. Youth need not forfeit their participation in their own peer group experiences in order to begin to contribute as leaders in a church's ministries. They can and should have opportunities to assist in leading in special projects, church committee assignments, and other activities where their gifts are not only useful but needed both for the sake of the church at large and for the sake of the ones who render the service. This is not to suggest that adults should fail to perform their leadership responsibilities in order to allow youth to have opportunities to lead. Nor is it to suggest a "youth takeover" of a church. It is to suggest that youth who are part of the membership need opportunities, in keeping with their individual readiness, to grow while leading, and to feel that they are members in fact and not just in theory. A church can benefit greatly by their leadership contributions. Further, it appears that having opportunities for genuine service during the youth age span is a significant factor for many youths in hearing God's call to commit themselves to vocational ministry.

Basic job training which enables a person to serve well in a specific leadership role is an essential part of this task of equipping church leaders for service. A church's training organization or, in a small church, the individual training leader or committee should work with other organizations in a church to plan and conduct training opportunities which will fit persons to serve effectively in positions for which they have been enlisted.

There is also the area of general leadership training which needs to be part of a church's training ministry. This is the training in leadership beyond that which is specifically required for a particular job but which enhances and improves a person's leadership skills. This often neglected area of training is essential if a church is to continue to mature beyond its own adolescence and become the church it has the potential to become.

The *fourth task* of a church's ministry of discipleship training is the task which is shared by all other program organizations in a church: *Interpret and undergird the work of the church and the denomination.* The same suggestions which we made in the previous chapter about this task apply to the training organization. But in view of the *second task* of the training organization (which calls for the teaching of denominational doctrine, church polity, and organization) the training organization has unique opportunity to relate to this interpreting and undergirding task. Its curriculum should carry appropriate helps to educate and to lead church members in their understanding of and support for their church and denomination.

Use the Church Training Organization

Probably the most likely way for most churches to conduct their ministry of discipleship training is to establish and maintain on a continuing basis a Church Training organization. This would seem best even for the very small church which might have only one person or a small committee who could lead the training tasks. The principal activities of this organization could be conducted in connection with the Sunday evening worship service, either before or after the service. Most churches do far better by having the training prior to the evening worship service. This time can be protected from other conflicts, and having members present for training can contribute significantly to attendance in the worship service.

1. ***Establish the Church Training organization.*** A church whose members are informed and convinced of the values of a ministry of discipleship training will more likely respond to efforts to establish such a ministry. This becomes the *first step* in establishing a Church Training organization. Through sermons, testimonies, special Sunday School lessons, articles, bulletin and newsletter inserts, invitational meetings with the pastor and prospective leaders and participants to discuss the idea, and other means, the members must be informed and convinced that they need a church training organization. If this step is successful, then the church leaders should proceed with the other suggestions. If, after a reasonable time of informing and convincing church members, there is a definite sense that they will not at least give the idea a good experimental try, it would be wise to wait and try again at a later time.

A *second step* is to request the church officially to endorse the forming of a Church Training organization, to establish the principal time for its operation, and to assert that that time is to be protected from conflict with all other interests and groups in the church's life. This is an indispensable part of the church's decision to form the organization. Even the Sunday School, which is usually given the prime time on a church's calendar—Sunday morning—would not do as well if it had to compete with church committee meetings, church council meetings, lack of church staff presence, meetings of music groups, mission education groups, or others. Such conflicts draw persons out of possible participation in the Church Training program, and indicate that the church is not quite serious about the importance of its ministry of discipleship training. Many Church Training programs have been weakened greatly, and in some cases eliminated, by the failure of the church to give it almost absolute priority during its allotted time. Exceptions to this exclusive priority for Church Training time must be genuine exceptions and should be allowed only rarely. The same support should be given to any other church organization which is conducting an all-age ministry at a regularly stated time in the church's calendar.

The *third step* is to select and enlist a Church Training director. In a very small church this person might be the only one leading in the

Church Training program. This leader would do all one person could do to encourage individuals to use training materials for their growth and development. The director assists the pastor in scheduling and promoting the discipleship training for new church members. The director might personally lead an ongoing group of adults or youth and adults. The director might also supervise individual training plans for church leaders, placing training materials in their hands and following through with individual encouragement. The director could also promote training emphases to be included in Sunday School class monthly business meetings and in similar meetings of other groups.

In larger churches the Church Training director works with the pastor and others to lead the organization in carrying out its tasks.

The *fourth step* is to identify the needs for training and discipling in the church. The pastor, other ministers, the Church Training director, and other leaders such as the Church Training council and the church council can use various means to identify individual and corporate needs for training. Surveys and individual conferences are helpful in identifying the needs.

The frequency of the addition of new church members will suggest the needs for their discipleship training. Each one should have individual attention immediately after coming into the fellowship. Continuing training of new members in an ongoing group might be needed in churches with frequent additions of new members. The sessions can be designed so that new members can enter and complete the cycle of sessions at any point, and then move into ongoing training groups for regular membership training. In churches with few additions, the group training of new members should be conducted as needed.

The *fifth step* is to decide on the most practical ways to organize to meet the needs and interests which have been identified. There are many alternatives. A very small church might have only a Church Training director as described earlier. Larger churches will have more elaborate organizations to meet their training needs.

The Sunday School roll serves as a source of prospects for enrollment in Church Training. If there are two groups in Sunday School for a given age, there might be one in Church Training, with the enlistment efforts focused on those on the Sunday School roll. Provision should be made for short-term training groups. These are usually undated units of study which supplement ongoing training, and are designed to meet special interests or needs. In a large organization, the ongoing groups would likely keep right on with their dated curriculum materials, while certain ones participate in short-term training groups. In small churches the short-term training probably would substitute for the ongoing training for a time. Members then go back to the regular ongoing training once the undated studies are completed.

The *sixth step* is to select and secure training materials and record-keeping materials. Denominational publishers' catalogs should supply the information needed to accomplish this important step.[1] Be specific in ordering the items chosen, and allow sufficient time for materials to arrive and for those who will lead in their use to become familiar with the study materials.

The *seventh step* in establishing a Church Training organization is to enlist and train leaders. The Church Training director, with guidance from the pastor and any other ministers related to the program, should work with the church's normal procedures for enlisting the leaders needed. Many churches use a church nominating committee to match persons with the leadership needs, and to approve the enlistment of certain potential leaders. After approval by the church's nominating committee, such enlistment is best done by the person who would be closest to the potential leader in the organization, the one who would lead that leader in the work. This simple procedure sequence avoids the confusion of having a person contacted for enlistment as a leader by two or more persons. This creates confusion and often does not achieve the desired matching of individual gifts with church leadership needs. Many churches then formally elect these leaders to their "office," and some even have an appropriate installation service which includes a charge to the leaders regarding their responsibilities.

It is indispensable that the new leaders begin or continue their training for leadership. At the start, an orientation workshop might be all there is time for. If so, do it well. Then follow up with continuing education and training for the leaders, frequently consulting with them about their progress and needs for more training. On-the-job training should continue for as long as one serves as a leader.

The *eighth step* is to launch the new organization well. Publicize it through every good channel. Secure individual commitments to participate. Use the other church organizations to interpret and to support the promotion, even as the Church Training organization stands ready to assist other program organizations in their similar needs.

It is important to time the beginning of a new organization well. Usually a church organization is begun best with the beginning of a new church year. Another good time is at the mid-year point. If the program is to be only seasonal, then any season can be suitable to begin. Also, it is important to get enough time at the right time of day for an effective Church Training program. A full hour could be well used, and probably should be set prior to the evening worship service. No other regular activities should conflict or take away from this vital ministry.

2. *Maintain the Church Training organization.* Once begun, a Church Training organization requires regular and routine maintenance to assure its continued effectiveness. This maintenance includes complete records information to inform the leaders of the progress of the organization and its members and groups. Regular meetings with the other leaders as a group are necessary to check on needs and progress, and to plan together to meet the needs. This is the work of the Church Training council. Further, leaders in a "supervisory" position should regularly confer with individual leaders and members to see that the work of the organization goes as it should. In all instances, the pastor and any other ministers related to the program need to be informed of the status and the needs of the organization. Church members should have regular reports in sufficient detail to keep them aware of the organization, its needs, and its plans.

Leadership vacancies should be filled promptly so that training groups might continue without serious delays. This need makes it all the more important for the leader training segment of Church Training to function effectively, and for supervising leaders to keep closely in touch with all leaders in order to anticipate needs for replacement or for expansion of organization which will require additional leaders.

Once a church has a well-operating, ongoing Church Training organization, great care should be taken regarding how short-term or other special training projects are correlated with the ongoing program. If such training opportunities are to be supplementary to the ongoing program, take the steps necessary to avoid displacing the ongoing training. For example, if a church has several groups of adults in ongoing Church Training with the use of dated units of study, consider offering only one group of a short-term or special-project nature to compete with the ongoing groups. Even then, care should be taken to assure that no ongoing group is permanently weakened. This can be done by limiting the number who enroll from any ongoing group, and offering to schedule the short-term or other special-training project later when others might participate. Persons completing these temporary sessions return to their regular ongoing groups, unless they become leaders.

If the need and interest in the short-term or special project warrant it, another procedure is to adjourn the ongoing group or groups *for a definitely specified time,* with firm plans for returning to the regular format. Let these plans be well known before interrupting the ongoing groups. Care must be exercised by not making a frequent practice of this formal adjournment procedure, lest the ongoing Church Training suffer irreparable damage. Good, regular educational groups are more easily weakened than they are strengthened or restarted. Eventually, all types of training suffer from the effects of continually starting over, and the accompanying confusion and uncertainty about what is to be offered.

Train Through Special Projects

There is a place in a church's ministry of discipleship training for special training projects. They should be chosen to meet special needs and interests, and carefully correlated with the church's ongoing training. As a matter of fact, the training program in a very small church might take on the appearance of being altogether made up of special projects. If that is what can be done, that is what should be done. In many churches, however, the special projects are chosen to be offered for a specified time only, and often for just certain persons.

1. *Seasonal training for new church members.* In a church which does not have a continuing training plan for new church members, such a group or groups (or even the training of individuals, if there are not enough to form groups) might be treated as special training projects. If possible, there should be a group for

each age division. This allows the training to be conducted in keeping with the human growth and development needs of the new members. True, they are all "babes in Christ" if they are all recent converts, but the learning readiness varies widely between children, youth, and adults. Such training groups usually include those who join the church by transfer of membership from another church, though some special provision might be made for them if it is useful to do so.

2. *Church leader training for special groups.* There are numerous special groups in a church which need training for their leaders. Much of this training can be provided by the leaders in a church who specialize in setting up and conducting training events. For example, an annual training event for church committees is a good way to launch the new church year's work that is done through committees of a church. A short series of training sessions can be scheduled for those who serve in this way. Other special needs, such as training ushers, media personnel, and persons to witness and to lead others to witness can be met through leader training sessions. These training projects are in addition to the other leader training which a church might conduct.

3. *Special training projects for all ages.* From time to time, such as once or twice a year, a church can enrich the training for its members by offering special training opportunities for all ages. For example, the subject areas of doctrine, ethics, or other Church Training areas can be good training subjects for an emphasis in which provisions are made for all age groups. The format might be to begin the study on Sunday and to continue through Wednesday, meeting each evening for training. Other schedules might suit some churches better. Insofar as is possible, such studies should be in addition to the regular training offered to members, rather than being in lieu of their regular studies. Great doctrines like the doctrines of God, the church, salvation, missions, and others could greatly support discipleship growth among members.

Curriculum for Discipleship Training

It may surprise some to know that the basic text for discipleship training in a church is the Bible. The use of the Bible in Sunday School is largely for exegetical studies. In discipleship training the studies are more topical, or more skill oriented, with the Bible related often as supporting and elaborating data. Often in skills training, the skills themselves require apt use of the Bible. In all cases, what is being taught in discipleship training must be compatible with biblical truth. The place of the Bible in discipleship training must not be overlooked.

Church leaders, especially those who make up the leadership of the Church Training council, should lead in choosing the curriculum materials for this ministry. The "Curriculum Selection Checklist" could help in evaluating and selecting curriculum materials for discipleship training. Catalogs of denominational publishers should be among the first resources to examine. There are numerous dated and undated materials from which to choose. Generally, dated materials should form the base of materials a church uses. Undated materials are used to supplement and to enrich the program.

Professional quality curriculum materials for discipleship training of all kinds are usually far to be preferred to any other kind. Members participating in the training groups need materials of their own which involve them in study and preparation for the sessions and for participation in the learning activities. Otherwise, the leader of the training becomes the only resource of the learning experience, and, even at best, this limits the possibilities for most effective learning. Use of quality curriculum materials helps to assure that the training will come much nearer realizing its potential.

Conclusion

Discipleship training is an indispensable ministry in a church. To make it optional is to neglect the training of new Christians, other new church members, church members, and church leaders. A church cannot have a vital present nor an assured future without it. The bare survival of many churches is testimony to the need for effective discipleship training.

With carefully correlated ongoing church member training, new church member training, and church leader training, a church can have an effective ministry of discipleship training which will enrich its present life and work and help to assure its future. As someone has said, "Christian conversion is the end of the Christian experience— the *front* end." New members must be nurtured. Church members must continue to grow in orderly development. Church leaders must learn to serve more effectively. This is the challenge of the ministry of discipleship training.

Concerns for Further Study

Consider these questions as you continue to reflect upon the ministry of discipleship training.

1. To what extent do you share the author's view that the area of discipleship training as described in this chapter is probably the most neglected area of educational ministry in the history of churches?

2. What difference do you think it might make in your church if you had an effective ministry to train (1) new church members, (2) church members, and (3) church leaders?

3. What do you see as some advantages of using professional quality curriculum materials in a church's training program?

Note

1. For churches cooperating with the Southern Baptist Convention, the Church Training Department of the Baptist Sunday School Board will provide limited quantities of *free* materials for a church which is beginning an organized Church Training program. This offer is available for a given church only once, and includes curriculum and administrative materials chosen by the church. The address for information about these materials is 127 Ninth Avenue, North, Nashville, Tennessee 37234.

8
Ministry of Missions Education and Action

A church is a fellowship of Christians on mission. Its mission is to make known the manifold wisdom of God—the gospel of forgiveness, grace, and salvation through Jesus Christ, the Lord and Savior. What a church does to express genuine Christian love for those persons outside its membership, those who are not presently enrolled in its programs or in its fellowship, is the external mission of a church.

Mission means "a sending forth." It implies that there is a commission for which those who are sent forth are responsible. The Great Commission is to be obeyed:

> And Jesus came and said to them, "All authority in heaven and on earth has been given to me. Go therefore and make disciples of all nations, baptizing them in the name of the Father and of the Son and of the Holy Spirit, teaching them to observe all that I have commanded you; and lo, I am with you always, to the close of the age" (Matt. 28:18-20).

This compelling command of Christ is for a church not only with regard to itself, but to all who have not yet received him.

> Missions is what the church does in keeping with the Great Commission of its sovereign Lord to extend the witness and ministry beyond itself (its community of faith) to bring all persons to Christ and thereby glorify God.[1]

A church is to send forth those who will go both near and far to do the work of fulfilling the commission. There is a correlation between knowing and going. There is a correlation between missions education and mission action. A person is not likely to be willing to do missions about which nothing is known. From a rational viewpoint, this justifies a church's ministry of missions education. Out of missions education comes mission action.

It is redundant to speak of a missionary church. By nature, a church that is a church is missionary. Being missionary is inherent in being a bona fide church. While some churches are more active than others in missions, a church is not fully a church that is not obedient to the command of the Lord of the church in this area. It is imperative that a church manifest life in missionary terms. It is also imperative that a church do all it can to advance the knowledge and understanding of its members regarding missions. This emphasis on missionary education is a major strategy for leading members to become involved in missions.

Of major concern to many Christians is the relatively small number of church members who are regularly involved in missions education. We should rejoice that many are engaged in Bible teaching and learning, for example, but wish to see comparable numbers engaged in the study and the practice of missions. Fortunately, one cannot be engaged in Bible teaching and learning without being exposed to the missionary message of the Bible. The need for a sharper focus upon the missions aspects of biblical truth is obvious. Church leaders would do well to reflect upon their personal needs for a stronger participation in missions education and action.

Structures for Missions Education and Action

In numerous denominations the work of promoting and support-ing missions (both direct missions and representative missions) has been led by the mission-minded women of the church. They have led in missions education. They have done a disproportionate share of mission action. They deserve the deep respect and gratitude of all. In some denominations men have joined the women in this effort. The most common expression of organized effort in many churches today is in the form of separate organizations for women and for men. Regardless of who does the work, it is a church's responsibility to advance the cause of missions.

A church should provide ample opportunities for those who are informed and concerned for missions to work together in coopera-tive ways to get the job done. Perhaps in some churches this would mean a single, churchwide organization. In others this might not be advisable. It would seem wise first to attempt to work together even from different organizational bases, and then, if the occasion warrants, merge into a single structure. Pursue that path very carefully.

For our purposes of presenting a model of missions education and action, we shall describe a women's organization and a men's organization— Woman's Missionary Union and Brotherhood, both of which are recommended for churches cooperating with the Southern Baptist Convention. Their tasks are very similar. Their approaches to their work are similar. Often they work together from their separate organizational bases.

Woman's Missionary Union

Woman's Missionary Union is an organization for women, girls, and preschool boys and girls. Its stated purposes are to promote and support missions, to help the church fulfill its mission, and to lead in missions education. This church organization does its work through four tasks.

The *first task* of Woman's Missionary Union (abbreviated stylistically as WMU) is: *Teach missions.* The authors of *A Church on Mission* wrote:

> The in-depth study of missions helps a church achieve its reason for being, encourages church members to understand their world responsibility, cultivates concern, and motivates the investment of life and resources in missions.[2]

The content for this teaching task includes four dimensions. The first content area is a study of the biblical basis of Christian missions. The organization is committed to the concept that the study of the missionary message of the Bible forms the basis for any understanding of missions. The second area is a study of the progress of Christian missions. This study of missions history shows how churches have progressed in carrying out the Great Commission, leading them to understand better the plans and methods of contemporary missions. The third area— the study of contemporary missions— receives by far the most attention. A study of missions in the present tense enables persons to respond and to relate personally to missions. The fourth content area is that of the spiritual development of the learner, especially as it relates to missions. "It includes prayer guides, helps for personal meditation, stewardship, personal witnessing, mission action, career mission service, non-career mission service, and the role of women in missions."[3]

In addition to teaching missions in a variety of groups within the organization, WMU joins with Brotherhood in certain joint study projects. They promote special mission study projects for the whole church, or for one age group in the church.

The *second task* of WMU is: *Engage in mission action and personal witnessing.* Mission action is ministering and witnessing to persons of special need or circumstance who are not members of the church or its programs; and it is also combating social and moral problems. This task illustrates the integral relationship between effective teaching and resultant action.

Some of the persons of special need or circumstance to whom a church, led by WMU, ministers are: prisoners, military personnel, alcoholics, drug abusers, poor, unchurched groups, language groups, internationals, migrants, travelers and tourists, nonreaders, aging, unwed parents, juvenile delinquents, the sick, nonevangelicals, and minority groups.

Some of the target issues of a social or moral nature to which mission action might be addressed include family problems, gambling, pornography, obscenity, alcoholism, drug abuse, racial problems, and economic and political problems.

The personal witnessing aspect of this second task focuses on persons often overlooked by the church. Christians are taught and led to share the gospel with others, and to encourage them to confess Jesus Christ as Savior and Lord.

The *third task* of WMU is: *Support missions.* Support for missions is fostered by regular prayer for missions and for missionaries. Prayer is coupled with educational programs to provide an information base for more specific praying. Prayer is seasonally joined with the promotion of special offerings for missions. These annual special offerings for missions (the Lottie Moon Christmas Offering for Foreign Missions and the Annie Armstrong Easter Offering for Home Missions), each accompanied by a week of study and prayer, provide approximately one half of the total financial support for these denominational mission programs. Regular giving to missions through the church's budget is also advocated by the missions organizations, as they encourage tithing and support of the Cooperative Program (the denomination's unified financial support system). Again, approximately one half of the Cooperative Program funds are earmarked for missions.

A vital feature of this third task of supporting missions is an emphasis on persons becoming involved personally in career and noncareer mission service. There is a vast and growing response to this emphasis among church members. Members are also encouraged and led to provide personal ministries for missionaries and their families. Letters, calls, caring for children and parents, providing transportation and housing, and other ministries as needed are illustrative of this important part of task three.

The *fourth task* of WMU is the same as for all other program organizations in a church: *Interpret and undergird the work of the church and denomination.*

Age-graded missions groups for women, girls, and preschool boys and girls is the structured approach for Woman's Missionary Union. Recommended groupings are: Baptist Women, a unit for women ages thirty and up; Baptist Young Women, eighteen to twenty-nine years; Acteens for girls ages twelve to seventeen (or school grades seven to twelve); Girls in Action for girls ages six to eleven (or school grades one through six); and Mission Friends for boys and girls from birth to five years (or to school entrance).

A *very small church* can have an effective program of mission education and action. Many small churches excel in this regard. In all size churches, the mission organizations advocate a close working relationship with the pastor and with any other staff ministers a church might have. Figure 4 shows two ways the organization might look in a very small church.[4] A larger church might have a WMU organization like that in Figure 5.[5] The organization in a very large church could be quite complex.[6]

In addition to working through its own structures, Woman's Missionary Union makes special efforts to relate appropriately to the educational plans for all other program organizations in a church: Sunday School, Church Training, Brotherhood, Music Ministry, and Pastoral Ministries. It is important for all church organizations to work together to help a church fulfill its mission and perform its functions. The tasks of all church organizations must be programmed in relationship.

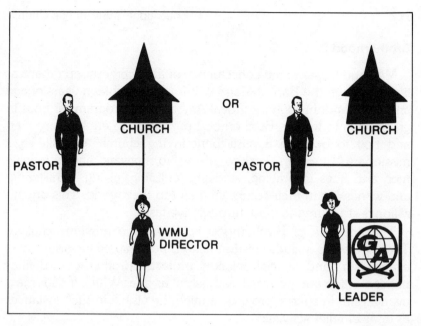

Figure 4

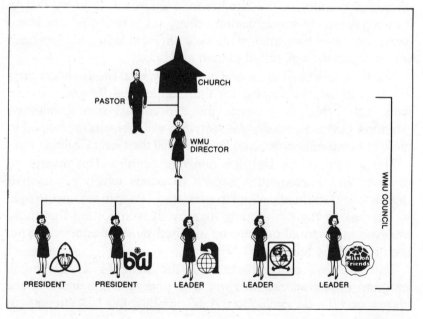

Figure 5

Brotherhood

Men and boys are the constituency of the Brotherhood organization. Through the Baptist Men's unit for men eighteen years of age and older and through the Royal Ambassador program for boys in grades one to twelve, Brotherhood purposes "to equip every man and boy to become a participant in the church as a life-style missionary."[7] Leaders work to inform, to motivate, and to involve men and boys in praying, studying, enlisting, giving, ministering, and witnessing in their community and to their world. This organization is structured to work through five tasks.

The *first task* of Brotherhood is: *Engage in mission activities.* These activities include mission action, personal evangelism, mass evangelism, and special mission projects. Brotherhood defines mission action and personal evangelism as does WMU. It adds mass evangelism. In special projects, it might be visible in such instances as disaster relief activities.

The *second task* of Brotherhood is: *Teach missions.* The content areas are the missionary message of the Bible, the progress of Christian missions, and contemporary missions. A somewhat unique dimension of the Brotherhood approach is to try *first* to involve persons in some mission activity (as in task one) and *then,* having activated their interest, move them into study. This approach seems especially well suited to men and boys.

The *third task* is: *Pray for and give to missions.* Brotherhood gives major emphasis to support for the Cooperative Program. It also joins with WMU to promote the two annual special missions offerings. Giving to missions is seen as a way persons are helped to grow in being missionary and help to fulfill the Great Commission.

The *fourth task* is: *Develop personal ministry.* This means "to discover and implement a service to others which a person is uniquely and spiritually gifted to perform."[8] Pastors are encouraged in this task in their equipping ministry. It is important that those involved in personal ministry be affirmed by the pastor and other members of the fellowship.

The *fifth task* of Brotherhood is the same as for all church program organizations: *Interpret and undergird the work of the church and the denomination.* Accomplishing this task strengthens not only Brotherhood work but also that of the church and the various agencies of the denomination.

Figure 6 indicates the suggested leadership structure of a well-organized Brotherhood. Significant work can be done with a smaller organization pattern scaled down from this chart. For example, a Brotherhood might function for a time with only a Royal Ambassador section. In this instance, the Brotherhood director would serve as the Royal Ambassador director and personally lead the work with the boys.

Other Mission Education and Action

The association of education and action in missions is intentional. Missions education manifests itself in mission action and in other forms of mission support. Two of these we mention here.

1. *Establishing new churches* is usually best accomplished through the church missions committee. This committee has five to seven members, including leaders from the mission organizations of the church and the Sunday School. This committee has an educational and action assignment which includes (1) orienting the church missions committee; (2) selecting the area of need; (3) preparing the church; (4) cultivating the mission field; (5) starting a home fellowship mission; (6) organizing a mission chapel; (7) financing the venture; (8) planning a building; and (9) constituting the church.[9]

2. *Developing missions support through Christian steward-ship*—especially with regard to the areas of earning, spending, giving, and the final distribution of possessions—is of vital importance in missions education and action. While all church organizations should assist in communicating stewardship concepts and information, a church stewardship committee should lead this work. This committee of five to seven members should work year round to help develop Christian stewards and to support the ministries cooperatively undertaken by their church with other churches. For Southern Baptists this translates to support for the Cooperative Program.

Mission action is supported by human resources and financial resources. Education in missions depends upon education and development of human resources and financial resources in order to

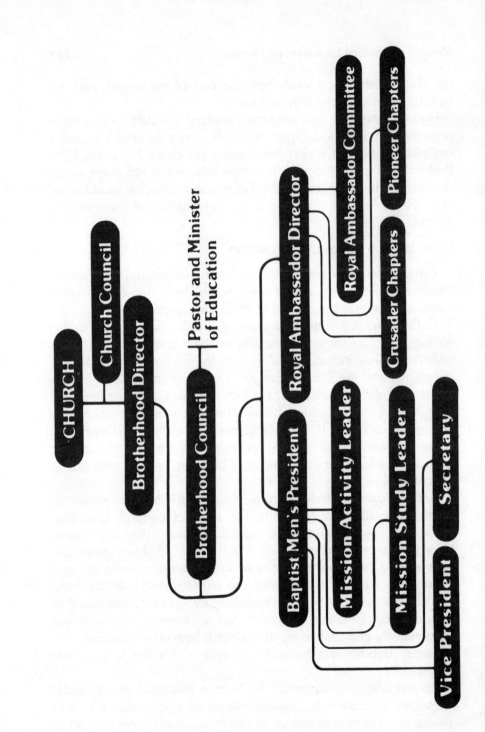

Figure 6

move into mission action directly on the home front, and through representative missions—others going where all cannot go—in other lands around the world.

Curriculum for Missions Education

Several basic curriculum areas are the focus of missions education. The beginning point is a continuing study of the missionary message of the Bible. As with all church organizations, the biblical basis is the foundation for the educational ministry in a church.

The history of Christian missions is the next major area for teaching and learning in missions. The point is not to stop with the past, however, but to set the stage for better understanding and participation in contemporary missions. Issues, conditions, obstacles, strategies, needs, and trends in contemporary missions are among the areas examined.

The spiritual development of the learner is an area of concern for the missions education ministry. Of particular importance with regard to missions are things like guidance in one's prayer life, personal meditation, stewardship, personal witnessing, mission action, career mission service, noncareer mission service, and the role of individuals in missions. Education and activity in personally ministering to persons in need are also part of the educational concern.

In missions, as perhaps in few other areas, it is important in the curriculum experiences to see the connections between education and action. Whichever comes to an individual first, education or action, each stimulates interest in the other, if the experience is authentic. Genuine education in missions results in a desire to help make some needed things happen. Getting involved in helping make some needed things happen stimulates interest in knowing more about the situation. Education is change. Involvement in mission education and in mission action changes persons. This is a powerful combination of forces in the lives of persons.

Guided curriculum experiences, whether the beginning point is in a study group or on some mission action occasion, are significant in the ministry of a church. The leadership councils of a church's missions organizations should give careful attention to study plans and resources, as well as to mission action experiences. In the model structures in this chapter, these groups would be the WMU council and the Brotherhood council. In cooperative undertakings between these organizations, their councils jointly should plan and select curriculum materials and experiences.

The denominational sources should be the first place the leaders look for help. Leaders should contact the appropriate sources within their own denomination to secure catalogs and sample materials to consider in their planning. The "Curriculum Selection Checklist" in chapter 16 of this book could be useful in choosing the resources which are best.

Conclusion

It is the mission of a fellowship of Christians who form a church to make known the manifold wisdom of God, near and far. This must be done within a church for those who are part of a church and its families. It also must be done beyond the "walls" of a church, for those who are not presently enrolled in a church's programs or fellowship. This latter area is usually understood as missions. A church needs a ministry of education and action in the area of missions. It is an expression of the bona fide nature of a church to involve itself in missions education and action.

In missions there are strong ties between study and action, when either is authentic. Missions uniquely infers doing something about concerns of which one knows. A church comes very near fulfilling its mission as a church when it conducts an effective ministry of missions education and action.

Concerns for Further Study

Consider these questions as you continue to reflect upon the ministry of missions education and action.

1. What is your response to the statement that "by nature a church that is a church is missionary"?

2. In view of the relatively small number of persons involved in regular missions education and action in many churches, what do

you think a church might do to involve more of its members in these vital activities?

3. What are some ways in which missions education and action might appropriately be included in the activities of other church program organizations?

Notes

1. Bobbie Sorrill, *WMU—A Church Missions Organization* (Birmingham: Woman's Missionary Union, 1981), p. 15.

2. Reginald M. McDonough, compiler, *A Church on Mission* (Nashville: Convention Press, 1980), pp. 115-16.

3. Sorrill, p. 42.

4. Ibid., p. 91.

5. Ibid., p. 92.

6. See ibid., p. 94 for a suggested pattern.

7. McDonough, p. 119.

8. Ibid., p. 122.

9. Ibid., pp. 123-27.

9
Ministry of Music

Music is an integral part of making known the manifold wisdom of God. Just as one may speak or listen to another speak, so may one sing or listen to another sing the good news. And one may listen to musical instruments as they express the devotion, skill, and commitment of the performer (the doer of music, not just a presenter of a show of music) and as they aid the listener to have experiences pleasing to God. Music is a medium with a message. Christian music is a medium of Christian messages.

The people of a church need a ministry of music. Those outside a church whom a church seeks to reach need a ministry of music. All need the messages communicated by appropriate Christian music. There is an eloquence in the use of good music which, when presented to God and to one another with the right spirit and attitude, transcends barriers of communication and understanding which might not be overcome by other mediums.

God would have his children make use of music. Paul wrote the church at Corinth, "I will sing with the spirit and I will sing with the mind also" (1 Cor. 14:15b). "The mind" is also translated "the understanding." This suggests "that the singing should be Spirit-filled and that the singing should be understood by the singer. . . . If there is no understanding, the singing has no meaning."[1] All who hear need to be able to understand. Again, Paul wrote,

> Let the word of Christ dwell in you richly, teach and admonish one another in all wisdom, and sing psalms and hymns and spiritual songs with thankfulness in your hearts to God. And whatever you do, in word or deed, do everything in the name of the Lord Jesus, giving thanks to God the Father through him (Col. 3:16-17).

The authors of A Church on Mission suggested that this passage outlines the direction, dimension, declaration, and desirability of a church's music ministry.[2]

The ministry of music in a church has many possible facets. First and of foremost importance to many is the *congregational* music. Music of adoration, praise, prayer, proclamation, invitation, confession, forgiveness, faith, love, hope, victory, joy, thanksgiving, commitment, and other offerings and responses are significant in the life of a congregation. *Music performance groups,* such as choirs and instrumental groups, can be meaningful both to the participants who perform and to those who hear and see them. *Music activity groups,* like preschool choirs and others whose primary purpose is the experience they might have with music (as over against performing), have their place. *Music study groups,* working together to learn musical skills, history, appreciation, and other music interests, contribute. *Individual musicians* — vocalists, music directors, pianists, organists, other instrumentalists — can render vital services while they themselves grow and develop. *Music in other church organizations* led by trained musicians and that which is employed as an educational method by persons who are not necessarily musicians in a highly technical sense are areas of potential value hitherto only slightly realized. Churches have only begun to utilize the vitality and strength of good church music, and to use it boldly and skillfully in the church's mission.

Church leaders and members, musicians and nonmusicians alike, should take a vital interest in the ministry of music. The gifted and trained musicians should be depended upon to give worthy leadership in this ministry. But, as with all other areas which are important parts of the faith—Bible teaching, theologizing, nurture, proclamation, witnessing, for example—music is too important to be relegated exclusively to the professionals. The priesthood of all believers applies to music as it does to the other vital areas of concern in the faith.

Music as an Educational Method

The place of music in worship has been firmly established not only in New Testament Christian history, but also in the Old Testament. The place of music in education is not yet as clearly seen, apart from the educational values to those who lead and perform for others. Surely this latter value is no small educational consequence. The arduous hours of rehearsals, private practice, and performances certainly have their impact upon the diligent musicians.

Harry Eskew and Hugh T. McElrath, in their impressive introduction to Christian hymnology, give high priority to hymn instruction in the music ministry of a church.

> Through hymn instruction one is able to teach the message of the church, to help persons worship, to provide guidance in Christian living, and to present the vast heritage of the church, including knowledge of outstanding leaders in its history and a significant portion of its devotional literature and music.[3]

They go on to suggest hymns in the curriculum of each of a church's educational organizations. They also recommend learning new hymns through a variety of ways, including a hymn of the month, hymn study classes, and hymns in the home. They cited James R. Sydnor's suggestions in *The Hymn and Congregational Singing* (now out of print) for encouraging family hymn singing.

> 1. The church office can keep a supply of hymnals to be sold to members.
> 2. A list of suggested uses of hymns in the home can be published in the church bulletin.
> 3. Children can be provided music appreciation and training (e.g., recordings, private music study, and membership in a children's choir) which will result in improved hymn singing.
> 4. Parents may request piano teachers to include hymn playing in the private music studies of their children.
> 5. A hymn stanza frequently can be used as a table grace (e.g., the Doxology, "For the beauty of the earth," "Now thank we all our God").
> 6. Parents can use an evening hymn as they tuck their children into bed.
> 7. Families can enjoy informal hymn singing, either by themselves or with invited friends.[4]

"The music experiences which the church provides for preschoolers and children (grades 1 to 6) are largely educational in purpose."[5] The preschool groups are seldom involved in performing in congregational services. But both groups form concepts related to Bible truths about God, Jesus, the Bible, church, the family, self, others, and the natural world as they participate in the regular music activities of a graded choir program. They experience wonder, joy, feelings of well-being and personal worth, beauty, relaxation, rhythmic response, outlets for emotions, and personal creativity.[6]

For youth there are added educational values in music education. "Choir retreats and choir tours are new areas of keen interest involving musical, social, witnessing, and mission endeavors that build strong morale."[7] Many receive Christ through their participation in music. And adults have these experiences and others through music, including unique opportunities by special adult groups—single adults, singles again, and senior adults.[8]

The graded choir program offers the fullest opportunities for the educational use of music in a church. However, we would voice as strong an appeal as possible to the music leaders and to other members of a church to work together to capitalize upon and to maximize the opportunities for using music in the other organizations of a church. This appeal involves extending the present use of music leaders and instrumentalists into every possible group where music would be appropriate. But even more strongly, the appeal is to educate and train the workers of other church educational organizations in ways music can be used to teach and to lead the growth of their constituents.

Obviously, it would be desirable for everyone who uses music in teaching to be able to do a highly acceptable job musically. Yet almost any teacher or leader who can "make a joyful noise" could find ways to employ this marvelous method to instruct, and to have other growth experiences in education. For example, almost anyone could use a recording! Music leaders who supply curriculum materials for the graded choir programs for churches, and others of influence in the programs of education in the churches, must do more to bring together the resources of music in the educational ministries of churches. Already they have bridged the gap of using superior educational methods in music groups. Let the flow between music and education go in all directions. Let there be not only good educational methods in music groups, but also good music in educational groups—even that which is done by nonmusicians.

Structures for the Ministry of Music

There are tasks of the ministry of music in a church. These are basic continuing activities of primary importance in helping a church fulfill its mission.

The *first task* of the ministry of music in a church is: *Provide musical experiences in congregational services.* This means that the music ministry has responsibility for planning, rehearsing, arranging, performing, and leading music for the congregational services.

Several actions are essential for those who lead the music ministry in performing this task. They include: (1) assisting the pastor in planning the congregational services; (2) leading in selecting, rehearsing, arranging, and performing music for congregational services; (3) leading the congregation in relevant, meaningful, inspiring musical experiences that contribute to the thrust and mission of the church; (4) motivating the church constituency to want to be involved in the musical experiences and to grow in their understanding of the role of music in the congregational services; (5) providing resources for musical experiences of the congregation; and (6) assisting church organizations in enlisting and training song leaders and accompanists for their departmental and organizational meetings.[9]

The *second task* is: *Develop musical skills, attitudes, and understanding.* This means that music ministry leaders must "plan and carry out a definite schedule of teaching, training and performance activities to develop positive attitudes toward church music, increase understandings of the full dimension of church music, and guide persons in developmental learning and performance experiences."[10]

The *third task* is: *Witness and minister through music.* This task relates the music resources of a church to the needs of persons for witness and ministry both in the church and in the community, both believers and nonbelievers. This requires the discovery and analysis of needs for witness and for ministry, and the development of plans for and involvement of members in the needed projects.

The *fourth task* is the ministry of music in a church is the same as for all the church program organizations: *Interpret and undergird the work of the church and denomination.* Music leaders should find ways appropriate to the ministry they lead to implement this important task.

Churches of all sizes have a ministry of music. A *very small church* might have only a pastor, a volunteer (nonpaid) music director, and a volunteer pianist. These, together with the congregation, from whom there might also be individual vocal or instrumental contributions, make up their music ministry structure. Obviously, larger churches require more organization.[11]

For churches in which there is the possibility of graded choirs, the recommended basis for grouping and grading is the same age divisions as for the other program organizations in a church: Preschool, ages four and five; Children, ages six through eleven (or school grades one through six); Youth, ages twelve through seventeen (or school grades seven through twelve); and Adult, ages eighteen (or high school graduation) and up.

A church might have almost any number of other music groups, depending upon the resources among the membership and in the community. And, with or without the possibility for much group work in the music ministry, almost any church can give encouragement and other help to individuals who have the interest and the potential for music development and growth.

Curriculum for the Ministry of Music

Curriculum for the ministry of music in a church calls for uniquely complex sensitivities. Added to the many considerations regarding the texts of the music are many other criteria regarding the music itself, and, of course, the text and the music together. Add to these considerations the suitability and acceptability of the many situations in which music is called for, and it is not difficult to see the complexity. There is diversity of musical tastes among churches. There is often diversity within a given church. With the help of the Holy Spirit, leaders in a church's music ministry must find ways to use appropriately and effectively the talents and the resources available to them, thus meeting the needs of the members and of others who are their concern.

Music texts should be compatible with biblical truth, and not contradictory. In many instances they are passages of Scripture. The texts must be theologically and doctrinally sound, especially in light of the educational values of music. Relevance to past, present, or future experience is often a desirable feature of good texts.

The texts should communicate meanings which are clear and

accurate, suited to the purpose of a church and to the occasion of their use. The language should be appropriate to the abilities of the participants, both the performers and others involved. Highly abstract, figurative language is usually inappropriate with children or others who might be very literal-minded. Good grammar and poetic form are important in most instances. The overall literary quality of the music text should grace its message, and not distract from it.

The music itself should be technically acceptable, not sloven or calling forth responses inappropriate to the text or to the witness of the church. It should be within reasonable range of the capabilities of the performers to perform and of others to receive with appreciation. It needs to be interesting. At times it should be stimulating. It helps if the music is pleasing to an appropriate extent. Appropriateness as to taste, rhythm, beat, tempo, difficulty, and length are among other considerations for the music.

The curriculum of a church's music ministry must take into account the many areas of knowledge, skills, attitudes, and understanding in which both performers and others need education and experiences. Writing of this need, the authors of *A Church on Mission* called for a curriculum with a balanced approach to music education and music performance.

> This material involves sequential and progressive learning and performance activities based on mental, physical, and spiritual readiness of individuals. This task leads participants in the music ministry to make use of their musical skills through structured educational and performance activities that result in personal development, Christian growth, and the use of talents to support the mission of the church. The curriculum is contained in leader and member age-graded periodicals, Church Study Course materials, and related products.[12]

Music ministry leaders, such as the Music Ministry Council, should oversee and supervise the selection and use of music curriculum in a church. Often they would need to work cooperatively with leaders of other church organizations and with church staff members in this. Probably the single most important choice of materials, assuming the Bible is already a church's basic text, is selecting the principal hymnal of the church. According to Eskew and McElrath, "the teaching of the hymnal has yet to become a sig-

nificant part of the educational program of most congregations."[13]
These music scholars make an excellent case for teaching hymns in
a church. In addition to the fact that hymns communicate the
message of the church, they stated that some hymns are based
upon specific Scripture verses, and others are paraphrases of
Scripture. Hymns effectively convey theology. Singing hymns involves the congregation in active participation. Hymns are sung
over and over again, year after year, and teach effectively through
repetition. Their melodies linger in the memory and carry the
thoughts connected with them into the mind and the heart. In
worship, they help individuals express their feelings which they
otherwise might have difficulty expressing.[14]

In addition to the regular use of hymns for singing, there are
available hymn study sheets which are excellent aids in teaching
hymns. These sheets usually explain how a hymn came to be
written, what the text means, something of the background of the
tune, and refer to particular Scriptures which might relate to the
hymn. One plan that involves the systematic integration of hymns
into the children's choir curriculum consists of two three-year hymn
cycles, one for grades one through three, and another for grades
four through six. This plan is being used by the Church Music
Department of the Sunday School Board of the Southern Baptist
Convention, and is in their periodicals: *Music Makers* (grades one
through three), *Youth Musician* (grades four through six), and *The
Music Leader* (for leaders of children's choirs).[15]

Other music supplies and equipment, ranging from recordings,
record players, and teaching aids of various kinds to musical
instruments which may be simple to complex, are of interest and
importance to a church's music ministry. In all a church provides by
way of its ministry of music, the power and the promise of potential
should be taken seriously by those who lead.

> God in his Word exhorts us to praise him, to "come before his presence
> with singing." In his church, in all its activities, music is a vital experience. It
> voices praise, it testifies to the power of the gospel for salvation, it bears
> witness to the vitality of the Christian life. It reaches the unreached, it goes
> beyond closed doors, it communicates Christian love and understanding, it
> calms and heals and comforts. Those who have leadership responsibility in
> all areas of church life will wisely seek ways to use musical resources to help
> the church achieve its mission.[16]

Conclusion

A church's ministry of music is an integral part of its mission to make known the manifold wisdom of God. People in and out of the church need this ministry. Its tasks are complex. Its participants, performers, and those who receive the performances, vary greatly in their needs and readiness and tastes. A ministry of music must give attention to the needs of all the members.

One of the major areas of yet untapped potential is the fuller use of music as an educational method, not just for those who are to be the music leaders and performers, but for all the people of a church. Not only must music leaders be found and trained to lead them, but the "nonmusician" people who teach and lead in church program organizations must receive help and training in the use of music as a method. Musicians already make large use of educational methods in music; nonmusicians need to make good use of music in education.

Churches of varying sizes have a ministry of music. The organization of a church's music ministry should be suited to a church's needs and resources. When possible, the use of graded choirs should be a major part of this ministry. Music ministry leaders have an opportunity to structure the organization and to lead in the selection and use of appropriate experiences and materials in music. Wise leaders in a church's ministry of music can help a church in significant ways as it achieves its mission.

Concerns for Further Study

Consider these questions as you continue to reflect upon the ministry of music in a church.

1. What is there about music that makes it, perhaps above all the other arts, such an important aspect of the Christian faith?

2. What do you see as some advantages and some disadvantages in attempting to minister to the variety of musical taste among church members?

3. How would you seek to increase the use of music as an educational method by the "nonmusicians" who work in other church program organizations?

Notes

1. Reginald M. McDonough, compiler, *A Church on Mission* (Nashville: Convention Press, 1980), p. 131.

2. Ibid., p. 132.

3. Harry Eskew and Hugh T. McElrath, *Sing with Understanding* (Nashville: Broadman Press, 1980), p. 245.

4. Ibid., p. 257.

5. McDonough, p. 134.

6. Ibid., pp. 134-35.

7. Ibid., p. 135.

8. Ibid., p. 136.

9. Ibid., p. 137.

10. Ibid., p. 138.

11. For detailed help regarding the total church music ministry, see Bruce P. Powers, editor/compiler, *Christian Education Handbook* (Nashville: Broadman Press, 1981), pp. 168-80.

12. McDonough, p. 138.

13. Eskew and McElrath, p. 243.

14. Ibid.

15. Ibid., p. 247.

16. McDonough, p. 142.

10

Ministry of Enrichment and Support

Most churches have many ministries. They have a ministry of Bible teaching and learning. Many have a ministry of discipleship training. Many also have a ministry of missions education and action. Almost all have congregational music, and many have larger ministries of music. All have pastoral ministries. There are still other important ministries which enrich and support a church as it fulfills its mission.

Some of these ministries of enrichment and support are the concern of this chapter. Some of these are called "emphasis programs." Family ministry is an emphasis program. It is interpreted and channeled by all appropriate church programs. Some are called "service programs." They help a church operate and conduct its ministry more effectively. We shall focus in this chapter upon *four such ministries: family ministry, media services, recreation services,* and *administrative services.* Our approach to each shall be to describe or define what it means, relate the importance and the essence of its work, illustrate the kinds of things it might do, and observe ways it might go about its work.

Family Ministries

The family is God's first institution in time. He provided that man and woman meet each other's needs for companionship in marriage. He designed the family as the setting for procreation. When God wanted to convey his relationships with the highest order of his creation, mankind, he used the idea of family. He is the Father; Jesus is the Son; those who receive Jesus are the Father's children and are joint heirs—brothers and sisters—with Jesus; Jesus is the bridegroom of the church, the bride.

Both the Old Testament and the New Testament affirm the special place of family in the values of the Father. Parents were given clear and strong admonitions to train their children religiously. This responsibility has not been rescinded. In numerous ways Jesus sanctioned, blessed, and advocated the sanctity of marriage and family. The New Testament writers had much to say about the family. Paul was especially strong when he wrote to Timothy: "If any one does not provide for his relatives, and especially for his own family, he has disowned the faith and is worse than an unbeliever" (1 Tim. 5:8). This provision seems to be broad enough to cover all the needs of a family. Just as the Father ordained and commanded that man and woman in a family should "be fruitful and multiply, and fill the earth and subdue it" (Gen. 1:28), the Son extended the "Great Commission" (Matt. 28:18-20) to the family of God, the church. One should conclude that the family is of unique interest to God.

Families today are in severe stress. So serious are the evidences of family trauma that some have concluded that the family as a unit cannot survive. Some of the indicators of this stress were identified in chapter 5. Statements of the needs of families abound, such as are found in *A Church on Mission,* an important book for the decade of the eighties for leaders and others in the Southern Baptist Convention.[1] This denomination has determined to place priority emphasis upon family ministry during the eighties. The Roman Catholic Church has also designated the eighties as the decade of the family, with special programs to strengthen families. Along with these two largest of America's denominations of Christians, other church groups are working diligently to minister to the needs of families.

Individual congregations must bear the responsibility for most of what might be done to assist families. It is urgent that a church give major attention to its ministry to families. "The task of the family ministry program of a church is to minister to the distinctive needs of families, senior adults, and single adults."[2] A statement of two major groups of considerations which a comprehensive ministry to families must include will illustrate both the critical needs and the complexity of family ministry.

First is the dimension of *developmental and crises needs.* The Family Ministries Department of the Sunday School Board of the Southern Baptist Convention has identified fifteen areas of such needs. They are: development and learning tasks within a family system; capability skills, discipline, nurture, and meeting needs; sexuality needs and adjustments; Christian education, values, worship, service; relationship and communication skills; divorce, widowhood, separation adjustment; marital growth and development; parenthood skills development; financial management, vocational change adjustment; self-esteem and personal competency development; health and nutrition; personal and spiritual enrichment; affirmation, confrontation, forgiveness, reconciliation; remarriage adjustment; and physical, emotional, and terminal illness adjustment. This department seeks to assist churches with leadership development, program designs, materials, and other help in developing and sustaining a ministry to these developmental and crises needs of families.

Second is the dimension of the *life cycle.* A church's ministry to families must take into account all of the stages of persons in the family setting: birth, infancy, childhood, youth, young adulthood, median adulthood, older adulthood, and death. The family at each stage has its distinctive needs. Church leaders must be aware of these distinctive needs, and be prepared to help appropriately.

Often the occasion for special ministry to families arises just prior to, during, and just after the passage from one stage of life to another. Marriage, birth, and death are examples of opportunities for ministry to families. Always in these change points are some degree of crisis, some sense of urgency, and often some unique readiness to be ministered to. These change points are times when values might be reviewed, and vows and new levels of commitment made or strengthened. Timely ministries at these change points can help strengthen families, and often help them avoid having crisis turn to tragedy, such as the breakup of the family. Church leaders must be aware of the potential for ministry in the times of transition crises in families, and be prepared to minister to families effectively. Likewise, families need to be aware of the possibilities in their own needs, and be encouraged to look to their church for strength and support.

A church should minister to persons because persons need help. A by-product of appropriate ministries to persons often is a strengthening of the relationship between individuals and their church. This is not the motivation for such ministries, but the fortunate by-products for the individuals and for the church.

There are so many possibilities a church might consider when developing a ministry plan for families that it is essential to focus on priority concerns of families.

> Priority concerns of families usually include marriage preparation education, marriage enrichment, family relationship development, parenting skills development, family crises ministry, mid-life and empty nest adjustments, preretirement planning, and adjustments to retirement and to the later years of life. The family ministry program of a church may be a variety of special projects designed and conducted to meet these specific priority needs. Ongoing activities may also be a part of the program.[3]

An individual church leader, such as the pastor or another concerned person, might begin to awaken a church's sensitivities to the needs for a family ministries plan. One approach might be to conduct a family needs forum. This event could be conducted in one evening, and would be designed to secure ideas and suggestions regarding the needs in a church for family ministries. Such an event could result in the formation of a Family Life Committee to give leadership to the ministries suggested. If a church already has such a committee, this group could conduct the forum. Suggested duties of the committee might be (1) survey family life needs; (2) develop and recommend to the church council an overall family life plan; (3) plan and direct various family life projects; (4) lead the church to develop a ministry to singles, senior adults, and intergenerational groups as needed; and (5) coordinate plans and activities through the church council.[4]

Certain Sundays in the church year might be chosen for special emphasis days. Family Worship Commitment Day, Family in Bible Study Day, Couples Commitment Day, Parent Commitment Day, Senior Adult Day, and Single Adult Day, as well as Mother's Day and Father's Day illustrate occasions which might be used to focus upon families.

Conferences, workshops, retreats, and special study programs offer formats for more depth in ministry. These formats might be the vehicles for such concerns as marriage enrichment, parent enrichment, Christian education in the home, spiritual growth, personal relationships, ministry to others, stewardship of life, continuing to learn, and other needs to be met.

Christian Home Week, Growing in Oneness project, Parents

Building a Christian Home project, Family Fest, Your Family a Witness for Christ, and intergenerational projects are some of the projects a church might include in its family ministry plan.

A significant part of a church's ministry to families can be conducted by way of the Deacon Family Ministry Plan. In this plan a deacon is assigned responsibility for a specific number of church member households (ten to fifteen at most) with whose families the deacon establishes and maintains contact on a year-round basis. Special events in the lives of family members, and other occasions in the life of the church itself, give opportunities for the deacon to be aware of needs and to minister to the family members. In addition, the deacon can be the communication link between the family and the other resource persons and groups in a church. Since a large percentage of the membership of most churches does not partici-pate regularly in any of the church's organizations (even Sunday School), this pattern for organized ministry to all church members might be the only vital link between these members and the larger fellowship.

Other church organizations render valuable ministries to families. Sunday School classes, for example, often minister very effectively to their members at critical points in the members' lives. These groups are important in the overall ministry of a church to its families.

In view of the fact that most churches do not have a formal educational organization (more than a committee) for family minis-try or for family life education, perhaps a suggestion to the church's major educational organizations would help. In addition to provid-ing for family members in the regular major church organizations, special care should be given to planning for the extracurricular events and in the supporting events (planning meetings, special program events, and rehearsals, for example) to assure that families are considered. Otherwise it is possible, even likely, that church program organizations might become an inadvertent contributor to the problems families experience.

A practical expression of this special care for families would be to minimize the number of meetings which are designed to provide only for one family member, and to try to schedule essential and useful experiences for other family members when such meetings are necessary. This is not an easy concept to implement, but churches must come to grips with this problem. A church must not be part of the problems families have, but part of the solution to their problems. Perhaps every event's planning procedure should indicate the event's impact upon families and what provisions are planned to maximize the contribution to families.

Family ministry is a vital *emphasis program*. It is of primary importance to a church in achieving its objectives. Its program is most often interpreted and channeled through the other program organizations. (Other *emphasis* programs are stewardship, evangelism, establishing new churches, and vocational guidance).[5] Through a plan for family ministry, a church must minister to the distinctive needs of families, senior adults, and single adults.

Media Services

Several decades ago churches began seriously to use what was called the church library to enrich and support the various ministries of the church. The church library was a repository of books, for the most part. The church library ministry has grown tremendously, and its outlook has changed from that of a book depository to that of a media library.

This media library is located in a media center in a church. It might have a very small staff, such as a director, a technical processes director, and a promotion director. In very small churches, one person might do all of these basic jobs.

Churches use a variety of media in their programs. Some of the materials included in a full-service media library ministry are: *printed materials* — including books, periodicals, newspapers, tracts, leaflets, and clippings from newspapers or magazines. *Projected visuals and audiovisuals* are among the first additions beyond printed materials. These include slides, filmstrips, overhead transparencies, motion pictures, videocassettes, videodiscs, and microfiche. *Audio materials,* such as disc and tape recordings, are part of a full-service media library. So is a variety of audiovisual equipment, such as 8mm, 16mm, and 35mm projectors, opaque projectors, overhead projectors, tape recorders, record players, cassette duplicators, video monitors, portable public address systems, and microfiche readers. *Nonprojected visuals* — including maps, charts, flipcharts, sentence-strip charts, posters, flat pictures, framed art pieces, games, and globes—contribute significantly to a media library ministry. Other *miscellaneous materials* are useful, such as multimedia kits, costumes, permanent flower arrangements, "props" for drama groups, and other objects. *Music resources* might also be requested by the music ministry.[6]

Many churches operate their media library with the small staff listed earlier. Some have a larger staff. They might add to the three positions already stated these others: a circulation director, a media maintenance director, a media education director, and a special services director.

A church's media services has two basic tasks. The first task is to educate persons in the use of media. Media services staff persons need to have an ongoing plan of media education for church leaders and members to keep them informed and updated regarding materials and services available and their optimum use. *A Church on Mission* offered these suggestions:

> The media services staff performs this educational function in many ways. Individual conferences, special workshops, and presentations in regularly scheduled meetings offer opportunities for media education. Promotional avenues such as posters, bulletin boards, displays, announcements, skits, and other visual and oral means may also be used to inform church members and leaders of media and their use.[7]

It is important that media resources be seen as valuable aids in learning, growing, teaching, ministering, and witnessing.

The second task of a church's media services is to provide media and media services to support the church in the achievement of its mission. The media field is complex. Materials and equipment can be expensive. It would be poor stewardship generally for individual leaders or church organizations to provide their own media, even if they could do so. It makes good sense for media services to be provided through a media services staff and a media library.

Media services staff assist by selecting, securing, processing, cataloging, storing, and circulating media. They also help to identify opportunities and needs for media services. Working with church leaders and program leaders they set up systems for service. They work to secure space, money, personnel, and other essentials. They institute, maintain, and refine the media services.[8]

In Bible study, missions education, discipleship training, outreach, music ministry, and in many other interests of a church, media can be used to stimulate interest, maintain attention, and generate better learning experiences. The challenge of the times calls for the use of every appropriate means to reach people for Christ and to help them grow and develop as Christians. A vital media services program can be a significant part of a church's efforts to fulfill its mission.

Recreation Services

Recreation is the use of leisuretime for activity which is "designed to create, to restore, and to refresh the individual."[9] Leisuretime as a generally available "commodity" is a recent phenomenon. Most people have not had large blocks of unoccupied time when they were free to do what they chose. For most of the ages, people's energies have been required to eke out an existence. This fact remains true today for many in the world.

Technological developments since the beginning of the industrial revolution have afforded an increasing number of persons in developed nations, especially in the United States, increasing amounts of discretionary or leisuretime. Many have chosen to use their discretionary time to busy themselves in alternate occupations for added pay, to increase materially their standard of living, or to support more adequately the standard they already try to maintain. Many others have chosen to use some of their newly found leisuretime to create, to restore, to refresh themselves in recreation activities.

The fact that most church members and their families can choose to use portions of their leisuretime for recreation has given rise to a vibrant and growing ministry opportunity for churches, the ministry of Christian recreation. In addition to the positive factors which favor a church's involvement in ministry through Christian recreation, there are forces almost too numerous to catalog which vie for the recreation time and other resources of society at large as well as church members and their families. Many of these forces add to the misery and suffering of Christians as well as of the total society. Church members, their families, and those whom churches are trying to reach need some constructive and Christian recreation alternatives which churches can provide.

"The task of recreation services in a church is to provide recreation methods, materials, services, and experiences that will enrich the

lives of persons and support the total mission of the church."[10] In
serving to enrich and support a church's ministries, recreation
services can be a catalyst in outreach, a vehicle for ministry and
mission action, a tool for teaching, an environment for fellowship,
and an avenue to abundant living.[11]

Churches engage in a variety of recreational activities as part of
their recreation services ministry. *Social recreation* has long been part
of a church's leisuretime option. Parties, banquets, fellowships,
picnics, and other similar activities can contribute to quality interac-
tion of people with people. *Sports and games* offer enjoyment,
competition, fellowship, and exercise. As stated in *A Church on
Mission,*

> Christ-centered sports programs will include opportunities for the individual
> to give or receive a positive Christian witness, and to develop the personal
> qualities of honesty, dependability, patience, self-control, perseverance,
> courage, responsibility, sportsmanship, and teamwork.[12]

Drama— storytelling, puppetry, monologue, improvisation, creative dramatics, choral drama, pantomime, tableau, music drama,
play production, fun drama, readers' theater, and multimedia — can
be a powerful recreational force for those who "present" and for
those who "spectate." Relatively few churches have maximized this
potent medium, but more and more are beginning to realize what it
can do. It is one art form which churches should investigate with
confidence and care. Rightly used, there are few methods which
equal its possibilities for good.

*Camping, recreation music, retreats, arts, crafts, hobbies, physi-
cal fitness,* and *therapeutic recreation* are other forms of enrichment
and support which recreation services in a church can provide.
There are other forms which leaders in a church might develop.
Some denominations, such as the Southern Baptist Convention
through its Sunday School Board, provide considerable resources
to help leaders in the field of church recreation.

A church might conduct a recreation interest survey, such as the
one detailed in Ray Conner's book, *A Guide to Church Recreation,*[13] to determine the interests and needs for particular forms of
recreation in its church and community. The types and amount of
recreation activities, the different age groups and target groups to be
included, the number of persons available to train and qualify as

recreation leaders, and other resources together would indicate to a church just how they should organize for this ministry.

The pastor, or other appropriate person, should lead the church to secure a recreation director. This person might be unpaid, or employed part-time or full-time. Someone might be called as minister of recreation. A very small church might have only one person leading its recreation program. Other churches might have, in addition to a director, others who direct one or more areas of recreation — crafts, camping, drama, retreats, social, sports, for example. Some churches might find it useful to have age-group or special target group representatives to assist directors in interpreting needs and opportunities of their groups. The best organization is the one which best accomplishes the work needed and desired by a given church. Those who lead a church's recreation services should work through their relationships to other church organizations and through the church council to enrich and support the total mission of their church.

Administrative Services

A church as a whole can rarely attend to all its administrative needs. Most often the church body should limit its work to making decisions, and should delegate to individuals and to groups the responsibility to study, plan, and recommend procedures and solutions to administrative problems. Those individuals, sometimes called church officers, and those groups, sometimes called committees, render *administrative services* to a church. They

> share the common task of assisting the church to plan its program, manage its resources, and govern its life and work. The duties of each officer and committee grow out of and are a breakdown of this general task.[14]

Some might wonder about including administrative services as part of the educational ministry of a church. Perhaps they see administrative services only as certain responsibilities, or even disdainful chores, which need to be performed so the church can get on with its ministry. Such a view fails in at least two ways to notice the significant possibilities for ministry within administrative services. First, it fails to see that administrative services, support services though they are (in contrast to being programs with ends of their own), are integral to the successful completion of the church's programs themselves. The church needs assistance in guiding, governing, and maintaining itself. This assistance is provided by administrative services in a church. Without these services, a church will not function efficiently.

Second, there is tremendous educational value in the experiences persons have while serving in some administrative service capacity. For one thing, persons usually need and sometimes receive special training for their task. This training itself can be a very worthy contribution to the growth and development of the individual. The very acts performed while serving often occasion growth and development of significant value to the individual. Insights about themselves and about others, as well as knowledge, skills, and relationship opportunities often are the real compensation one receives for serving. There is also the joy of knowing a service has been rendered to others, to the church, and to the Lord. Such personal growth and development opportunities should be pointed out to those who are asked to serve, and to others, to the end that administrative services are seen for what they are really worth both to the church and to individuals. They should not be unduly magnified, but they should never be maligned.

Church committees, elected by and accountable *only* to the church, represent one of the major types of administrative service groups. The nominating committee, church property and space committee, stewardship committee, family life committee, flower committee, food service committee, history committee, missions committee, evangelism committee, personnel committee, preschool committee, weekday education committee, public relations committee, ushering committee, and audio services committee are among those commonly found in churches.

Perhaps through a temporary study committee, a church should identify the areas in which it needs committees. Appropriate committee titles should be chosen, and the responsibilities of each committee clearly stated in writing. The church nominating committee or a committee on committees should enlist the chairperson of each committee, and work with each chairperson to select committee members to be enlisted by the chairpersons themselves. Chairpersons and members should be elected by the church. Committee members should serve on a rotating basis, perhaps on three-year terms. The first year one third of the members of a given committee would be elected to serve for one year, one third for two years, and one third for three years. Those completing their tenure would be replaced by newly elected members, thus providing a revolving service and growth opportunity for more church members. Normally it is wise to choose new chairpersons from among those who have served one or more years as a committee member.

Each year there should be a church committee workshop to train all committee members. One good format for this workshop is to have a general meeting of all committees for a presentation suited to their needs as they begin a new year of work for the church. Following a general session, individual committees should meet briefly to get acquainted and to set the time and agenda for their first working meeting of the new church year or calendar year. Training helps for this workshop are available.[15] The continuation of this kind of service and training, with new personnel coming into service each year, provides opportunities for growth and learning by committee members which no other means provides. It should be a worthy part of a church's educational ministry.

Some of the same suggestions might be applied to officers of a church, such as the moderator, trustees, church treasurer, and church clerk. The idea of annually rotating members who serve in these offices should not apply. Rather, there might be fixed tenures with additional terms allowed by election. Their training might best be done on an individual basis.

Conclusion

Many churches have multiple ministries they attempt to maintain. They have Bible teaching and learning, discipleship training, missions education and action, music ministry, and pastoral ministry. They also have other significant ministries which, while not as "basic" as these, are nonetheless essential if these others are to be successful. They are emphasis programs, like family ministries (and stewardship, evangelism, establishing new churches, and vocational guidance, which are not enlarged upon here); and service ministries, like media services, recreation services, and administrative services.

The educational opportunities in these emphasis and service ministries are abundant. In family ministries it is urgent that churches consider very carefully the impact upon families of fragmented scheduling, as well as considering the positive needs of families which they might plan to meet. These needs can be seen in terms of developmental and crises needs, and must be viewed from the life cycle perspective. A family life committee should give leadership in this emphasis area.

The service ministries — media, recreation, and administrative — are organized differently. The media and recreation services function like a staff organization. Administrative services work through committees and individual church officers. Each of these services offers indispensable service to other church programs, while providing growth and development for those who serve. Hence, these are vital parts of a church's educational ministry, and should be seen as such.

Concerns for Further Study

Consider these questions as you continue to reflect upon the ministries of enrichment and support.

1. What do you think a church might do to maximize its ministry to families?

2. Assuming you had an interest in and a commitment to being the media library director in a very small church, what are some of the things you might do to establish and maintain this important ministry?

3. What rationale would you give to support the idea of a comprehensive program of recreation in a church?

4. What would you suggest as possible ways to put more education into the administrative services — church committees and officers — of a church?

Notes

1. Reginald M. McDonough, compiler, *A Church on Mission* (Nashville: Convention Press, 1980), pp. 53-56.
2. Ibid., p. 54.
3. Ibid., p. 56.
4. Ibid., p. 155.
5. Ibid., p. 70.
6. Ibid., p. 144.
7. Ibid.
8. For more details about the ministry of media services see Jacqulyn Anderson, compiler, *How to Administer and Promote a Church Media Center* (Nashville: Broadman Press, 1978); and the books previously cited, compiled by McDonough and by Powers.
9. McDonough, p. 148.
10. Ibid.
11. Ibid., pp. 148-49.
12. Ibid., p. 150.
13. Ray Conner, *A Guide to Church Recreation* (Nashville: Convention Press, 1977).
14. McDonough, p. 152.
15. See current listings on the "Undated Materials Order Form," and in the current "Church Materials Catalog," both from the Materials Services Department, 127 Ninth Avenue, North, Nashville, Tennessee 37234.

Part III
Leadership Personnel

Prologue

The educational ministry of a church requires leadership. Very little that is prized or cherished is accomplished in the ministries of a church by accident. Someone, or preferably several someones, must lead intentionally.

A leader is one who has others following. What the leader does intentionally to get others to follow is leadership. There are certain things to be done for which churches historically have sought leaders who have experienced a call from God to minister. The vast majority of churches have only one staff position for which they seek such a person—the position of pastor. Usually a church determines who will be its pastor. Hence, the pastor has a call from God and a call from the church. What the pastor does to enable the church to be the church and to do the work of the church we call ministry.

Some churches grow to the point that they call others who also have experienced a call from God to share the pastoral responsibilities to minister. They might also minister where the pastor alone could not possibly have time, knowledge, or energy to do. What these other ministers do is just as surely ministry as that which a pastor might do. Ministry is ministry because of what is done rather than by whom it is done. Fortunate is a church which has the services of a team of gifted and called ministers who give their best energies to leading the church to fulfill its mission.

There are others who lead in a church's ministries. Their name could be "Legion," for they are many—though not yet enough. They are volunteers. The volunteers are ministers, too, though churches seldom formalize them into a status with the designation of minister. These volunteers are the leaders who are asked by the church to serve without financial compensation. They teach classes in Sunday School, lead individuals or groups in discipleship training, missions education and action, music ministry, or work in one of the emphasis or service programs. There is a sense in which all who serve are volunteers. But those who serve with no financial compensation form the classic category for whom we use the term *volunteers.*

Part III has three chapters in which we shall present the work of the pastor, other ministers, and volunteer leaders in education in a church. One of the major organizational approaches to leadership, leadership through a church's councils, will be presented. The objective of Part III is to help persons clearly to understand the roles and working structures of those who lead the educational ministry of a church.

11
Pastoral Role in Education

A church needs to be guided, protected, and nourished in order to grow, develop, and reproduce itself in the world—to fulfill its mission. God has provided ways acceptable to himself for these needs for loving, caring concern—pastoral ministries—to be met. His way is through the variety of gifts he has given to the church.

> And his gifts were that some should be apostles, some prophets, some evangelists, some pastors and teachers, to equip the saints for the work of ministry, for building up the body of Christ, until we all attain to the unity of the faith and of the knowledge of the Son of God, to mature manhood, to the measure of the stature of the fullness of Christ (Eph. 4:11-13).

God has given to some, from among all who respond to his call to discipleship, certain essential functional abilities which are to be used within the church. The abilities are gifts. Those persons who are recipients of his gifts become his gifts also, as they develop and use worthily the functional abilities they are given. The gifts are not personal accomplishments; they are to be used to minister, not to exalt or to achieve status among those who comprise the church. God has given pastors and teachers, deacons, and other ministers—servants—who are to bless the life and work of the church by exercising their gifts in ministry. Many churches have only a pastor and deacons to lead them in the church's pastoral ministries. Other churches have a larger staff of ministers. Often volunteer workers lead some of these ministry areas. Whoever make up the ministry team, theirs is the opportunity and responsibility to work together to lead the pastoral ministries of a church.

An Overview of Pastoral Ministries in a Church

There are four basic tasks for pastoral ministries in the ongoing life of a church: (1) lead the church in the accomplishment of its mission; (2) proclaim the gospel to believers and unbelievers; (3) care for the church's members and other persons in the community; and (4) interpret and undergird the work of the church and the denomination.[1]

The task of leading the church in the accomplishment of its mission is a pastoral task. It involves working with other church members and leaders to determine what ministries are needed. It may be accomplished by working with the church council, organizational councils, officers and committees of the church, and the church itself, to plan, conduct, and evaluate short-range and long-range church activities. Those who lead pastoral ministries help the church to discover and secure the proper persons for jobs which are to be done. They set up and maintain adequate communications systems among leaders and members. They encourage and inspire responsible participation in the life and work of the church. They try to lead the church to be the church, and to do the work of the church.

The task of leading the church to proclaim the gospel to believers and unbelievers is a pastoral responsibility.

> Those who lead are expected to develop skills to achieve maximum effectiveness as proclaimers. They seek to lead all church members to become proclaimers to the extent of their ability and opportunity. They seek to discover and use all possible avenues in communicating the gospel.[2]

Preaching is the primary approach in public proclamation of the gospel. There are other approaches through which proclamation might occur. Discovering and developing the interests and skills of church members in the use of all legitimate means and media for proclamation is the challenge of this task.

Pastoral ministries should lead the church to care for its members and other persons in the community. "A church is at its best when it is known as a community of believers who express the love of Christ to persons in need."[3] Some needs call for the personal attention of those with special abilities and training, because of the complex or delicate nature of the needs. Other needs can be met by almost anyone who cares enough to take the time to reach out to persons in need. Still other needs should be referred to appropriate persons or agencies outside the church. Church groups, such as Sunday

School classes, WMU groups, Brotherhood, and deacons (especially through the Deacon Family Ministry Plan) can be significant in a church's plans to care in specific ways for those in need.

As with all other ministry programs in a church, pastoral ministries has the responsibility to interpret and undergird the work of the church and the denomination. Following reasonable achievement and maintenance of success as a Christian person, and as a married person, and a parent person (for those who experience these relationships), a leader in pastoral ministries succeeds when the church succeeds. "Good preaching or competent counseling alone will not build a church. Part of the success of pastoral ministries depends on interpreting and undergirding the work of the entire church."[4] It is important to all concerned that pastoral ministries leaders maximize the opportunities appropriate to them to advance the work of the church and the denomination.

The Unique Leadership Role of the Pastor

From the days of the early churches, the role of the pastor has been vital. In pastoral ministries the pastor is the leading servant of a church. The pastor has the primary individual responsibility, privilege, and sometimes burden of being the one person to whom the church looks for significant guidance in the life and work of the church. There are times when the complexities and the magnitude of the office of pastor weigh heavily upon the person in that office.

The predicament of the pastor often is like that of Moses as he was leading the children of Israel from Egypt to the Promised Land. Moses' father-in-law, Jethro, said to Moses, "You and the people with you will wear yourselves out, for the thing is too heavy for you; you are not able to perform it alone" (Ex. 18:18). Jethro then proceeded to tell Moses how he could be the leader and share the responsibilities with other qualified and trained persons. Together they could get the job done, the people could go their way in peace, and Moses and the people could endure. There are many worthy lessons in this biblical experience for those who minister.

There are certain aspects of ministry which the pastor normally must perform. For example, the pastor must be the chief proclaimer and the leader of others who proclaim. Through proclamation the pastor not only presents the truths of the gospel, but also the vision of the implications of the gospel for the church in its ministries. Through proclamation the pastor leads the church to do the work of the church. Such proclamation is the cutting edge of pastoral leadership. Without it a church is not likely to come close to reaching its potential as a church.

Effective pastoral ministry by the pastor cannot end with proclamation. The pastor must also lead the church in the doing of its work. A major part of that work is the educational ministry of the church. The pastor is also the chief educator of a church. One of the biblical qualifications for one who aspires to the office of pastor is to be "an apt teacher" (1 Tim. 3:2). But again, what pastor can do all that is needed in teaching a church? Not even the pastor of the very small church can do it all. It would not be wise or right to attempt to do it alone.

The basic approach which seems to offer hope for a pastor in the unique role as leading educator in a church is threefold in its dimensions. First and of most vital importance is for the pastor to be a growing Christian person. In the arena of spiritual and moral leadership, this is fundamental. One promising model for this dimension is described by Ernest E. Mosley in *Priorities in Ministry*. In order for one to be an effective pastoral leader Mosley suggests the arrangement of priorities according to the chart in Figure 7.[5] He offers four basic principles in priority management by using concentric circles. (1) The control, or constraints, in priorities must always be from the inside out; (2) whenever an inside circle is weak, the potential in the circles outside is limited; (3) whenever an outside circle takes priority over an inside circle, look out for trouble; and (4) when the order of priorities is maintained, greater satisfaction is experienced in a minister's life, and greater effectiveness is experienced in work.[6]

With regard to the idea that the pastor must first be a growing Christian person, Mosley suggests a simple but profound acceptance of the areas identified in Galatians 5:22-23, the "fruit of the spirit," as the criteria for evaluating one's growth: "love, joy, peace, patience, kindness, goodness, faithfulness, gentleness, self-control."

The personal example of the pastor as a growing Christian is an important element in the effort to help others grow. And, to be sure, the need for being a growing person cannot be limited properly to the pastor. But no pastor can lead effectively in the growth of others

Figure 7

without trying to set an example.

A second dimension for a pastor in the unique role as the leading educator in a church is that of being an enabler of others. The pastor must not attempt to carry the responsibility alone. There are others in a church who have gifts of teaching. They can be identified, trained, and given the responsibility. The pastor can remain faithful to the admonition to teach and, at the same time, focus major attention on the strategy of being an *enabler* of others who teach.

Some ministers have difficulty sharing what they perceive to be their responsibility for the gospel of salvation. Seward Hiltner spoke to this concern.

> There is no reflective Christian who has not at some time asked the question, "Was God out of his mind to entrust this most precious treasure to people like us and churches like ours?" And if he has answered the question rightly, he has finally said, "Yes, we are as bad as that; but God was willing to risk it, and he must know what he is doing."
>
> If even God felt it wise and right and essential to risk his purposes and his love through fallible human instruments, who is a minister to be unwilling to

acknowledge that his ministry must be risked through fallible human beings who are, in actual fact, no more fallible than he?[7]

The pastor must encourage and lead in the discovery and development of others who can help in the educational ministry.

The third dimension is that of the pastor's personal leadership and support. The pastor must actively demonstrate leadership and support for the educational ministries. This is not to say that the pastor should make all of the decisions or try to do all the work. Harry Piland illustrated how a pastor can relate to the Sunday School in order to demonstrate leadership and support on a weekly basis. These suggestions might be applied to all educational organizations in a church.

(1) He can study records to determine whether each teaching unit is functioning and where worker vacancies exist. (2) He can walk through the building(s), evaluating present use of space and location of possible new units. (3) He can walk through the building on Sunday morning and observe in the various departments or he may visit Sunday School classes at different times. (4) He can attend and participate in the Sunday School council and weekly workers' meetings. (5) He can recognize Sunday School workers during the worship hour. (6) He can preach on the mission of the church and relate the place of the Sunday School to that mission. (7) He can attend various Sunday School department activities, such as fellowships, banquets, and retreats. (8) He can be involved in training Sunday School members in how to witness. (9) He can participate and lead out in planned visitation and witnessing through the Sunday School.[8]

The Pastor Without a Staff

Each pastor must develop an approach suitable to the situation in light of the needs and resources peculiar to a given church. Most churches have only a pastor to give leadership from the perspective of the minister. They do not have other ministers. They look to the one person who is their minister to lead them in the major ministries the church attempts to carry out. In addition, many churches (approximately one third of the churches in the Southern Baptist Convention, for example) have a pastor who is bivocational and earns part of the family's essential livelihood from a job other than the pastorate. The number is increasing. Yet some of the pastors who have no other ministers with whom to work are very effective in their ministry. How are they able to do it?

There is no single formula for success for the pastor without a staff, or for any other pastor, for that matter. It is possible, however, to identify some marks of the pastor who is effective. Most often *they live personally disciplined lives.* This usually includes developing a personally productive pattern for when they will work and when they will do other things than work. It means that they take reasonable care of themselves in terms of work, exercise, rest, eating, family time, study and personal development, and other essentials for a productive life. Such disciplined living becomes even more essential for the bivocational pastor.

They recognize their own humanity and the limits which that realization suggests. It is unrealistic to expect that a person will do each task as though it were the only task for which one is responsible. A person does not have to capitulate in order to acknowledge that there is a time for working and a time to refrain from working. Unwillingness on the part of some pastors to acknowledge their human limitations, coupled with unreal expectations of some church members, can make the things one does accomplish become devoid of joy. It can lead to lowered productivity and on to "burnout." One must come to terms with the fact that there can be more items on one's "do list" at the end of a busy and productive day of ministry than there were at the beginning of the day, due to the many things which arise during some days of ministry. One's workday must end at some reasonable time. The effective pastor seeks rest and restoration and saves the remaining tasks for another time. God does not expect the impossible from humans. He only expects the possible, and he knows our limits.

They see and utilize the potential in other persons. This means that the effective pastor sees in others the capacities to grow and to share in ministering. The wise pastor develops a sensitivity to the gifts God has given to others and learns to envision what these gifts might mean if challenged, trained, and put to use in the work of the church.

They develop volunteer leaders through whom the ministry can be multiplied. Often this requires one-to-one relationships with individuals who have potential to render needed service to the cause. It includes helping individuals to see their own gifts and potential, and to become interested in relating to the worthy endeavors of the church in the expression of their gifts. It requires that ministers truly care about individuals, and not just about humanity in general. Individuals respond to this kind of pastoral leadership and will go to great lengths to help in their church's ministries with this kind of leadership. The pastor who relates well to individuals is likely to challenge a church's potential, with or without other ministers to help in the task.

The pastor without a staff must learn to work with key volunteer leaders of major church programs as though they were staff members. It probably doesn't help to title them "staff," because in fact they are not staff. Still, these leaders should be a pastor's first level of relationship as together they lead in the church's ministries.

The Minister of Education and Other Staff Leaders

One of the phenomena of churches in the twentieth century has been the growth of the number of churches who have ministers in addition to the pastor. While the concept of multiple ministers is as old as the New Testament churches, the vast majority of churches in history and at present have but one minister, the pastor. In churches cooperating with the Southern Baptist Convention, for example, approximately 62 percent have fewer than three hundred members. These churches have 24 percent of the members in that denomination. "The pastor is usually the only employed staff member in a church with fewer than three hundred members."[9]

It is interesting to note, however, that most of the churches with more than three hundred members have one or more persons serving either part time or full time as ministers, in addition to the pastor. The total memberships of those churches with multiple ministers exceeds considerably the total memberships of the churches with a pastor only. Several thousand churches (approximately 4,000 in the Southern Baptist Convention) have employed persons to serve as minister of education. Many others have additional persons employed as educational specialists with age groups. Many churches also have employed persons to serve as associate pastors, assistant pastors, ministers of music, ministers of recreation, and various other specialized ministries.

The pastor is the leader of the ministries team. The minister of education and other ministers should be seen as persons who are called to minister in the same occupational sense as the pastor. Of particular concern to our subject is the minister of education, along with other educational ministers a church might have. What is the role of the minister of education in a church? What does this mean with regard to the pastoral role in education?

The pastor is the pastor of the educational ministries of a church. The pastor is the chief educational minister. The pastor should be seen as the "chief among equals." The minister of education and other educational ministers share the pastoral ministry responsibilities of a church. Those ministries are not the property of any one minister person. They belong to and are the responsibility of the church itself. The minister of education can and should render many specialized educational services to the church, in keeping with the overall leadership role of the pastor. The chart in Figure 8 is a sample of what a minister of education might do.[10]

It should be obvious that those things a minister of education does regarding the educational ministries of a church need not be duplicated by the pastor. They should be performed within the bounds of the pastor's guidance as prescribed by the church. The pastor with educational ministers with whom to work should take the initiative to keep informed about those essential parts of the educational ministry that will enable the pastor to be effective in maintaining the unique leadership role given by the church.

Part of the work of the educational ministers is to keep the pastor informed, especially of the critical points regarding the educational ministries. These critical points can be determined by those involved in leadership roles. Minimally they should include information about possible new ministry plans, possible major adjustments or other changes affecting educational efforts, important organizational problems or changes, particular personnel needs or problems, major indicators of progress or of potential difficulties, and any other matters felt by either party to be of interest or concern to the pastor. It is important that this information for the pastor be communicated early enough to allow him adequate time to exert appropriate influence upon the situation in light of his responsibility to the church.

THE WORK OF THE
MINISTER OF EDUCATION
AN OVERVIEW

THE WORK OF THE MINISTER OF EDUCATION

MINISTER
- ★ Perform services ascribed to ordained ministers
- ★ Aid in worship services
- ★ Help in hospital ministry
- ★ Minister through church member visitation
- ★ Counsel

ADMINISTRATOR
- ★ Keep organizations balanced to meet needs
- ★ Participate in program design
- ★ Request and manage finances
- ★ Lead in recruitment of volunteer workers
- ★ Promote church's program through all education organizations
- ★ Inventory church members' skills
- ★ Guide nominating committee in its assigned work
- ★ Work with church council and other church committees

EDUCATOR
- ★ Lead in selection and research of teaching curriculum
- ★ Stay informed about educational trends
- ★ Know age-group teaching-learning processes
- ★ Supervise paid education staff
- ★ Train potential leaders
- ★ Develop teachers through systematic training program
- ★ Secure teaching equipment
- ★ Offer library and media services

GROWTH AGENT
- ★ Create new units for reaching people
- ★ Project and encourage the building of needed physical facilities
- ★ Help in the design and accomplishment of long-range plans
- ★ Lead in evangelistic outreach
- ★ Assume responsibility for prospect and new member visitation
- ★ Promote good public relations

Figure 8

The pastor and other ministers of a church should be a team, as contrasted with a loose collection of individual ministers concerned only with their personal concepts of their ministry as individuals. They are indeed individuals. It is quite normal and natural that each would have personal concepts about ministry. The overriding consideration, however, is that a *church* has ministries to conduct, and its ministers are to be its servants in leading the church to fulfill its mission. When a church has several ministers to serve the church, fortunate is the church *and* the ministers when they work *together,* subordinating their individual differences for the good of the body.

Conclusion

A church has needs which are to be met by persons through pastoral ministries. God has given some for this purpose. Pastors, deacons, and other ministers have responsibilities for pastoral ministries in a church. The pastoral ministries of a church involve the mutually supportive assignments of leading, proclaiming, and caring.

The pastor has a unique and vital role in the pastoral ministries of a church. In addition to the singular kinds of ministries the pastor must personally perform, there are responsibilities and needs for the pastor to help others as they share in the ministries of a church. It is indispensable that the pastor develop the capacity to share with others the responsibilities which they can accept and perform. In very small churches, this means sharing the load with volunteer workers, especially those who lead major organizations of the church. In larger churches it also means sharing the load with other ministers called of God and by the church to join with the pastor in serving the church to the end that the church can fulfill its mission.

The minister of education and other educational ministers work, with the pastor's guidance, to minister to the educational needs of the church. It is vital that the pastor keep informed regarding the educational ministries of the church, and that the pastor give appropriate leadership and support to these ministries. In case there are other educational ministers, a team concept in which all team members work together for the best interests of the church must be developed.

Concerns for Further Study

Consider these questions as you continue to reflect upon the pastoral role in education.

1. What do you see as some of the implications of viewing the first three basic tasks for pastoral ministries — lead, proclaim, care — as interlocking and mutually supportive?

2. How can a pastor become an enabler of other persons, and give appropriate energies to other significant responsibilities of a pastorate?

3. Why should a pastor be concerned with the educational ministries of a church if there are other ministers on the staff who are called, trained, and employed by the church to lead in the educational ministries?

Notes

1. Reginald M. McDonough, compiler, *A Church on Mission* (Nashville: Convention Press, 1980), pp. 78-83.

2. Ibid., p. 80.

3. Ibid., p. 82.

4. Ibid., p. 83.

5. Ernest E. Mosley, *Priorities in Ministry* (Nashville: Convention Press, 1978), p. 18.

6. Ibid., pp. 13-18.

7. Seward Hiltner, *Ferment in the Ministry* (New York: Abingdon Press, 1969), p. 85.

8. Harry Piland, *Basic Sunday School Work* (Nashville: Convention Press, 1980), p. 50.

9. Bruce Grubbs, *Helping a Small Church Grow* (Nashville: Convention Press, 1980), p. 3.

10. Will Beal, compiler, *The Work of the Minister of Education* (Nashville: Convention Press, 1976), p. 30.

12
Volunteer Leaders in Education

A church is an association of volunteers. Those who make up its fellowship are persons who of their own free will chose to come together, in obedience to divine expectation. They have voluntarily responded to the call of God to discipleship. They have voluntarily and individually sought to identify with a body of believers of like faith commitment, and have been received into the fellowship of the body. They share in the privileges and in the responsibilities of membership in a church.

Among the privileges of belonging to a church fellowship are having a voice and a vote in the decision-making processes and the government of the church. Another privilege is being eligible to be considered for an elective office or a job, some place of responsibility in the life and work of a church. There are other privileges, and there are other responsibilities. The concern of this chapter is with the privilege and responsibility of serving, as invited by fellow members (the church), in some needed capacity in the educational ministries of a church.

The Church Depends on Volunteers

It is easy to observe that there are many things to be done in a church which attempts to establish and maintain a comprehensive plan for ministering to those in its fellowship. Add to these responsibilities those which are essential in the ministries of a church to those persons not yet reached for Christ and church membership, and the number of jobs is almost overwhelming. There are Bible classes and departments which call for teachers and other leaders. There are discipleship groups or individuals who need guidance and training. There are mission study and mission action groups which require leaders. There are choirs and other music ministry groups which need leaders. The ministries to families, the media ministry, the recreation ministry, the deacons, the administrative service groups and individuals (church committees and church officers), and other ministries a church might foster make it necessary to call upon the members to accept responsibility for much of the work.

Occasionally there are sincere persons who suggest that the church should stop kidding itself about doing its work with volunteers, and simply employ qualified persons to do the teaching and educational ministries. These advocates usually cite the modern technological capabilities now available for education. One qualified teacher could teach many pupils, they feel. They speak of how hard it is to get people to agree to teach or to lead. Some say that only the less capable are likely to be available to teach on a volunteer basis in the church. They envision great strides of progress in education in the church by way of a staff of employed, paid educators. Their sincerity should not be mistaken for good judgment. There is not the slightest possibility that a church could fulfill its educational mission with an all-paid staff of educators.

First, there are few, if any, churches with sufficient money to employ enough qualified people to staff a well-organized educational ministry. Second, there are not enough persons qualified to answer the invitation to such a monumental task. Third, the kind of teaching and learning which could be made to occur through a paid teaching corps would most likely be limited to the cognitive domain — learning the facts and figures, the names of people and places — to the neglect of the affective domain — changes in attitudes, appreciations, feelings, and commitments to act. Both domains are essential to quality education. Furthermore, there is no guarantee that because one is paid to teach one will perform with more effectiveness.

To be sure, there are mounting problems with the effective use of volunteer teachers and leaders. The very task of discovering, recruiting, and training a volunteer work force sufficient for the challenge is a continuing problem. A majority of women now are employed outside the home, and are no longer available for volunteer service as formerly. Many men are occupied with two or more jobs. Families are feeling financial pressures which preoccupy their energies with the need to provide more income. Distractions accompanying the proliferation of media entertainment, spectator sports, individual mobility, and other contemporary realities make it harder than before to get the attention of people, much less their support. The age-old concern with how to motivate volunteers still lingers. But many of these very same problems are present (only slightly altered in some instances) with persons who are paid. Churches can ill afford to put their hopes on a paid work force only to discover that there also are consuming problems with paid personnel. If there are difficulties to be overcome whether paid or nonpaid, it seems for the church that the choice is clear: insofar as is possible and feasible, go with volunteer workers!

Strictly speaking, a volunteer is one who enters into or offers himself for a service of his own free will. A freedom and spontaneity of choice or action without external compulsion is implied. This does not mean the volunteer always comes forward without solicitation or recruitment and begins working. Some do. But most are enlisted by someone. Usage has added the connotation that the volunteer receives no financial compensation. Except for the difference regarding compensation, the paid church staff member might have as much claim to being classified a volunteer as the worker who receives no financial compensation.

Certainly there are some differences in working with a volunteer and in working with a paid professional. Still, in ministry there is the reality that one who performs the tasks *because* he is paid to minister is grossly overpaid at whatever the rate of pay; while one who performs ministry well and without monetary motivation could not be paid enough.

The church depends on volunteers. A church might compensate some so that they can give full energies to leading in ministry. For the most part, it is wise and right for the members to share meaningfully in the work of the church. Many think the survival of effective ministries in a church properly depends upon volunteers.

Two Tracks of Education in a Church

One of the best reasons for engaging large numbers of church members in leadership roles in the educational ministries of a church is that those who lead have opportunities and experiences which enable them to grow far more in the faith than they would if they were not in a leadership role. Who learns more, the teacher or the members of a Bible class? Normally, who works more in preparation for the study session, the teacher or the members? Who feels the need to learn, the one who is the leader in the learning session or those who are taught? Who feels more keenly the need to improve teaching and learning skills, the teacher or the members?

Churches in which the organizational model for their educational groups calls for a small teacher-pupil ratio actually have the possibility for an advanced track of teaching and learning. The ministers and other leaders have the opportunity to focus on equipping the many teachers in a much higher level of growth and development than that which is possible for the study group members whom these volunteer teachers teach.

Given the choice, for instance, of organizing a hundred adults into one large Bible-study group under the teaching of a masterful and interesting teacher or organizing the same people into five groups of twenty with five possibly less-qualified teachers, the choice might well be to go with the five groups. Then there are five teachers who might be challenged and led to train and work to become more effective teachers. These five would grow far more than if they were only class members. In addition, there would likely be far more meaningful individual participation among those who attended a given session. The important personal ties between the teachers and pupils would more likely develop. This is especially vital in teaching spiritual and moral truth. It is essential to learning in the affective domain. There also would likely be more interest in reaching out to recruit other students in order to expand the class membership. In reality, one should find ways to choose both alternatives. The masterful, interesting teacher could be called upon to help the five in their growth and development; and from time to time this exceptional teacher could lead the entire group in special Bible-study projects which would provide enrichment and additional study opportunities.

There should be two significant tracks of educational ministries in a church: the leader track and the member track. Each track is vital. It is the leader track which should claim the larger share of assistance from a church's ministers and organizational leaders, as together they work to provide more effective ministries for the maximum possible number of persons who might take part in these ministries. Such a strategy offers hope for a more nearly adequate mobilization of a church's resources and for the essential multiplication of the work force which must occur if the gospel is to be shared with the masses of the world. The harvest still is white; pray that the Lord of the harvest will send forth laborers. Determine to be part of the answer to such praying.

Motivating Volunteer Leaders in Education

The problems which tend to obstruct or limit the use of volunteers in a church's educational ministries are more numerous and complex than they were in the first half of the twentieth century. In a time when persons should have more discretionary time, many seem to be harder to interest in volunteer service. And it is a figment of the imagination to assume that everybody has more discretionary time. This is especially the case of the women in the work force, many of whom have jobs outside the home added to their already demanding responsibilities in the home. How can a church cope with these and other difficult problems?

Part of the answer lies in more effective and realistic planning of the church's ministries — highlighting priority ministries, consolidating and coordinating schedules, and other reflections of sensitive leadership.

How to motivate persons looms as perhaps the largest area of concern in any age. How does a leader interest others to act or to react in relation to the church's educational ministries? How does one get another to serve, to give time and other resources on behalf of a church's work? Let us look briefly at the matter of motivation.

In another volume, this writer described motivation:

> Put simply, a motive is what causes a person to act or to react. Motivation is the act of unleashing that within the individual which incites him to act or to react. When the unleashing is stimulated from within a person we call it intrinsic motivation. When the stimulus is generated from without, as would be the case with the use of incentives, we call it extrinsic motivation. Intrinsic motivation, which many feel to be the purer kind, is like impulses or springs, often unrecognized or unconscious, providing impetus or driving power arising in oneself. Extrinsic motivation, considered by some to be less preferred in terms of ethics, is like an inducement, a spur, a goad, or an incentive, stimulating from outside oneself the internal impetus, causing one to act or to react.[1]

In any case, motivation comes from within a person. What leaders can do is to try to create conditions which will touch the inner mechanism in a person.

The Christian leader must exercise special care and high ethical sensitivity in attempting to create these conditions. The one being motivated must be fully respected, and must not be led into that to which he could not give full, conscious assent. No person has the right to violate another. Each is made in God's image and is of ultimate value. It is right to inform of needs, to present challenge and opportunity, and to speak of legitimate compensations or benefits to all concerned. Undue coercion, appeals to fear, withholding vital information, and other such actions are out of order for the Christian leader in attempting to get others to serve.

It is helpful to study the literature regarding motivation. Research is plentiful. One of the most interesting and useful books is *Keys to Effective Motivation* by Reginald M. McDonough (Nashville: Broadman Press, 1979). Another good source is *Christian Education Handbook,* compiled and edited by Bruce P. Powers (Nashville: Broadman Press, 1981), especially the chapter by Jerry M. Stubblefield entitled "How to Staff and Motivate." McDonough's volume, *Working with Volunteer Leaders in the Church* (Nashville: Broadman Press, 1976) is another worthy contribution.

A classic in the field of motivation is the book by Abraham H. Maslow, *Motivation and Personality* (New York: Harper and Row, 1970). His "hierarchy of needs" has become a standard symbol in motivational references. He identified needs of persons as physiological, safety (security), social (affiliation), esteem (recognition), and self-actualization. Beyond these are the need to know and understand and aesthetic needs. He postulated that a person's behavior at a given moment is usually determined by his greatest need. Satisfied at that need level, one might move to a higher level need. It is useful to know the make-up of persons and to work within the light of such knowledge, guided also by the concerns mentioned earlier with regard to respecting one's personhood.

At some risk of oversimplifying an admittedly complex matter, we should like to suggest a very uncomplicated basis for appealing to church members to serve as volunteers: *biblical love.* The encyclopedia to the *Master Study Bible* defines love:

An emotion, sentiment, or feeling of pleasurable attraction toward, or delight in, something, as a principle, a person, or a thing, which induces a desire for the presence, possession, well-being, or promotion of its object.[2]

Biblical love probably has no equal in terms of strength or worthiness. And one of the facts known about motivation is that there is a positive correlation between the worthiness of a cause and the willingness of persons to give themselves and their resources to it.

The appeal to biblical love as the motivation for volunteer service needs to be presented in balance. There are at least four dimensions which must be included. They are *love for God, love for the church, love for other persons, and love for self.* These dimensions must not be placed against each other, but must be seen as compatible and mutually supportive.

Love for God is commanded in Scripture. It is expected. In the light of his great love for us, it is a natural and normal response to him. We are admonished by Jesus himself to love him with all our being (Mark 12:30). Our love for him takes priority over our love for family and self. We are in such debt to him that there is no way to repay him with service, but it is through obedience and service that we express our love for him. It is valid to offer (not coerce) believers opportunities for meaningful service to God.

Love for the church is a worthy and right basis for appealing to persons to serve. Christ, the head of the church, "loved the church and gave himself up for her" (Eph. 5:25). Followers of Christ are instructed repeatedly in the Scriptures to love one another. Such love is taken in the Scripture to be a sign of the genuineness of one's love for God, the mark of a true believer. Members of the fellowship of believers should enjoy one another's presence. They should feel that they belong to one another. They should be concerned for the well-being of one another. They should desire to advance the interests of one another. This adds up to *love.* A member who says he loves the Lord of the church but who demonstrates no love for the others of the fellowship casts doubt upon the validity of his professed love for the Lord of the church. It is possible for one to feign a love for others in the church who does not in fact love or know the Lord of the church; it is not possible to love the Lord of the church and have no love for his body, the church. One way members can manifest the reality of their love for the Lord and for his church is to serve. One way to serve is to help others grow and develop through the educational ministries of a church. Such an appeal is a valid part of the approach to motivating volunteers.

Love for other persons is a sound basis for appealing to members of a church to serve voluntarily. Some of this dimension is related to the prior point, love for the church, since the church is made up of people. But in this love for other persons is included all persons in or out of a church. This dimension not only speaks to the love which members of the fellowship should have for one another, but to the love which any Christian should have for any other human being.

An unfortunate reflection upon some church members is that sometimes persons who make no claim to the love of God appear to demonstrate more of the "milk of human kindness" toward others than do some who claim to love God and the church. In terms of the alleviation of human misery and need, it is fortunate that there are persons other than Christians who are willing to give of themselves on behalf of others. Many do this, and some to heroic proportions. How much more their service might mean if it could be done for the glory of God! With respect to the self-interest of the one who serves others, the service should come more because of the need of the persons being served than because of what the one served might come to mean to the church. The goal should be unselfish service. If there is a response beneficial to the church, well and good. If no such response is forthcoming, the serving goes on, because we care — we love.

Love for self is an essential dimension of appealing to persons to serve as volunteers. This aspect of a balanced approach to getting persons to serve has been neglected. The apostle Paul wrote that one must not think more highly of himself than he ought. Jesus said that the gauge for one's love for his neighbor is one's love for self. Jesus apparently assumed a normal self-esteem which would lead a person to want for others what one should want for self. It is imperative for one who serves best to have a genuine love for self, while avoiding the extreme about which Paul cautioned. In appealing for persons to serve, it seems right to help the prospective workers realize some of the ways in which they themselves might benefit from serving.

Present a balanced appeal which touches all these dimensions. Potential volunteers are being shown a way of serving God. They are being presented an opportunity to demonstrate their love for others of the fellowship of believers and for other persons for whom the church, the body of Christ, is concerned. In the process they themselves have opportunities for growth and development, education and training, self-improvement, happy fellowship, and the joy of meaningful service. Such a sincere and balanced appeal bears fruit in motivating persons to volunteer.

Ministers and other leaders should be careful, however, not to imply that those who do not respond to this or any other appeal to serve are defaulting on their professed love for God, the church, other persons, or self. There are other factors which are important in the dynamics of the situation. The individual needs to feel right and good about his own gifts and potential in relation to the service opportunity presented to him. Furthermore, there are times in people's lives when, due to prior commitments or other valid reasons such as health problems, the most "religious" response they could make would be to say, "Not now." When the response is negative, their choice to decline must be respected without categorizing them as uncooperative or unconcerned. Rather, they most likely will have other opportunities to consider serving in a place and at a time when they can happily give their consent. People should not work for long periods of time as volunteers or as staffers with a hesitant, grudging spirit due to having been overly persuaded or otherwise coerced into service for which they do not feel suited or called. There are plenty of kinds of service for almost everyone to be able to have a joyful work opportunity.

Ministers and Volunteer Leaders Working Together

There are some differences and some common denominators which affect the work of ministers and volunteers. Some are employed by the church, while others are not financially compensated. Some are ordained to their function, while others are not. Some are occupied as full-time workers in the church, while others have other occupations. All need to work together in the service of the church. All are chosen by church-approved procedures to serve the church. All are committed to the lordship of Christ in the church. They are concerned with helping others in Christ's name because others need help.[3] How should they work together, in light of these similarities and differences?

Among the attitudes and understandings which tend to make for the best effect when paid and unpaid persons are working together are these: (1) the particular tasks of ministry are indeed ministry without regard for the status or the terms of compensation of the person who does them; (2) all who serve must have some opportunity to do tasks which have meaning, not just the chores which others choose not to do; (3) all deserve respect since they serve of their own free will, based upon the love commitments which represent their response to God, the church, others, and self; (4) each desires and rejoices in the successes of the other, whether paid or unpaid; and (5) the strategy of the paid staff persons is to enable the volunteers to accomplish their tasks, with a reasonable sense of fulfillment, growth, service, and joy.

Some of the unproductive and usually unhappy attitudes in working relations among paid and unpaid workers stem from violations of the above suggestions. Others stem from such negative or discriminatory attitudes as (1) persons of either category presuming that others are there to serve by doing menial tasks which are beneath their own dignity; (2) their own role is to determine what those in the other category should do, and then leave it to them to do it and, in some manner, be accountable to them; (3) treatment of those who are paid as if they were hirelings, working only because they are paid. These and other such reflections of low esteem for others need to be deleted insofar as possible if ministers and volunteers are to work together happily and productively.

There are joys almost beyond description when there are useful and productive working relations among staff positions and volunteer workers in the educational ministries of a church. Bonds of love, friendship, and fellowship come into being. All of this is in addition to the joy of accomplishing the work which fulfills the purpose of a church in its educational ministries.

Conclusion

All who serve in a church's educational ministries are, in some sense, volunteers. The church depends upon volunteers in addition to its ministers. There are many jobs to be done for which volunteers can be discovered, recruited, and trained. There is no suitable way for paid persons to do all that needs to be done, without the meaningful collaboration of many volunteer workers.

Those who work as volunteer leaders in a church's educational ministries comprise a very significant educational ministry opportunity themselves. They are the "graduate student" level of local church education. They learn and develop as a normal and natural part of their preparation and serving to help others learn and develop. This is a very good reason to make extensive use of their services, even in preference to an educational design in which only elite educators serve as instructors.

Ministers and other leaders should try to learn about motivating volunteer workers. A simple basis for motivating which could incorporate all the best that is known about motivational theory is to appeal to biblical love. Though there are some differences in paid and unpaid workers, there is far more which they hold in common. With thoughtful and considerate attitudes, they can work together happily and productively.

Concerns for Further Study

Consider these questions as you continue to reflect upon the use of volunteer leaders in education.

1. Do you agree or disagree with the idea that a church should employ and pay qualified persons to do all the teaching and educational ministries? Why?

2. Do you think you could develop an appeal to persons to serve based upon the biblical love stimuli as suggested in this chapter? How would you apply such an approach in asking a specific person to consider teaching preschool children in Sunday School?

3. What is the biggest hindrance you have observed in the working together of paid and unpaid workers? What would you suggest to overcome this?

Notes

1. Lyle E. Schaller and Charles A. Tidwell, *Creative Church Administration* (Nashville: Abingdon Press, 1975), p. 67.

2. *Master Study Bible* (Nashville: Holman Bible Publishers, 1981), p. 2021.

3. Ernest E. Mosley, *Called to Joy: A Design for Pastoral Ministry* (Nashville: Convention Press, 1973), pp. 26 ff.

13
Organizational Councils in Education

A worthy and comprehensive educational ministry in a church requires the leadership efforts of more than one person. Even in a very small church there is need for consultation among several persons, preferably on a regular basis, regarding educational ministries. This consultation needs to take place in all three tenses of ministry: (1) before, in order to plan and prepare adequately for ministering; (2) during, in order to assure the proper conducting, including essential adjustments, of ministry plans; and (3) after, in order to evaluate — to determine the extent to which goals were achieved, to learn the lessons which would contribute to improvement, and to celebrate appropriately the progress made.

Many churches do not use a consultative approach to their educational ministries. In these churches, each leader does that which seems right in his own sight, within the limits of his own concepts of the church and of his own responsibilities. In these churches the results are often like one might expect of a team of athletes who never get together to work out their plays or strategies before the contest; who never huddle during a game to call the next play or plays; who never come back into the huddle to inform others of what is happening in their positions, and to suggest what might work better. These athletes seldom need any plans for celebrating after their games, because they seldom have anything to celebrate.

The Idea of Councils in a Church

A council is an assembly called together for consultation or advice. It is not an additional organization. It is a gathering of persons who are called together by virtue of positions or offices which they already hold.

In the early days of this century, Sunday School leaders here and there in churches met together from time to time to discuss the needs and problems of their Sunday Schools and to make plans for improvement. Some of these were called the Sunday School Superintendent's Cabinet. In the organization formerly called Training Union, a similar group within churches was called the Training Union Executive Committee. In Woman's Missionary Union the leadership group was the Executive Board. In the Brotherhood organization it was the Planning Committee. The music ministry leaders called their leadership group the Music Council. Some groups used committee or board terminology to identify themselves. Some pastors around the country began to meet with the leaders of these and other organizations in churches they served, and they called the group the Pastor's Cabinet, on the order of the President's Cabinet in our national government. Some called theirs a committee, a board, or a commission. In each instance the idea was to bring together the key leaders of an organization for consultation, advice, and planning.

Southern Baptists, as well as United Methodists and some others, use the term *council* to identify some of the leadership groups within a congregation. The major ministry planning and leadership group in United Methodist congregations is the Church Ministry Council. For Southern Baptists the title church council has come into use; and each of the organizations for programming within a church has a similarly named group: the Sunday School council, the Church Training council, the Woman's Missionary Union council, the Brotherhood council, and the music ministry council. The church council is formed by the leaders of each of the organizational councils, along with certain other leaders, usually under the direct leadership of the pastor. The result has been to improve considerably the effectiveness of the ministries churches perform.

The Church Council Leads the Way

A church needs leaders who will work together to lead the church in developing and implementing a comprehensive, coordinated, effective ministries plan. Churches look to the pastor more than to any other person for guidance in this arena. Wise pastors call upon the key leaders of organizations and groups in the church to work together on this important and ongoing need. This is what a church council is all about. As Truman Brown, Jr., wrote: "The church council is the servant of the congregation. It exists not to make decisions for the congregation but to help the congregation make its decisions wisely."[1] He continued:

> The church council is the logical setting in which priority needs of the total church can be identified and plans made to reach them. The church council's duties include the basic steps needed to lead the church to catch a vision and implement a plan to achieve that vision. The basic duties of the council are to: (1) Help the church understand its mission and define its priorities. (2) Coordinate studies of church and community needs. (3) Recommend to the church coordinated plans for evangelism, missions, Christian development, worship, stewardship, and ministry. (4) Coordinate the church's schedule of activities, special events, and use of facilities. (5) Evaluate progress and the priority use of church resources.[2]

In performing these duties a church council leads the way in effective ministry planning, coordinating, and evaluating.

In almost all instances the pastor serves as chairman of the church council. Among the duties of the chairman are these: (1) lead the church council to perform its tasks; (2) prepare and distribute an agenda for each council meeting; (3) notify council members of the time and place of each regular meeting; (4) preside during church council meetings; (5) present plans and action suggestions to the council; (6) call for recommendations from the council during regular church business meetings; (7) plan for training of church council members so they can perform their duties effectively; and (8) supervise the preparation and distribution of church council minutes, reports, and plans that are necessary to the proper operation of the group.

Leaders of any of the basic programs in a church should be members of the church council. This could include the Sunday School director, Church Training director, music ministry director, Woman's Missionary Union director, Brotherhood director, and the director of pastoral ministries (usually the pastor). The deacon chairman, the directors of media services and the church recreation ministry, and the chairpersons of certain committees of the church (evangelism, missions, stewardship, nominating) are among others who might be asked to serve. In addition, any church staff members who are responsible for assisting in the total development of one or more of the basic programs of a church should be members of the church council. A member of the church council may serve as secretary to the council.

It is possible for the church council to get too large and cumbersome. It is a good idea to limit the regular membership to those who really need to be part of the church's total planning by virtue of being the leader of a church program. Any other person, leader or member, could have free access to the agenda and to a place on the agenda should the need arise.

The pastor and other leaders of a church are expected to be fair in their use of whatever power comes with being on the church council. The field of responsibility is that of ministry planning, coordinating, and evaluating—not church discipline, church government, or some other area of concern. It does not require a large number of persons. For example, rarely would the chairpersons of some committees of the church need to be in church council meetings. When they do need to be present, they certainly should be. But one of the dangers of a very large group is that the group might become too preoccupied with its own authority. So consider working with a relatively small church council.

The church council should plan well ahead of any of the other councils or groups in a church, in order to make it possible for the other groups to coordinate their plans with those of the church at large. The church objectives and goals which the church council develops and recommends become guidelines for the total ministry plan of a church. The organizational councils and other church groups relate their specific tasks then to the objectives and goals of the church. In this way it is possible to coordinate the work so that all the parts fit together harmoniously into one design for ministry. There is no more significant work of its kind in the life of a church than that which an effective church council performs.[3]

Organizational Councils Lead in Detailed Planning

Each of the educational program organizations in a church has a leadership group. In many churches these leadership groups are called councils. The organizational council is made up of the director of the organization, whatever general officers the organization has, plus the leaders of the major units within the organization. For example, in a very small Sunday School the council might consist of the Sunday School director, possibly a general secretary, and the teacher of each of the departments (Preschool and Children) and classes (Youth and Adult).

In larger Sunday Schools the council would have department directors as members rather than teachers. Division directors are used in even larger Sunday Schools, especially where there are three or more departments within an age division. Division directors should be on the Sunday School council, and, in most instances, the department directors should continue as council members. Figure 9 illustrates the idea of the organization recommended for the councils of any of the church program organizations. The charts in chapter 8 for Woman's Missionary Union and for Brotherhood indicate the suggested membership of their councils. Council members for other organizations are chosen in a similar manner.

The work of each council is to lead in planning, coordinating, and evaluating their organization's ministries. Each organization has certain tasks to perform on behalf of the church. Each council must see that plans are made that will enable their organization to fulfill their responsibilities in the life of the church.

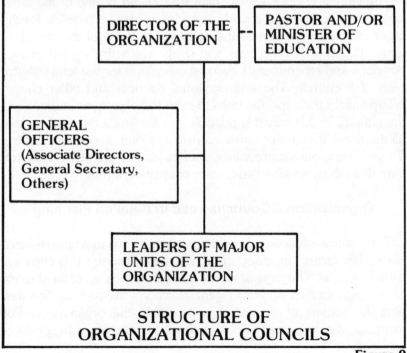

Figure 9

Sometimes organizational councils plan activities and projects which are not directly related to the overall church goals or action plans, but which are consistent with the roles of their organizations. These plans also need to be coordinated with the general church calendar proposed by the church council.[4]

The church council usually determines the major action plans which each organization is responsible for implementing through activities and projects. The tasks of each organization guide the church council in its decisions regarding which group should be responsible for planning activities and projects for a given action plan. Ordinarily an organization should expect to plan the activities and projects for those action plans which obviously involve its distinctive tasks. Some activities and projects require that leaders of more than one organization plan together. The idea is to develop a coordinated church ministries plan in which each organization contributes and relates in the light of its own tasks.

Once the activities and projects of all organizations have been proposed within the organizations, the leader of each group brings the plans to the church council for coordination into a unified annual program plan. Unnecessary duplication can be eliminated, conflicting requests for resources can be resolved together, and the church calendar can be developed with the best interests of the total church given priority.

Organizational councils plan for the resources they will need to carry out the activities and projects their organization will direct. Among the resources they anticipate and try to provide are organization, leaders, training, materials, equipment, space, and publicity. Needs and plans in these areas, as well as anticipated needs for funding, are shared in the church council as part of the planning process.

The following suggestions offer guidance to an organizational council in resource planning.

(1) Plan additional organization or organizational adjustments needed to carry out ministry plans for the coming planning period—usually one year. The pastor and possibly other staff members can advise and suggest resource materials at this point.

Organizational changes usually indicate that more leaders are needed and where they are needed. Once the organizational changes are determined, the organizational council prepares a list of additional workers needed, including any adjustments in the positions filled by present workers. The church nominating committee then fulfills its worker enlistment responsibility.

(2) Plan for leader training. The leader training needs depend on the actions scheduled and the skills leaders already possess. The organizational council needs to work closely with the Church Training director and those who assist that director to determine the training needs of the persons who are to receive training. Those responsible for leader training should develop specific training plans for the leaders who need it. These plans should include the type of training to be offered, the possible dates for the training, the materials that will be needed, and the person or group who should conduct the training. The church council should review these plans before they are presented to the church.

(3) Plan to secure materials, equipment, and space. The needs in these areas should be listed. Assignments should be made to secure or reserve these well in advance of their date to be used. This includes not only the needs for special, short-term projects or events, but also for the year-round needs.

Curriculum materials should be selected carefully. Resource persons, like those who work in the media library, should have opportunity to work closely with the planners in selecting materials and equipment for learning and teaching. Lists of items to be purchased should be made available for the church council and the budget planners in order to assure adequate funding in the planning stage.

Requests for available space can be worked out by the church council, based upon the requests from the various organizational councils. Occasionally certain actions might have to be delayed or deleted, pending the availability of adequate space. Increasingly churches are learning that by flexible and creative scheduling they can make better use of present facilities and other physical resources, with resultant savings which can be used in other ways. Churches of the near future can ill afford to continue expanding their buildings and coping with rampant utilities expenses without first making the optimum use of the buildings they already have.

(4) Plan to inform appropriate persons of the ministry plans — the activities and projects, and other items which are included. The organizational councils should identify the audiences, determine the

kind and extent of information to be communicated, set up a schedule for the publicity, and consider the media that are most suited to promoting the work. In some churches there are committees, officers, church staff members, or other persons who can be called upon to give major assistance in communicating the information to those who need to know.

There are other things the councils do as they lead their organizations. Powers described their duties briefly in *Christian Education Handbook:* Help the program understand its mission and define its priorities in the light of church priorities; conduct studies of church and community needs related to program tasks; coordinate the program's activities and schedules; and evaluate progress, effectiveness, and the priority use of church resources.[5]

As the church council and the organizational councils go about their work they are contributing significantly to the educational ministries of a church. Almost all of that which they plan, conduct, and evaluate has direct bearing on the effectiveness of the teaching and learning a church experiences. Many who otherwise might not have the opportunity for quality teaching and learning of the faith do have this opportunity because of the diligent work of church leaders through the councils. In the process, the members of the councils themselves have experiences which cause them to grow and to develop as Christians. A church needs some structured way for its leaders to lead. Councils are proving to be a good way for many.

Conclusion

Churches need the leadership of more than one person. It seems folly to attempt to engage in a comprehensive educational ministry without drawing upon the wisdom and energies of many.

Increasingly, churches are planning, conducting, and evaluating their ministries with the use of councils. Many churches use a church council for leadership in their ministries. Persons who are already in places of responsible leadership in the church's organizations usually comprise this church council, under the leadership of the pastor. A relatively small church council can lead effectively in a church's ministries. Others who need to relate to the church council should be able to do so easily. It is not a closed group.

Each of the basic program organizations of an educational nature in a church should have a council of its own. The organizational director, any general officers, and the leaders of major organizational components should be included in an organizational council. Following the lead of the church council, the organizational councils plan, conduct, and evaluate their work in the light of their unique tasks. The church council determines objectives and goals to recommend for the entire church ministries plan.

By using such group processes of leadership, it is possible in many churches to have more effective educational and ministry experiences than would otherwise occur. In the process, too, the members of the councils have unique experiences which help them to grow and develop in the faith.

Concerns for Further Study

Consider these questions as you continue to reflect upon a church's councils and the educational ministry.

1. What would you suggest are the advantages of a church council to the church which has only one minister?

2. What reasons could you suggest for meaningful use of a church council in a very large church with multiple staff members in its educational ministries?

3. In keeping with the suggestions of this chapter, what would be the specific composition of the church council and the organizational councils in the church of your membership?

Notes

1. Truman Brown, Jr., *Church Council Handbook* (Nashville: Convention Press, 1981), p. 6.
2. Ibid., p. 10.
3. For additional information about the work of the church council, see the relevant sections in Reginald M. McDonough, compiler, *A Church on Mission* (Nashville: Convention Press, 1980) and Bruce P. Powers, editor/compiler, *Christian Education Handbook* (Nashville: Broadman Press, 1981).
4. Charles A. Tidwell, *Working Together Through the Church Council* (Nashville: Convention Press, 1968), p. 51.
5. Powers, p. 54.

Part IV
Vital Processes

Prologue

Certain processes are essential to the effective life of the educational ministry of a church. Certain actions or series of actions must take place in order to realize the hopes and aspirations of a church. Thus far in this book we have presented and underscored the importance of the educational ministry of a church in several dimensions. *Why* an education ministry is necessary constituted the focus of Part I. *What* comprises the basic components of an educational ministry was the concern of Part II. *Who* are the personnel in the educational leadership of a church was described in Part III.

Part IV deals with *how* a church educates—the major kinds of things leaders and members do in order to move a church from where it is to where it wants and needs to be. Of course, a church never really arrives. Any church which arrives has in reality begun the return trip. It is vital that a church keep on advancing.

It is a vital process for a church to plan. Leaders must design actions to reach certain goals. They must plan to meet the needs, and perhaps some desires, of the members and others for whom they are concerned. They must plan and organize for quality and for quantity in the educational ministries. Organizing is also a vital process. How a church plans and organizes to perform its educational ministries is the concern of chapter 14.

Earlier sections of this book have stressed that the work of a church's educational ministry can best be accomplished by using the gifts and services of many persons. For many persons to be included in the work force of a church on a continuing basis there should be some procedures for discovering, recruiting, and training on a year-round basis. These procedures cannot be occasional interests; they must have almost constant attention. How a church does these is the focus of chapter 15.

An adequate educational ministry requires many resources, in addition to the personnel resource. Chapter 16 deals with providing such resources as a spirit and climate for educating, curriculum materials, supplies, equipment, furnishings, space, and financial support.

A church must implement and evaluate its educational ministries. Worthy and effective promotion, proper supervision, adequate recording and reporting, and comprehensive evaluation are needed. These are considered in chapter 17.

The objective of Part IV is to help those who lead the educational ministry of a church to know some effective ways of planning, conducting, and evaluating this ministry, and how to relate resources to the effort.

14
Planning and Organizing to Meet Needs

Planning and organizing are vital processes which are essential to the educational ministry of a church. Those who are in positions of leadership in a church's educational organizations need to give frequent attention to these processes. The purpose is to anticipate the needs of those for whom ministries are intended and design plans, including proper organization, for meeting those needs. It is true that neither good planning nor good organization or both together will guarantee success. It is also true, however, that without good planning and good organization, failure is a real possibility.

Planning Educational Ministries

Leaders of a church's educational ministries do not have the option of choosing whether or not to plan. The needs are too great to leave to chance. The urgency of the needs calls for the best thinking, the best data gathering, the best analyzing, the most creativity, and the best decision-making leaders can give.

It is not only essential to plan, it is also right. It is a natural thing for man to plan. God made man with the capacity to think about the future. It is one of the ways man is made in the image of God. God himself has modeled the role as a planner. His plan of redemption is the plan of the ages. Man must be a good steward of the God-given capacity to plan. Like all gifts, it was not given merely for our possession, but for our use according to his purposes.

Some Principles of Planning

Here we shall suggest some principles which seem to be particularly appropriate in planning a church's educational ministry.

1. *Lean on God.* "Trust in the Lord with all your heart, and do not rely on your own insight" (Prov. 3:5). God knows what the future holds, and he can help us plan for the future. The founda-

tional dimension of planning is to try to discern the will of God and to relate to his will. To learn of his nature and of his concerns for the needs of persons and to counsel with others who are intent on the same approach are among the ways we learn to lean on God.

2. *Include implementers in planning.* Everyone may have access to God. None has exclusive rights or powers of access. Those persons who are expected to have some part in helping to carry out plans should be included in the planning. Better plans usually result from group thinking. Support for such plans comes more readily because the plans are perceived to be better, and they usually are. Participants in planning are more likely to identify personally with that which they had some part in planning. Communication of plans is more effective when implementers are included in the planning.

3. *Plan from ends to means.* First, determine the purpose and objectives—the ultimate reason and the final outcomes which are the objects of the plans. Then, plan the programs, the organization, human resources, physical resources, financial resources, and the administrative guidance needed. Avoid end-means inversion—planning the what, when, where, who, and how before determining the why.

4. *Put the church first.* In the event of conflict between the best interests of the total church and those of any individual, group, or organization, the interests of the church should prevail. Furthermore, there is an attendant responsibility for those who plan the overall church program to plan far enough in advance for others to have opportunity to coordinate their plans with those of the church. The right to priority on the part of the church should be used judiciously. The church is the individuals, groups, and organizations collectively. This principle intends to avoid having the church plans preempted by any of its components or subordinated to them.

5. *Plan to meet priority needs.* Take the time to get valid data about who needs help and what kinds of help they need most. There are many good things a church might plan to do, but some are imperative. Determine these priority needs, and plan for them first. If anything is to be deleted, let it be the low priority item.

Be definitive, not just general. For example, do not plan according to an indefinite generality like, "There are *numerous* youth in our community and in our church who need to be reached for Bible study." Instead, find out their names, addresses, phone numbers, school grades, relationship to Christ and the church, family circumstances, and other pertinent information which would possibly help those who will attempt to minister to the youth. Consider what approaches offer most promise in reaching the youth (or whatever age you are planning for), and choose the best from these approaches.

Avoid letting planning degenerate into cataloging problems. One of the banes of some churches is that some find it easier to list the obstacles, the reasons why a thing cannot be achieved, than to work to find solutions. In order to be effective, it is important to develop solution-minded planners. Learn to counter the obstacle raisers with approaches like, "Yes, but now how can we find some ways to meet these needs? We have a new day and a new opportunity. What do you suggest?" Don't allow perpetual indulgence in looking back. Look to the present and to the future, and try to meet those needs.

6. *Aim for the range of challenge.* In setting goals, set them so as to suggest that success is possible with good effort. At the same time, set the goals high enough that success is not a foregone conclusion. Between these points is a range of challenge which requires good effort, with the promise of possible success. If goals are set so high that no one thinks they can be reached, people lose heart for the effort. If goals are too easy, people tend to lose interest or to be indifferent.

7. *Allow for flexibility.* Good plans are marked by their allowance for change. Changed conditions often require changed plans. For example, it is much more pleasant to planners when they are planning for growth and improvement than it is when they are planning to adjust to reductions, but there are times when each might be warranted. Unexpected changes of circumstances, good or bad, usually require flexibility in the plans. Expect this, and don't be defeated or unduly upset by it.

8. *Provide resources for planning.* This is a leadership responsibility. There are materials and information which help in planning. There are organizational principles and leadership skills which planners need to know. Reliance on the Holy Spirit for wisdom and strength is a vital resource in planning. Leaders help to keep these and other resources available to and before fellow planners in order to enable them to do their best possible work.

9. *Keep plans reasonably simple.* Even sophisticated people often respond best to uncomplicated plans when it comes to group activities and other such relationships. Many seem to have overestimated the sophistication of the masses of people. In an article in *Horizons* magazine, published by Cambridge Associates, Boston, January 1973, the following statistics were presented about the American people: Eighty-four percent have not flown. Seventy-nine percent own no stock. Seventy-five percent have never traveled outside the United States. Fifty percent do not use credit cards. Through the media many are aware of much of which prior generations were not aware; but there are many who have yet to experience themselves some of the marks of sophistication which others take for granted. Plans do not have to be fancy to be good. They do have to be targeted to meet bona fide needs; and it helps if the plans are fairly simple.

10. *Put plans in writing.* This is especially important should the need occur to refer to plans as action progresses. It also provides a record for any future use, and helps in evaluating. It is possible, of course, to do some good planning without writing the plans. The elaborate writing of plans need not become a major part of planning. Nevertheless, there are good reasons for writing the salient features and facts about plans.

Kinds of Planning

Many possible kinds of planning call for the attention of leaders of a church's educational ministry. While it is not so important to know all the theories and the procedures about planning academically as it is to lead the people effectively in doing good planning, it helps for leaders to have some knowledge of planning theory and technology. A leader is more apt to lead well who knows something of the possibilities.

One of the ways of viewing kinds of planning is to see planning as (1) operational, (2) annual or short-range, and (3) long-range. As might be surmised, the operational planning is that which is closest in time to the day-by-day, week-in and week-out, month-by-month, quarter-by-quarter happenings in a church. Almost all churches have some planning going on in this category, even if it is only the reactive decision-making required to move from one event to another. Many churches regularly do annual planning, producing a calendar of church activities for a year. Some churches have found long-range planning, planning beyond next year to three, four, or five years and more into the future, to be not only helpful, but essential.

In theory, every church should have a long-range plan first. This plan would be a concept the church hopes and plans will materialize within a definite time span. Goals and strategies for ministry are "painted with broad strokes." Then annual planning and operational planning place the long-range plan into specific allocations of resources—dates on the calendar, personnel, budget, and other resources—and the actual initiating, adjusting, and conducting that which was planned. Following this concept, let us look briefly at these kinds of planning.

1. *Long-range planning offers a church benefits.* Through the careful and prayerful study of the nature and purpose of a church, and the stating of these in terms which have meaning to the people of a congregation, a church can know more clearly where it is headed in the long term, and the kinds of actions which are imperative. This helps the church have a clear sense of its identity and direction.

Through the examination of the real and specific needs of the church and the community in which it ministers, and with priority planning to meet these needs, members may experience genuine relevancy to life which otherwise might elude them. What a church does should be relevant to life.

Through the wise and sincere utilization of large numbers of members in the planning and the implementation of plans for ministry, a unity of concern develops which touches members and their resources in ways which are not likely to happen otherwise. The sense of belonging and of being engaged in most worthy ministries which are relevant and which help the church to be the church are significant values for a fellowship. These serve to increase the motivation among members to work more and more effectively to relate their resources as good stewards.

Through long-range planning, a church which initially has the potential for growth can have a means of continuing to grow intentionally, both in quantity and in quality. It is as though they were making a trip to a distant place. They determine where they wish to arrive, identify probable points along the route, and plan to provide the means required to move them from point to point in the direction of their ultimate destination. There is a sense of real partnership with the Master Planner. One of the by-products is that members will experience the joy that comes from such feelings of relationship to the work of the Lord and the church.

The church should have an overall long-range plan, a major part of which will be accomplished through the educational ministry. There is a natural sequence or flow of planning which a church long-range plan should follow. It includes steps like (1) getting started; (2) discovering needs; (3) setting long-range goals; (4) planning long-range strategies; and (5) presenting the long-range plan to the church.[1] A church long-range planning committee, working closely with the pastor and staff, should be responsible for the arduous assignment of developing and presenting to the church a plan which, upon acceptance by the church, will guide the church for the years ahead.

In educational planning in a church, the plans can hardly be projected for more than five years, lest they be off target due to changing needs. Even these should be subject to revision as circumstances and needs change within that time frame. The church council has responsibility for adjusting and leading in implementing the church's ministry plans in ways compatible with the church-approved long-range plan.

The long-range plan is the general framework which guides the many components of a church. The long-range plan itself must be kept current. It must not become an inflexible design which inhibits the church in its responses to needs. Its purpose is to help make possible more relevant priority ministries, not to hinder them. A good plan, however, would rarely deserve to be scuttled completely. It must be revised and updated, at least on an annual basis. At this time it would ideally be extended by adding another year to the plan. A major review and new plan would probably be warranted each decade.

2. *Annual or short-range planning is essential to effective ministry in a church.* This planning is usually initiated by the church council. It extends to the organizational councils. It also involves church committees and their planning. Pastor, church staff, and the volunteer leaders of church organizations and committees work together and produce such annual guides as the church

calendar of ministry events, the church budget, and other tools which enhance and support the various ministries through the year.

With the church long-range plan as a primary guide, the church council reviews and confirms priority needs. Other information should be considered, such as current denominational emphases, new data from the community and the church membership, and other significant factors related to circumstances and conditions at the time. Short-range goals, a coordinated calendar for the church year, and a proposed budget related to the ministry plans become the practical expressions which help to transpose long-range plans into specific annual plans for a given year.

The church council becomes the planning forum through which leaders of church ministries, including church committees as needed, can develop a total plan for the church which relates all of the ministries and support systems appropriately. Leaders of basic church programs, such as the Sunday School director, the Church Training director, the directors of Woman's Missionary Union, Brotherhood, and the music ministry, and chairmen of committees lead their organizations to plan to contribute through their unique tasks and gifts to the church's overall plans. The church council also provides a helpful forum for the organizations to share information, and to seek counsel if needed, about the actions and events unique to their responsibilities. This communication network leads to better understanding, more appreciation, higher trust, and better coopera-tion among the various interest groups and ministry organizations in a church.

A variety of materials, training events, and other helpful items are available to assist the annual planning process in a church. There are church development guides, achievement standards, resource kits, program organization planning books (such as the annual *Sunday School Plan Book*), program organization leadership maga-zines, denominational calendars, and other materials which leaders can secure. There are training events related to church annual planning which are offered at various locations, such as the Baptist associations or state conventions, and conference centers. Annual planning is a vital cog in the wheels of effective planning for the educational ministries of a church.

3. *Operational planning is that which is required as plans previously made come to the implementation stage.* Many

decisions and other planning actions remain as leaders fill in the final details and make the essential adjustments as prior plans approach reality. There will be unexpected developments that call for schedule changes and other responses as the time for action approaches.

The organizational councils, as well as committees of the church, do the detailed operational planning related to their respective assignments. When it is helpful or needed, the leaders relate their operational planning to the church council. It is usually adequate for organizational councils to meet on a monthly basis, at a regular time. In churches with a very full agenda of events, some organizational councils, such as the Sunday School council, might meet briefly on a weekly basis for exchange of information, clarification of plans, problem-solving, or other good reasons. Even these groups, though, probably need an extended session on a regular monthly basis for planning. Some groups, such as the church council or organizational councils, have planning retreats during which they work on plans of several types related to their assignments.

Illustrative of other operational planning meetings is the weekly workers' meeting which many Sunday School leaders consider to be indispensable to an effective Bible teaching ministry. Kenneth M. Dean, an experienced teaching improvement consultant, wrote, "In order for a church to provide and maintain a challenging Bible teaching program that is reaching prospects and adding new members to its Sunday School, it must have a well-planned weekly workers' meeting."[2] This meeting can help Sunday School workers accomplish planning, promoting, problem solving, preparation, personal support, and prayer for one another, for the members, for department activities, for church concerns, and for other objects.

Some of the most effective weekly workers' meetings are in small churches with small Sunday Schools which are not departmentalized. One agenda for such a meeting in a small Sunday School suggests a general period when all workers are together for about twenty minutes to handle the school's administrative concerns, to plan for reaching, witnessing, and ministering, and to pray together. There follows a teaching-learning period with all workers together for directed planning of age-group units and lessons (about thirty minutes). It concludes with about ten minutes for special age-group time to prepare the room or area of the building for Sunday's session.

In larger, departmentalized Sunday Schools a better plan would be a three-part meeting, with about fifteen minutes for department directors to meet together, followed by a very brief time (five-eight minutes) for all workers together for general concerns to be cared for, and concluding with each department meeting separately for the agenda like that of the entire meeting of the small Sunday School. This latter segment requires about fifty to sixty minutes to be most effective. Each Sunday School should determine the best format to meet its needs. Going on the assumption that Sunday School workers are committed to doing the best possible job, such a meeting each week is an economy of their time and can result in many good accomplishments.

Sunday School leaders, including department directors, need training which will equip them to lead successful meetings with their workers. There are denominational materials to help with this important meeting. When recruited, Sunday School workers need to understand that the weekly workers' meeting is part of the responsibility they are being asked to accept. The meeting must have priority scheduling in a church, and other organizations need to avoid duplication of leaders and schedules which would weaken this meeting. Many churches find that a time before or after the mid-week prayer meeting of the church is the prime time for a good weekly workers' meeting.

There are numerous other planning needs. Committees, classes, task forces, and other groups need to function well in planning in order to provide effective ministries in education. There are meetings to preview and to select curriculum materials, usually on a quarterly or an annual basis, or both.

Organizing for Growth

There is ample biblical and historical evidence to support the thesis that a church should desire to grow. Almost all churches do wish to experience growth. They want to experience "the divine-human process of adding to a church those who are saved through Jesus Christ, equipping them for responsible discipleship resulting in witnessing, ministering, and establishing new fellowships of believers."[3] Few ideas in the field of practical theology have received the attention of theoreticians and practitioners alike during recent years as has the idea of growing churches. Studies have been made to discover what makes churches grow. Seminaries and other institutions have established centers for the study of the subject. Many churches and some entire denominations have given growth a priority place in their ministries. It is a vital concern for those who would lead a church in its educational ministries.

The Southern Baptist Convention, which has grown to be the largest non-Catholic denomination in America, has been interested in and knowledgeable of how to grow churches for many years. The more recent interest of others has helped churches of this denomination to sharpen their thinking and to expand their understanding of important additional factors which contribute to growing churches. Others have helped Southern Baptists place more emphasis, for example, upon acquiring and using more thorough demographic data in planning and providing for churches to grow. Likewise, others have drawn heavily from Southern Baptists in their knowledge of what makes churches grow.

There are two rather fundamental conditions, however, which must precede any effective methodological approach for a church to grow. First, people must be potentially available to a church. Even in a world of burgeoning population, some churches are not located among pockets of people, and they are not likely to experience great numerical growth, regardless of their desire for it. Such churches must focus on other vital dimensions of a growing church, and not be made to feel untrue to the commission if they do not have unusual numerical growth.

Second, there must be a willingness to grow. This sometimes is a subtle factor. Few active members of a church would admit to not being willing for their church to grow. But the real truth behind this willingness to grow is the willingness to *change*. Growth requires change. Many who would nod in apparent assent to the pastor's preaching about reaching out to others balk at the suggestion of possible change which must precede or accompany growth. Unless there are people potentially available to a church, and unless there is a willingness to grow (and to *work* at it), there is no formula which will produce growth. Wise church leaders who wish to lead their church to grow must be aware of and deal with these two conditions.

Marks of a Growing Church

What are some major characteristics of a growing church? An ad hoc growth study committee from the Sunday School Board and the Home Mission Board of the Southern Baptist Convention studied this question for a period of two years. They observed and felt several common marks in growing churches. These characteristics are not listed in a particular order, and they are emphasized in different ways in different growing churches.

1. Pastor and staff leaders are committed to and involved in growth.

2. Lay persons are committed to and involved in growth.

3. There is a priority commitment to winning lost persons to faith in Jesus Christ.

4. New believers and other members are equipped for personal growth, witness, and ministry.

5. They regularly experience worship, including music and preaching that are dynamic, challenging, joyful, and expectant.

6. They are a fellowship that expresses acceptance, concern, and love.

7. The Bible is central in preaching and study.

8. They use the Sunday School as the major growth outreach arm of the church.

9. They have a caring concern for meeting the needs of all persons.

10. They make specific plans to grow in the context of their setting.

11. They express a world concern through scriptural giving and individual participation.

12. There is a prayerful sensitivity to the leadership of the Holy Spirit.[4]

Growing Through the Sunday School

Each of the educational organizations of a church is the most important organization in the church in the area of its responsibilities. All of a church's educational organizations contribute to a growing church. But the Sunday School has been found, by

Southern Baptists and others, to be the most effective growth outreach arm of the church. There are good reasons why this is true.

1. *Why the Sunday School is the best organization for growth of a church.* The Bible is the principal textbook of the Sunday School. Curriculum materials are not the text, but are helps in understanding and teaching the text, the Bible. The Bible has a unique appeal to students, both in and out of the church. It is the Sunday School's task to lead in the church's Bible teaching.

Reaching persons for Bible study, witnessing to them about Christ, and leading them into church membership are major tasks of the Sunday School. It is natural that the organization with these tasks should be the leader of a church's efforts in these growth activities.

The Sunday School has the largest organization and the largest number of workers of the organizations in a church. Its workers can most readily lead in the outreach activities to prospective new members. In so doing they are simply putting their teachings into practice.

The Sunday School has the greatest potential constituency of all church organizations. Among its members are the youngest infants, even before they are brought to the church building, to the oldest persons, even if they are unable to attend. All persons in all conditions or age groups are potential members of a Sunday School.

The Sunday School meets fifty-two weeks per year. Someone is present, teaching people the Bible, as surely as Sundays come and go. This fact is important. No organization in a church can do so well as can the organization which has no cancellations of schedule. Other organizations might do well to follow this example.

The Sunday School in America is the most readily recognized organization of the church to those outside the church. Even the least knowledgeable person outside the church has *some* degree of awareness of Sunday School, however vague it might be. This recognition can be an asset in outreach.

Sunday School has the prime time in most church programs for attracting unreached persons—Sunday morning, prior to the major worship service (or just after the service, in some instances; or between morning services, in some churches which have grown to need more than one morning worship service).

Historically, among Southern Baptists, one person out of three enrolled in Sunday School has been reached for Christian conversion. This compares with one person in approximately two-hundred forty who have made professions of faith in these churches without having been enrolled in their Sunday Schools. It seems clear that the major strategy for a church to reach the unreached would be to enroll them and engage them in Bible study through the Sunday School.

2. *Essential actions producing growth.* Through decades of church growth by growing Sunday Schools, knowledge about how to use the Sunday School to grow churches has developed. Shortly after the turn of the century, an energetic layman, Arthur Flake, developed a five-step procedure for growing a Sunday School. Later, when he had become a national leader of Sunday School work among Southern Baptists, he published the "formula." The 1922 version was stated: (1) the constituency for the Sunday School should be known; (2) the organization should be enlarged; (3) a suitable place should be provided; (4) the enlarged organization should be set up; and (5) a program of visitation should be maintained.[5]

Later the "Flake formula," as it came to be known, was streamlined in its language and put in the active voice: (1) know your possibilities; (2) enlarge the organization; (3) provide the space; (4) enlist and train the workers; and (5) go after the people. This formula became the procedure for thousands of churches which followed its steps to reach millions of unreached people. Coupled with the compatible use of the "laws of Sunday School growth," developed and expressed by J. N. Barnette, an assistant and later successor to Flake, the Southern Baptist Convention more than doubled in the ten year period between 1945-55, a feat which had taken the century before 1945 to accomplish. The contributions of these advocates of growing churches through growing Sunday Schools can scarcely be measured.

Barnette's "laws" were seven in number. Stated briefly and with limited commentary here, they are as follows:

(1) The law relating to number of workers: Enrollment in Sunday School increases in proportion to workers at the ratio of ten to one. This suggests that one way to take a growth stance is to increase the number of workers in keeping with the ratio. There is a natural

tendency among some to prefer to combine classes or departments in order to have larger groups in attendance. Rather, enlisting more workers who will minister to the members and potential members should build attendance.

(2) The law relating to size of units: Units (classes, especially) normally reach their maximum growth within a few months after they are started. Classes should begin the church year with a healthy nucleus, but with room to grow before reaching the optimum size. For example, a class of youth whose optimum membership should not exceed fifteen should begin the year with eight to twelve members, with some known potential members. More than likely they can grow to reach fifteen members during the year, but only if they allow for growth when the organization is begun.

(3) The law relating to new units: New units grow faster and win more people to Christ and provide more workers. Generally the first year is the most productive growth year for a Sunday School class. Hence, a measure of newness can be arranged each year by reorganizing the classes and departments, allowing room for growth.

(4) The law relating to grading: Grading by ages provides the logical basis for adding new units. While there are other ways to group, age is the most common denominator for a continuing organization. It is generally best suited to teaching which is directed to the life needs of members.

(5) The law relating to promotion: Promotion on the age basis follows the natural laws of growth and development. Annual promotion is necessary in a growing Sunday School. To get away from annual promotion is to invite limits in the growth rate.

(6) The law relating to visitation: Enrollment and attendance increase in proportion to visitation (the number of personal visits). Cards, letters, and phone calls are useful, but none of these can be as effective as visits to absentees and to potential members.

(7) The law relating to the building: The building sets the pattern for Sunday School growth. A Sunday School cannot successfully grow beyond the capacity of its building. Some have learned to use the buildings more efficiently through multiple scheduling (having Sunday School during more than one period, or otherwise getting multiple use of the space). But the law holds. We shape our

buildings, and then they shape us. A church will never need the room it does not provide and use wisely.

A close examination of almost all growing Sunday Schools would reveal signs of "Flake's formula" and of Barnette's "laws." They are foundational to growing Sunday Schools. There are new ways of saying some of the truths they embody, but the truths endure. Given the potential people to reach, and a willingness to grow (including a willingness to change and to work), these concepts can guide a church to grow.

Harry Piland offered a very effective set of basic actions for growing a Sunday School. Leading a conference entitled "Pastor and Staff Planning for Church Growth" at the launching event of the World Missions/Church Growth Center at Southwestern Baptist Theological Seminary in the fall of 1980, Piland listed these as essential: (1) make a commitment to growth; (2) identify and enroll prospects; (3) start new classes and departments; (4) enlist workers; (5) train workers; (6) provide space and equipment; (7) conduct weekly workers' meetings; (8) conduct weekly visitation; and (9) teach the Bible to win the lost and develop the saved.

3. *Some special tools for growth.* There are many other approaches and devices which are potentially useful to a church in planning and organizing for growth. Here we shall mention but a few.

The approach offered by a veteran educational leader in growing churches, R. Othal Feather, is the plan described in his book, *Outreach Evangelism Through the Sunday School* (Nashville: Convention Press, 1972). Essentially a detailed plan for cultivation evangelism through the Sunday School, the genius of the concept (in addition to accurate information about those who are prospective Christians) is the careful matching of prospects with witnesses. Sunday School workers who know the person about whom there is a concern for reaching and winning to Christ consider the person in all the church (in or out of the Sunday School work force) who would be most likely to relate to the prospect effectively. This person is asked to accept the assignment for an extended relationship with the prospect and, through a continuing thoughtful cultivation of genuine interest and friendship, to try to reach the prospect for Christ.

A unique approach to enrolling persons in Bible study through the Sunday School was developed by Andy Anderson, a pastor in Florida and later a national worker in Sunday School growth. The approach, called "Action Plan," is both a short-term campaign/blitz of a community and a long-term basic enrollment technique which operates on the strategy of enrolling in Sunday School Bible study "anyone, anywhere, anytime, so long as they give their consent." Historically, persons have come to the church to be enrolled in Sunday School. The uniqueness of this plan is that members may enroll persons in their homes, at work, at school, in shopping centers, or wherever they desire, as long as the enrollee consents. Statistics indicate that, with appropriate follow-up, the attendance percentages of persons so enrolled is scarcely different from the attendance percentages of those already on Sunday School rolls by the more traditional methods of enrolling members. Some churches have used the campaign/blitz "Action Plan" with phenomenal increases in their enrollment. Some churches have enrolled as many in a few weeks with this strategy as they had in a previous decade or more.

One of the planning tools which has grown out of the recent emphasis upon growth through the Sunday School is the Sunday School Growth Spiral. A copy of the spiral is shown in Figure 10. This tool for planning for growth is based on traditional growth principles and procedures and is compatible with contemporary growth approaches. It offers a way of planning a systematic pattern of outreach and growth for a Sunday School and a church. Using the spiral, Sunday School leaders quarterly plan for year-round growth at a steady pace, in all the items listed on the spiral. They then work to reach their goals, and monitor their progress with the spiral.[6]

Conclusion

Good planning and organization are essential to a church's educational ministries if they are to be most effective. Leaders must lead in planning. They should study planning and learn to do it well. There are many helpful principles and procedures which they need to know and use.

There are various kinds of planning. We briefly considered three kinds: operational, annual (short-range), and long-range. Ideally a

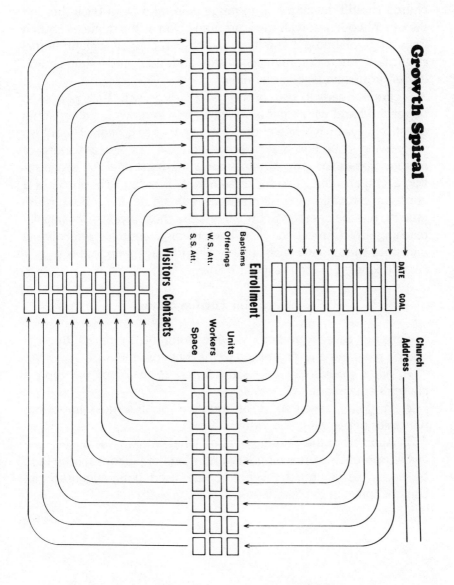

Growth Spiral

Enrollment

Baptisms
Offerings
W. S. Att.
S. S. Att.

Units
Workers
Space

Visitors Contacts

DATE GOAL

Church Address

Figure 10

church should develop a long-range plan, and work back through the other two kinds, with the long-range plan as the guide. A church long-range planning committee, the church council, organizational councils, church committees, pastor and staff, and other church leader groups engage in planning.

A church needs to plan and organize for growth. With people to be reached and with a genuine willingness to grow, there are some effective ways by which a church can experience growth. The marks of growing churches are now well known, as are a variety of methodologies for growing. For many, the most effective organization a church could use for growth is its Sunday School. All of a church's educational organizations contribute to good church growth, but the Sunday School offers the most promise for initially reaching the unreached. The leaders of a church's educational ministries should give careful thought and leadership to this significant dimension of their responsibility.

Concerns for Further Study

Consider these questions as you continue to reflect upon a church planning and organizing to meet needs.

1. What would you offer as a brief rationale for planning a church's educational ministries?

2. In your reflection, what are two of the most important principles of planning you would offer?

3. Apart from the Sunday School, what would you suggest as a viable approach to reaching large numbers of persons who would be added to a church? What if you used your suggestion in conjunction with the Sunday School for growth?

Notes

1. *Leading Your Church in Long-Range Planning* (notebook) (Nashville: Convention Press, 1975), p. 11.

2. Kenneth M. Dean, "Building a Sunday School Through Effective Weekly Workers' Meetings" (pamphlet) (Nashville: The Sunday School Board of the Southern Baptist Convention, 1980), n.p.

3. "Growing Southern Baptist Churches" (pamphlet), jointly issued by the Sunday School Board and the Home Mission Board of the Southern Baptist Convention, n.d., p. 3.

4. Several of these characteristics are discussed in detail in Bruce Grubbs, *Helping a Small Church Grow* (Nashville: Convention Press, 1980).

5. Arthur Flake, *Building a Standard Sunday School* (Nashville: The Sunday School Board of the Southern Baptist Convention, 1922), pp. 21*ff.*

6. Action and Sunday School Growth Spiral materials are available from Baptist Book Stores.

15
Discovering, Recruiting, and Training Workers

The work of a church is the work of God, performed through his people who make up the church. A church's work of teaching and learning requires the efforts of many of its members if the work is to be done well. It is the firm conclusion of many veteran church educators and pastors that a church has available to it the workers needed for what God wants that church to do. True, the workers do not just appear and begin to teach, to disciple, to minister, or to lead. Some in a church must lead the leaders, who must first be discovered, recruited, and trained. That task is the focus of this chapter.

Discovering the Gifts of the Members

Fortunately and interestingly, people differ from one another. They differ in many ways. One of the significant ways people of a church differ is in their abilities and gifts. They have varied talents and aptitudes, endowed by God. Each has some gift or gifts.

There are enough tasks to be performed in a church's educational ministries to make good use of almost any gift a person has received. A person who is gifted of God has a responsibility to develop that gift and to offer it back to him in obedient service. A church has a responsibility to be a means of helping individuals discover their gifts and of helping them use their gifts to relate with meaning to the work of God. The ministries of education in a church call for many gifted workers.

One of the most rewarding areas of ministry is the ministry of helping persons to discover, identify, and affirm their gifts, and to find ways to develop and use them. Church leaders need to give almost constant attention to the various ways they can help members in this discovery.

There are many ways to discover persons' gifts and their potential for meaningful service. Almost all of the ways, methodologically speaking, depend on the leaders being sensitive, caring, and observant. Nevertheless, most leaders, however sensitive, caring, and observant, can benefit by using some proven ways of finding the gifts and the gifted persons. Here we shall suggest some possibilities.

One way to discover persons who might be appropriate for consideration and guidance regarding their place in the work force of a church is to observe personally their participation pattern in regular and special church activities. Notice their responses. Look for indications of interest on their part in what is going on in the ministries of the church. Confirm their interest through conversations about their opinions and feelings regarding experiences in which they are involved. A simple question such as, "How did you like that . . . ?" or "What did you think of that . . . ?" can open the door for a leader to get an impression of the interest and readiness of a member. Don't pounce with an immediate recruitment appeal. Observe over some period of time, and remember what you are learning about each person. Make notes and keep a file on individuals, if necessary. If you go to this extent, date the notes and put down the gist of the conversation or their remarks. Later reflect on these impressions as you prepare to become more definite with individuals about their interest in serving.

Another way which is widely used by effective church leaders is to maintain an interest/talent/experience inventory on church members. There are forms available at denominational book stores and in other places. Many leaders make up their own questionnaires which they use to secure information about members for possible use in worker recruitment and development. There are forms to use in conducting a survey of members for this inventory, ranging from hand-tabulated cards, to pick cards, to computer forms. Keep the questionnaire as simple as possible, asking only the questions about which you might do something if members responded with the requested information.

Some leaders gather information for this inventory by surveying the membership periodically. Others call on new members of the church and secure information as part of the overall plan of assimilating new members. Some obtain the information during the new member orientation sessions. Some conduct mail surveys of the membership. Some find it useful to establish this data bank as part of the church's master membership profile and to keep the information updated rather than repeatedly asking veteran church members to fill out another questionnaire each year or two.

A wise and useful way which allows for a valuable personal touch in the discovery of persons with worker potential is continually to develop among all the present work force—teachers, directors, coordinators, church staff, and other leaders in the church—a sensitivity to the service potential and interests of members in their classes, departments, and groups of various kinds. Make it a mark of desirable achievement among present workers to alert the general leaders of the progress individuals are making in their growth and readiness for service.

An illustration of this latter approach would be to lead all teachers of adult Sunday School classes to set one goal each year in the area of identifying persons who might "graduate" into the work force of the church's educational ministries. Leaders of adult groups in other educational organizations could use the same approach. Periodically, perhaps twice a year or once a quarter at most, ask each of these teachers of adults to forward the names of those in their classes who should be considered.

Perhaps the readiness should be in terms of readiness for some preservice special training which is about to be offered. A form such as the one in Figure 11 might be used for this systematic harvesting of prospective workers.[1] Of course, keep the channels open at all times of the year for teachers and others to suggest what they have observed about prospective workers.

Keep track of the productivity of present workers in helping to discover other potential workers. Commend them, and recognize them appropriately in private and in public. In this and in other ways, the entire present work force becomes a network for discovering the gifts of others. Most teachers and other leaders experience unique joy when they are successful in helping in this effort of discovering the gifts of their pupils. A great teacher is known by the pupils who go on into more mature experiences than would be possible by staying forever in a class. Graduating into a service opportunity is such an experience.

There are other ways to help discover gifts. There are simulation games, such as NEXUS. During get-acquainted times, members

PROSPECTIVE STUDENT FOR SUNDAY SCHOOL WORKER TRAINING COURSE

(Teacher of Adults: Complete the card. Return the card via the record collection system, or give directly to the course director, who will make all recruitment contacts.)

One mark of a productive Adult class in Sunday School is the preparation of persons who are ready and willing to consider serving in the general work force of the Sunday School. Teachers and members should rejoice when a member moves into service beyond the class.

A new course to train potential workers for our Sunday School is about to begin. Please suggest confidentially one of your members you consider ready for such training. If you wish to recommend more than one, use a separate card for each.

Member's name _____ Phone_____

Your name _____ Date_____

Comment: _____

Figure 11

might be asked to present other members to the group instead of introducing themselves. These presentations to acquaint people with one another could follow structured questions about each individual—including information about their special interests, talents, and experience in church service. Such sharing should be treated as normal and desirable, as one way to express the interest of groups in the individuals who comprise their membership.

An important way to undergird the discovery efforts is for the pastor to speak forthrightly about the church's ministries and the opportunities they afford for members to serve. Such occasions should not be the generally futile appeals which almost beg persons to volunteer to serve. They must be on a higher level, citing the privileged nature, the growth experience, and the obedient offering of self which are represented in serving.

Rarely should there be public appeals for volunteers for specific jobs in the educational ministries of a church. Too often some who respond to such appeals tend to be the least qualified for the need. Such response could possibly create a very awkward situation. The work deserves more prayerful and thoughtful selectivity than dependence on public appeals allows.

It is important that the abilities, gifts, and aptitudes of members be discovered and appropriately matched with needs of the church. The latter consideration too often is the only factor considered. Better service can be rendered, lower worker turnover can be experienced, more job satisfaction can be gained, and other benefits can come from giving major attention to associating gifts and interests with the needs of the church for workers.

Recruiting Carefully and Systematically

Organization is only an idea until there are people in places required by the organization. People "make" an organization. A church might have a very well designed concept for a Sunday School organization, but the concept is only a good beginning. People must be selected, recruited, and confirmed by church action to fill each place of responsibility. The pastor and/or minister of education should work with the organizational councils to determine what positions each organization will have for the coming church year. Once these are determined, the recruitment process begins.

Selecting Prospective Workers

Many churches depend on a church committee to lead in the selection and actual recruitment of workers for the church organizations. In churches of the Southern Baptist Convention, the worker nominating committee is the primary method used. This is a committee selected by approved church procedure and accountable to the church for leading in staffing its organizations. In some churches the pastor appoints this committee and submits the names to the church for approval, subject to changes the church might make. In other churches the members of this important committee are chosen by ballot in a church business session. Each church should select its committee and determine the length of service according to approved procedures.

Many churches have a committee of three or five persons who are from the general church membership (not necessarily elected workers already serving in certain positions in the church). This committee nominates directors of organizations, who *upon* election relate to the nominating committee in the *ex officio* relationship.

These committee members and organization directors work together to coordinate the recruitment of all others who serve in the respective organizations.

The church nominating committee should serve as the clearing house for potential nominees for all church elected positions in the volunteer organizations (not the church staff positions). This committee leads the work of selecting and recruiting, and should call on many other persons to assist in the process.

An early matter for the nominating committee is to determine or review the qualifications required by the church for persons to be eligible for consideration for elected service. In some instances, the church itself might be asked to approve the qualifications upon the recommendation of the nominating committee.

There are many possible ways to state qualifications for selection. In addition to being a Christian and a member of the church in consideration, one very simple but profound statement is the threefold criteria of (1) faithful, (2) willing, and (3) capable. These simple labels should be expanded to fit the needs of each church.

A prospective worker should be faithful in obvious ways to the Lord. He or she should be faithful to the church, perhaps as demonstrated by reasonable regularity in attendance, positive attitudes toward the church and its ministries, and supportive of its chosen leaders. The prospective worker should be faithful to commitments which the accepted responsibility requires. A person considered should be faithful to himself, having a wholesome self-esteem, keeping promises, truthful, with genuine integrity.

Willingness should include a determination to work diligently to accomplish what the job requires. This might include visiting, attending planning meetings, and other specific activities. It should include willingness to work cooperatively with others and to consider fairly those changes which might be necessary to improve the work. It should include a willingness to work toward personal growth and improvement of skills.

Being capable might mean capable of learning and growing to be an effective worker. A worker prospect who is faithful, willing, and capable of learning and growing to be an effective worker is to be preferred over one who has "all kinds of abilities," but who is not faithful or willing to perform a task responsibly. The former can be helped to become capable by good training and supervision. The latter is hard to help because of not being faithful and willing. Of course, it is a delight to find a very capable person with abilities already well developed who is also faithful and willing.

Another concern of the nominating committee is to oversee the formulation of specific job descriptions for the positions which persons are to be asked to consider. The committee members need some awareness of what the jobs require, and those who are to make the recruitment contact need to be able to present the job clearly and briefly to the prospective worker. Most of the general church organizations have available in their leadership materials some model job descriptions for the usual positions the organizations require. Often these will be adequate.

With the job qualifications and the job descriptions in hand, the committee can then consider the information made available regarding the gifts, abilities, and interests of the prospective worker. Prayerfully they can relate the needs for workers with these other bodies of information and requirements and seek to match the right persons with the right jobs. Once there is agreement as to which persons should be asked to consider which jobs, the assignment for the recruitment contact should be made.

Often in this selection stage, an organization leader might present to the committee a request for clearance to contact someone whom the leader has already discovered to be a possibility as a worker in some position in the organization he represents. In many instances it would be wise to approve such requests. Among other reasons, it is a suitable way of commending the leader for the effective scouting done. But there is a concern here which is of critical importance: if the nominating committee is to be effective in coordinating the overall worker selection, recruitment, and confirmation processes, the committee must have the prerogative of determining in what positions certain ones will be asked to serve. Violate this fundamental principle, and the committee might as well be dismissed, for it cannot fulfill such a responsibility without the authority commensurate to the assignment.

Sometimes an aggressive and concerned leader will get ahead of the nominating committee and recruit a worker, and then come to ask the committee to endorse such action. In such instances it could be best to let the recruitment stand, but definitely reaffirm the committee's requirement that in all future instances clearance must be obtained prior to recruitment. Continual violation of this understanding undermines the entire concept of a church committee trying to help match the best potential workers with the service position which most needs their gifts.

Recruiting the Workers

The nominating committee, at times assisted by the pastor or the minister of education, recruits the heads of organizations. From that point, the persons who should make the contact with the person selected should be the one who would be the new worker's supervisor in the event the recruitment is successful. This person should be in the best position to talk realistically with the potential worker about exactly what the job requires and how they might work together.

The enlistment interview should be the beginning of a bond between the parties involved that results in a mutual commitment to try to do the work as it deserves to be done. The enlister should find a time and place to visit with the prospective worker when they can have an unhurried private conversation about the invitation to serve.

The need, the challenge, the requirements, the potential problems, the training opportunities, the curriculum materials and basic approach to their use, the membership and possible membership of the group, the essential activities the job calls for, the resources available, and whatever other information pertains to a realistic understanding should be discussed with the prospective worker. Time should be allowed for the prospective worker to think and to pray about the decision before giving an answer. Before the initial interview is concluded, the enlister should ask when the prospective worker thinks the decision can be made. He should invite the prospective worker to contact him with any questions that might arise pertinent to the decision. A contact from the enlister to offer to clarify any matter would sometimes be in order. The outcome of the enlistment effort should be reported promptly to the nominating committee.

Confirming the Workers

The church should have opportunity to approve those recruited to teach and lead in its organizations. This approval should include the leaders of the units of organization, such as the teachers and outreach leaders of Sunday School classes, the leaders of training groups, the chairpersons of committees, and possibly others. Generally the internal leadership of subgroups, as within the classes and committees, can be chosen by the classes and groups themselves. Church election or approval of workers serves to establish the church's oversight of its ministries, and is an appropriate and needed relationship. Furthermore, it is a way of affirming those chosen to serve.

In some churches elected workers are asked to make a commitment to a covenant statement related to their service. Samples of this type of statement are in some of the organizations' leadership magazines and manuals. Use of these covenants ranges from a kind of contractual agreement which the worker will follow or resign to a body of worthy goals of work and conduct toward which workers promise to strive faithfully.

Still another way of confirming workers is through a commissioning service. A sample taken from a printed Sunday morning worship bulletin follows.

Commissioning Service for Workers of the Church

Minister: And I heard the voice of the Lord saying, "Whom shall I send, and who will go for us?"

Workers: Then I said, "Here am I! Send me."

Minister: Because thou hast called us to salvation and to Christian living,

Workers: We consecrate ourselves to thee.

Minister: Because thou has commanded us to witness to the gospel of saving grace,

Workers: We consecrate our lips to thee.

Minister: Because thou hast commanded us to teach the unsearchable riches of thy word,

Workers: We consecrate our minds to thee.

Minister: Because thou hast called us to minister to people wherever we find them in need,

Workers: We dedicate our hands in thy service.

Minister: Because we have been called of God, what can we give in service to him?

Workers: Take our lives and let them be consecrated Lord to thee.

Minister: And what else can we give thee?

Workers: Take our lips and let them be filled with messages from thee.

Minister: Because of thy love to us,

Workers: Take our wills and make them thine.
Minister: Because we are so often limited in our understanding,
Workers: We plead the direction of thy Holy Spirit, O Lord.
Minister: Because the work we face is often unpleasant and difficult,
Workers: Make us constant in our work.
Minister: Because our sins of selfishness often lead to misunderstanding and wrong attitudes,
Workers: Keep our hearts pure, O Lord.
Minister: Because of the magnitude of the opportunity to challenge and mold the lives of others,
Workers: Help us to reflect the character of Christ in our living and service.
All: O Jesus I have promised to serve thee to the end; be thou forever near me my master and my friend.

> We beseech thee, O Lord, to use the ministry of our works for the edifying of the body of Christ, the church, until we all come in the unity of the faith, and of the knowledge of Jesus Christ thy son, unto mature Christian workers, unto the measure of the stature of the fulness of Christ.

PRAYER OF CONSECRATION
All: Let the words of our mouths and the meditations of our hearts be acceptable in thy sight, O Lord, our strength and our redeemer.

A job well done in the careful and systematic recruitment of workers for the educational ministries of a church pays dividends in many ways. The fellowship in service among well-functioning groups of workers in church organizations is some of the richest and best in all the life of the church. Ministers who concentrate on helping to create and maintain the leader groups in a church multiply their own ministries through these good leaders.

Training Workers

To multiply the teaching and learning in a church it is necessary to multiply the teachers and leaders. As indicated earlier, improving the teacher and leader level in a church represents an educational ministry in itself. A church must provide and arrange for the growth and development of its teachers and leaders in educational organizations. A church which fails to train its teachers and leaders cannot expect to do well the teaching and learning tasks for its members.

Readers might refer to the chapter "Training Teachers and Leaders" in *Christian Education Handbook,* edited and compiled by Bruce Powers. For our purposes here we shall mention major kinds of teacher and worker training and indicate the kinds of resources a church can use in its teacher and leader training.

Kinds of Training

One way to examine the kinds of training a church might use for teachers and leaders is to view training as (1) preservice training and (2) in-service training. Preservice training is timed to equip those who are just about to go on duty in a place of service. Sometimes this training is made available before one has actually been recruited for a specific place of service. In some instances the trainee might have been suggested as a prospective worker by the class teacher where the trainee attends Sunday School. This is one good way to select candidates for preservice training.

Preservice training might range from a single conference session to orient persons to the particular work they have agreed to do to a rather intensive series of training sessions such as those outlined in *Training Potential Sunday School Workers*. This latter resource offers guidance in detail for conducting either a thirty-two session series over a sixteen-week period or a twenty-four session series over an eight-week period for persons selected as potential workers in Sunday School.

The single conference session could be profitable if that is all that can be done, though it is extremely limited. There are materials such as the "Getting Ready" series, published by the Baptist Sunday School Board, which could contribute immensely to the effectiveness of a one-session conference. Better still, such materials could be presented to the prospective worker with instructions to examine the contents and then come for a follow-up session to discuss the contents in detail.

Other formats for preservice training, as for inservice training, are as varied as schedule options allow. For example, the following schedule options for training sessions are adapted from "Using the Sunday School Leadership Diploma to Train Workers" by Joseph M. Haynes.[2]

Times to Accomplish Training

1. Friday night and Saturday morning workshops
2. All-day workshops
3. Consecutive night sessions or a week of study

4. Weekend training sessions, using Saturday morning and afternoon
5. Training retreat
6. Associational training school
7. Sunday night training time
   a. Ongoing Church Training groups
   b. Interest groups for Sunday School workers not attending a Church Training group
   c. Equipping center concept
8. Individual study, using "personal learning activities"
9. Combination of reading book and joining others for write-up session
10. Courses offered one night or day a week until completed
11. Duplicate sessions offered one day and night until completed
12. State and/or regional training endeavors
13. Leadership conferences at Glorieta and Ridgecrest Conference Centers
14. Sunday morning for potential workers
15. One night for three weeks with covered-dish supper in homes
16. One-night training blitz from about 6:00 to 11:30
17. Two nights (Monday and Tuesday) each week for two weeks
18. Wednesday afternoon or evening
19. Weekly workers' meeting time
20. Mimeographed questions for individual study
21. Job descriptions, directed reading/listening programs, directed observation/evaluation

The Church Study Course

Among churches of the Southern Baptist Convention, a most productive and even more promising approach to leader and member training is known as the Church Study Course. It is a system consisting of short courses for adults and youth combined with a credit and recognition system. Also available in the system are noncredit short courses for children and preschoolers. These short courses are for use in addition to the ongoing study and training curricula in the churches.

There are more than four hundred courses in twenty-three subject areas in the system. Almost all of a church's training needs,

especially regarding the training of workers in the church organizations, can be met through this system. Courses are flexible enough
to offer credit for either individual or group study. The system is
easily maintained by volunteer workers with limited time. It is
universal so that credit earned in one church is recognized in all
other Southern Baptist churches. Persons of any church or
denomination can secure the materials and use them.

An annual Church Study Course Catalog gives full details about
the whole system, and lists each of the courses.[3] Beginning in
October 1982 the records for the entire system are to be computerized, with numerous free services thereby available to individuals,
churches, and associations to enable them to plan more effectively
the training they will offer. This truly remarkable system has the
potential of long-term usefulness in training, especially for training
teachers and leaders in the church organizations.

Seminary Extension

There are many significant training opportunities available to
ministers and laymen through extension education. One of the most
successful of these is the Seminary Extension Department of the
Southern Baptist Convention. In some four hundred centers located in all fifty states and in a number of foreign countries, and by
correspondence studies, the Seminary Extension Department annually enrolls more than ten thousand persons in a variety of
ministry-related courses leading to one of several diplomas. In
addition, certain of their courses lead to college credits. Some
seminaries also apply their credits to the associate degree.

Almost all of the courses are available for home study. The
program is part of the ministry of the Seminary External Education
Division, and is conducted under the joint auspices of the six
seminaries of the Southern Baptist Convention. Information can be
secured by contacting Seminary Extension, 460 James Robertson
Parkway, Nashville, Tennessee 37219.

Leaders in a church should locate the nearest center for Seminary Extension courses, and examine the offerings there with a view
to encouraging teachers and leaders to make use of any suitable
training opportunities. These courses, along with numerous other
opportunities, afford a rich variety from which to choose in helping

teachers and leaders train for their work in a church's educational ministries.

Conclusion

Some of the most educational work of a church is that which goes on in discovering, recruiting, and training the workers who will teach and lead in the educational ministries. It is vitally important for a church to have effective ways of accomplishing each of these responsibilities. Church leaders must be sensitive, caring, and observant as they seek to select, recruit, confirm, and train workers.

Systematic approaches such as the use of interest/talent/experience inventories, the church nominating committee, planned training events and courses, the Church Study Course, Seminary Extension courses, and other approaches should be designed or selected and used to do a thorough and comprehensive job with the work force in a church. A church which trains its educational work force has some hope of doing the job that is needed in educating its members.

Concerns for Further Study

Consider these questions as you continue to reflect upon a church discovering, recruiting, and training workers.

1. Why shouldn't a church just concern itself with getting whoever will agree to work in a given job, without going to all the trouble of trying to match gifts of individuals with job needs?

2. Why shouldn't the pastor and other church staff members do the worker recruitment for all the church organizations?

3. What kinds of plans would you make if it were your responsibility to develop training plans for all the Sunday School workers in your church?

Notes

1. Charles A. Tidwell, *Training Potential Sunday School Workers* (Nashville: Convention Press, 1976), p. 13.

2. See Bruce P. Powers, editor/compiler, *Christian Education Handbook* (Nashville: Broadman Press, 1981), pp. 255, 258.

3. For a catalog, or other information about the Church Study Course, contact the Sunday School Board, Southern Baptist Convention, Materials Services Department, 127 Ninth Avenue, North, Nashville, Tennessee 37234.

16
Providing Adequate Resources

Those who work in a church's educational ministries need certain resources to do their tasks effectively. It is possible to do the work without all the desired material resources. It is usually impossible to wait until all the desired resources are available before beginning to work. Sometimes the ministries must be performed with inadequate resources. A church has some responsibility to try to provide the resources to enable teachers and leaders to do their best possible work. In this chapter we shall look at some of the resources that are essential for the educational ministries.

Providing a Spirit and Climate for Education

The chief resources for those who teach and lead are not material but spiritual. The chief spiritual resource is the Holy Spirit. The Great Commission, itself a mandate to teach and to observe all of God's commands, concludes with the assurance of the very presence of God. Christians know that the Holy Spirit dwells in them to instruct, to guide, to convict, and to comfort. Reliance upon the promised Holy Spirit is the first requirement as a resource for an effective teacher in the realm of spiritual and moral teaching. No other resource can substitute for his presence and power.

The presence and power of the Holy Spirit are not such that anyone or any group can acquire, store, or dispense as needed. Each child of God has equal opportunity of access to his presence and power. Each has the privilege and the capacity and the responsibility to communicate with God and to seek his help through the Holy Spirit. What leaders can and should do is to keep before the teachers and leaders the necessity of reliance upon the Holy Spirit and of each one seeking to be aware of his presence and asking for his power to help them in their work. A genuine sense of partnership between God through the Holy Spirit and devoted

271

believers who are faithful, willing, and becoming capable is a powerful force for the good work of a church, which is indeed the work of God.

A climate which is conducive to teaching and learning is also a major resource for an effective church educational ministry. This climate is greatly influenced by the attitudes of leaders and members toward learning and knowledge.

On the one hand, it is important to have a sense of knowing some things for certain, and knowing them well. For example, the sure desire of God for mankind's redemption needs to be well known among leaders and teachers, in keeping with biblical teachings such as 2 Peter 3:9, "The Lord is not slow about his promise as some count slowness, but is forbearing toward you, not wishing that any should perish, but that all should reach repentance."

On the other hand, it is also important to be aware and to acknowledge that there are some things which are not yet known, some of which are not likely to be known. For example, "But of that day and hour no one knows, not even the angels of heaven, nor the Son, but the Father only" (Matt. 24:36). It is usually a detriment to the best teaching and learning in a church for some teachers to claim to know the unknowable and to imply some spiritual caste system which exalts themselves and belittles others. Cults are the result of such know-it-all leadership. There is little room for genuine teaching and learning in such a setting.

A good climate for teaching and learning is one in which there is a sense that there are some things we know with certainty and there are some things which, try though we might, we cannot know; but there are many, many things which are knowable with our effort and the Holy Spirit's help. Knowing these things could make life more what it should be. These knowables add richness, perspective, and other meaning to life in Christ. They add the kind of freedom to living which was intended when the Lord said, "If you continue in my word, you are truly my disciples, and you will know the truth, and the truth will make you free" (John 8:31-32).

Leaders in a church's educational ministries should try to provide such a climate for teaching and learning. They can do this by continually manifesting an attitude of being learners themselves, as they help make it possible for others to learn. Also, they must continue to participate in learning opportunities, such as training events, study programs, and other activities which help assure that they are growing persons. Creative leaders will find other ways to provide a climate and spirit for educating.

Providing Curriculum Materials

We have attempted to make it clear that the Bible is the principal text of the educational ministries of a church. In Part II we have already seen some of the essentials about choosing curriculum materials and about the relationship of the extrabiblical materials to the Bible. Here we shall briefly present some of the processes related to providing the materials.

A church has the responsibility and the right to determine what its members will study under the sponsorship or in the name of the church. In order to help assure that the church fulfills this responsibility and reserves this right, there should be a procedure for selecting and approving curriculum materials. Consider these suggested items as a possible procedure.

(1) The church council shall recommend to the church the line or lines of curriculum materials for use in the teaching and learning organizations.

(2) Parties advocating a variation from the approved lines of curriculum materials shall first present their proposal to the respective organizational council for consideration, well in advance of the anticipated use of the materials. If the organizational council joins in advocating the variation, the organization director (who also is the director of the organizational council) shall present the proposal to the church council. Upon approval by the church council, the variation shall come as a recommendation of the church council to the church. If the church council should not approve, the organizational council shall determine whether or not to recommend the variation to the church for consideration.

(3) In the event a church educational group contradicts the church-approved policy and procedure for curriculum selection, the organizational council and/or the church council shall instruct the teacher or leader regarding the due process. From that point the process shall be followed as stated above. Teachers or leaders who persist in violating the church's position on curriculum selection shall forfeit their positions as teachers or leaders.

A church which is affiliated with a denomination having a publishing house for curriculum materials is wise to give full and fair consideration to its products first. Such consideration should include keeping abreast of what is offered by the publishing house through catalogs, pamphlets, brochures, and other means. From time to time these leaders should examine carefully selected publications their church is using, and compare them item for item with other lines of similar materials. Use the Curriculum Selection Checklist[1] in Figure 12 to help determine the curriculum line most suited to the needs of the particular organizations.

The regularly used curriculum materials should be provided for in the church budget, with allowances for the current enrollment, new members, special projects, and new items which might be available during the year.[2]

The curriculum materials should be used principally in preparation for the teaching and learning sessions. They should not be prominent in the actual session, unless they are contributing to the teaching method as a visual aid, or in some similar way. In other words, it is not the periodical or other material which should be taught, but the biblical truth related to the needs of the group. It is important that the Bible be brought, seen, and properly used during teaching and learning sessions. Members of a Sunday School class, for example, are not appropriately impressed about the importance of studying the Bible if their teacher teaches them from something other than the Bible itself. The use of a good teaching plan or outline and selected teaching and learning aids in the session should be all a well-prepared teacher needs in addition to the Bible.

In most churches the pastor must take the initiative to lead in the selection and use of curriculum materials, working with the church council and others. In churches with a minister of education, that person should have primary responsibility for this leadership area. In some instances a church with no educational staff might have a gifted and trained layman who could be the principal leader in curriculum matters.[3]

Media library personnel can render valuable service to the educational ministries in the selection, distribution, and use of curriculum materials. Leaders should consult and plan with the media library staff to assure that materials are placed where they will be used. This is especially helpful regarding materials to be used

Curriculum Selection Checklist

Use this checklist to compare lines of curriculum you might consider for use with a given age group. Secure samples of each line you wish to consider. Examine the materials carefully. Check each item on the list below. Indicate by ✔ which line is best on each factor. Compare the basic pieces of each line: the pupil's material; the teacher's material. Choose and use the curriculum that best meets your needs.

Factor to Consider	Curriculum Lines		
	A	B	C
1. There is ample, appropriate use of the Bible.	___	___	___
2. The teachings are doctrinally sound.	___	___	___
3. Doctrinal emphases are balanced.	___	___	___
4. Coverage of the Bible is comprehensive.	___	___	___
5. The educational philosophy is valid.	___	___	___
6. Concepts presented are suited to the age group.	___	___	___
7. Content addresses life needs appropriately.	___	___	___
8. Teachings encourage appropriate responses.	___	___	___
9. Methodology is properly related to content.	___	___	___
10. Methods are suited to our workers' skills.	___	___	___
11. Training materials are available to develop worker's skills.	___	___	___
12. Learning activities are right for the age group.	___	___	___
13. The materials support the church program.	___	___	___
14. Materials advance purposes of this organization.	___	___	___
15. Quality teaching/learning aids are readily available.	___	___	___
16. Supplementary commentaries are available.	___	___	___
17. Art use is in good taste.	___	___	___
18. The layout is attractive to the user.	___	___	___
19. The binding is sufficiently durable.	___	___	___
20. The paper quality is adequate.	___	___	___
21. The print size is right.	___	___	___
22. The print is clear and easy to read.	___	___	___
23. Uses of color in materials is attractive.	___	___	___
24. Service for ordering, receiving, paying is good.	___	___	___
25. Consultation in use of materials is available.	___	___	___
26. Volume (number of pages) in each piece is adequate.	___	___	___
27. The cost in relation to the benefits is suitable.	___	___	___
28. The cost per comparable items is least.	___	___	___
29. _____	___	___	___
(Other factor we consider important)			
30. _____	___	___	___
(Other factor we consider important)			

Based upon this comparison, curriculum line _____ seems best for us. It is available at the following address:

_____

_____

_____

Figure 12

across organizational lines, such as materials for the family.

The choices and decisions made regarding a church's curriculum plan and the materials that support it are some of the most vital in a church's life. There is far more to the matter than just filling out the order forms. It is with the help of curriculum materials that the real curriculum—what happens to help people learn and develop—is experienced. Curriculum materials that are based on the Bible, designed to meet the needs of persons, penetrate and undergird the total church program, and appropriately relate method to content, in addition to other criteria, are essential to help a church reach its educational objective: to help persons become aware of God as revealed in Jesus Christ, respond to him in a personal commitment of faith, live in conscious recognition of the guidance and power of the Holy Spirit, and grow toward Christian maturity.

Providing Other Essential Resources

There are other essential resources which a church must provide in order to be most effective in its educational ministries. Among these resources are such things as adequate space (usually one or more buildings), equipment, furnishings, supplies, and funding.

Just as there are known ratios regarding teachers or leaders and members, there are also known space requirements for optimum experiences in educating each age group. Contrary to some opinions, Preschool and Children's Division ages require more space for education than do youth or adults. This is true because of their need to move around, their inability to sit still for long periods, and because of the more fundamentally physical ways in which they learn. Consult Figure 13 for recommended space provisions for the various ages for educational purposes.

More and more churches are learning to get multiple use of educational space by varied schedule arrangements. Some have more than one "shift" of Sunday School in the same space, for example. This can be done in several ways. One way is to have one Sunday School meet while an early worship service is in session, followed by another Sunday School and worship service. This means that there is full occupancy of both educational and worship space for two consecutive periods.

Another schedule possibility is to have one Sunday School meet

Determining Space in Age-Division Rooms

Organization and Space Needs for Division Grouping and Grading

Division	Age	For Each Department			For Each Class			Suggested Floor Space Per Person			
		Maximum Enrollment	Average Attendance[a]	Capacity of Space[b]	Max. Enrol.	Aver.[a] Attend.	Cap. of Space[b]	Department Assembly Minimum[c]	Recommended	Classroom Minimum[c]	Recommended
Preschool	B-1	12	5-8	7-10	Not applicable			20 sq. ft	25+	None	None
	2-3	20	9-13	12-16							
	4-5	25	11-16	15-20							
Children	6-8 9-11[d]	30	14-20	18-24	Not applicable			20 sq. ft	25+	None	None
Youth	12-14	50	23-33	30-40	10	5-7	6-8	20 sq. ft	25+	10 sq. ft	12
	15-17	60	27-39	36-48	15	8-10	9-12			10 sq. ft	12
Adult	18-up	125	56-81	75-100	25	12-16	15-20	8 sq. ft	10	8 sq. ft	12

Space is provided for each person expected to be in the rooms of the building. Determining the number for which to plan this space is a result of a careful analysis of projected enrollment, organization, and attendance.

In determining the total number of square feet of educational space required, the church should add to the floor space mentioned above enough space for offices, corridors, stairways, restrooms, storage, service space, and other accessory areas. This will require a total square footage from 35 square feet to 45 square feet per person in the educational building. Many churches provide even more space.

[a] Average attendance in churches ranges from 45% to 65% of enrollment.

[b] Capacity space to provide is figured at 60 to 80 percent of enrollment to be adequate for high expected attendance. Percentage to be used should be determined by the individual church's record of enrollment and attendance.

[c] Minimum square footage may sometimes be necessary in smaller churches and mission buildings.

[d] Existing assemblies with classrooms may be used by departments in the Children's Division. Provide additional tables, chairs, and chalkboards as needed.

Church Architecture Department, The Sunday School Board of the Southern Baptist Convention, Nashville, Tennessee

Figure 13

early, followed by a single worship service, and then by a second Sunday School. This involves three consecutive periods. Another schedule is to have one Sunday School at the traditional time prior to the single morning worship service, and then have a second Sunday School during the worship service. This involves only two consecutive periods, and has the flaw of having the second Sunday School participants regularly absent from the worship service.

Still another variation which normally uses only two consecutive periods calls for those age divisions which use a department and class format (usually youth and adults only) to have approximately half of the classes conduct their sessions first, while the others are in the department room, and then at the mid-point of the period change places. This accomplishes full occupancy of both class and department space simultaneously during one period, followed by the church worship service.

There are other possible ways to get multiple use of space. Concern about these possibilities is likely to become more and more of interest to churches with the increasing costs of building materials, interest rates on money for building, and the rapidly escalating costs of energy to heat and cool. Still another factor is the cost to individuals and families in making multiple trips to the meeting place of the church. Church leaders must search diligently for new ways to get more of the ministries of the church accomplished with less consumption, proportionately, of the church's financial resources. Otherwise, churches face the prospect of reduced ministries locally and in missions, staff reductions, and reduced attendance for the educational, worship, and other activities at the church buildings. There is an urgent need for mature, responsible, effective experimentation regarding space use, energy efficiency, and ministry scheduling to help churches continue and grow in their effectiveness.[4]

Church leaders should seek counsel from proven advisers regarding building plans and possible variations in their use of buildings already existing. Denominational educational and building consultants are readily available to many churches, and should be consulted. Other experienced pastors and educational ministers can offer helpful counsel. Their counsel might also help in scheduling and in equipment and furnishings for good teaching and learning.

Equipment and furnishings are important provisions for a

church's educational ministries. The numerous possibilities might seem overwhelming to the inexperienced educator, if considered all together. The space for the smallest babies and creepers, for example, might need all of the following: hospital cribs, diaper bag shelf, diaper rinsing with flush bowl, record player, adult rocking chair, safety chair, sink-refrigerator combination, utility tables, wall supply cabinet, clear glass windows with low sills, an adult toilet, and a playpen.

Toddler space should be furnished and equipped with the following: an area for cardboard blocks, book rack with slanting shelves, diaper bag shelf, doll bed, child-size toilet, open shelves with closed back, record player, child-size rocking chair, rocking boat and steps, wall supply cabinets, and clear glass windows with low sills.

Two- and three-year-olds need space equipped and furnished with chairs with ten-inch seat height, cabinet sink, book rack with slanting shelves, child-size toilet, clothes drying rack, coatrack for adults and one for children, doll bed, open shelves with closed back, painting easel, puzzle rack, record player, child-size rocking chair, play stove, small table, wall supply cabinet, and clear windows with low sills.

Space for four- and five-year-olds needs equipment and furnishings including clear glass windows with low sills, toilet with child-size fixtures, wall supply cabinet units, picture file desk, children's coatrack, picture rail, tackboard, block shelves, nature shelves, art shelves, book rack with slanting shelves, painting easel, clothes drying rack, record player, studio-type piano, cabinet-sink, play stove, doll bed, chest of drawers, child's rocking chair, small table, art table, puzzle table, puzzle rack, picture file desk, rack for adults and for children's wraps, and one chair with either ten- or twelve-inch seat height for each child and each teacher.

Children have these equipment and furnishings needs in their educational space: one chair with twelve- or fourteen-inch seat height per child, one table for each six children, portable shelves with closed back, studio-size piano, book rack with slanted shelves, portable coatracks for children and adults, storage cabinets, combination chalkboard, tackboard, and picture rail, cabinet for pictures and posters, record player, toilets on the hall, and sink.

Youth and adult space should have stacking or folding chairs with eighteen-inch seat height, small table or lectern in the department area, secretarial table, studio-size piano, movable coat and hat rack, chairs with tablet arms, small teaching table, folding tables available, freestanding chalkboard, chalkboard-tackboard fixed to the wall, shelves, easel, and wastebasket.

Those who plan for new buildings should make a list of equipment and furnishings for each age group, and include the cost estimates for these as they plan. Some items are more essential than others and should be the first secured in the event the space cannot be fully equipped and furnished from the beginning. A planned schedule for adding needed furnishings and equipment is advisable, in order to bring the facilities up to recommended quality. These additions should be included in the annual church budgeting process.

There are many other items of equipment and furnishings, when the ministries are considered which cross organizational and age-group lines. Media library, recreation, music, and all other ministries need the best equipment and furnishings a church can justifiably provide. Leaders of these and other ministries should have opportunity annually to request budget funding for their needs.

Supply items, such as chalk, art supplies, teaching aids, paper, scissors, paste, and numerous other supplies are recommended and are useful in the educational experiences. A church should have a simple procedure for coordinating the purchasing, storage, and distribution of these kinds of items. Some churches use a simple request form which the intended user completes and submits to the church office. One person usually secures the items and informs the requester of their availability. In addition, the items which are commonly used in many areas can be secured and stored conveniently for the workers to use as needed, without a special request.

These essential resources require funding. They should be considered integral parts of a church's funding processes. All ministry activities and the resources needed to support them should be funded in keeping with the church's approved financial plans. For most churches, small and large, this would mean that plans should be made to include funds in the church budget.

Plans for ministry should be made in advance of the budget planning. The church council, the organizational councils, church committees whose work calls for expenditures, and other groups which are considered a part of the church's ministries need to determine their proposed activities for the coming year, rank them in priority order, and place a realistic cost estimate on the ministries. These are presented by the respective leaders to the church budget committee in the order of their priority.

In the likely event that the budget planners cannot anticipate sufficient funds for all of the requests, the requesters of funds should have opportunity to determine which of their requests shall be deleted or modified. It is the function of budget planners to (1) anticipate income from all sources, (2) recommend categoric limits for the various ministry areas in keeping with the church's budgeting experience as modified by expected ministry adjustments, (3) compile the allocation requests into a unified budget as fairly and openly as possible, (4) secure church approval of the budget, and (5) oversee the financial operation of the church budget during the year, making adjustments as directed by church action and policies.

It is not the proper function of the budget committee to be expected to recommend what ministries to delete or modify, whose salaries to raise, cut, or leave the same, and other such specific decisions which should be dealt with by other church groups. To expect such decisions of the budget committee is an unfair imposition on them and on the other planning groups in a church. Lead each group to do its own work, and to relate that to the work of other groups in the light of each group's proper responsibilities. Such a process shows due respect to all leaders and provides religious growth and development for those involved. Further, it sets a good example of a church working together with a minimum of concern for power and manipulation.

One other word of caution might be useful regarding funding church ministries and the activities related to them. Many consider it questionable ethically and legally for groups in a church, or for the church as a whole, to engage in on-site services and sales activities to raise money for church functions. Ethically, if the services rendered are indeed services, they probably compete to some extent with regular business enterprises which depend on their services for a livelihood. Legally, few churches are certified or have been examined to qualify to serve food to the public or to engage in other sales or services to the public. Also, the proceeds from such services or sales probably are not properly reported for tax purposes. A church should be a good neighbor and a good corporate citizen.

Find other appropriate ways to fund church activities. Call upon members to increase their gifts. Charge actual cost for participation in certain events and possibly help underwrite such costs from the budget receipts. Probably no ethic or law would be jeopardized if the names of youth or others interested in earning from their services were made known to the members, who then could use their services at their homes for baby-sitting, lawn care, car washing, or other such help. It seems out of character to have the church gathered at the church property to engage in business for a profit.

Conclusion

A church needs certain resources for ministry. Chief among these essential resources is a spirit and climate for education. Reliance on the Holy Spirit is foundational. A good attitude toward teaching and learning is also necessary. Suitable curriculum materials are vital. The curriculum materials selected and used in a church should be clearly under church guidance and control.

A church also needs such resources as space (buildings), equipment, furnishings, supplies, and money to make all these and other resources available as needed. Church planning groups, such as the church council, organizational councils, certain church committees, and other groups need to plan and work together to try to provide the best resources they can justify to support the ministries and their activities. The ministry needs should be determined, and costs estimated, and funds secured in a manner which manifests that a church is a family of God's children. Then even the "mundane" areas of administering resources become experiences for growth and development of those involved.

Concerns for Further Study

Consider these questions as you continue to reflect upon a church providing adequate resources.

1. What suggestions would you make regarding providing a spirit and climate in a church which encourages education?

2. Secure a set of Sunday School teacher's materials for one of

the age divisions from one line from your denomination and compare it with either another line from your denomination or that of
another source. Follow the "Curriculum Selection Checklist" in this
chapter. What are your conclusions?

3. How do the space provisions and the equipment and furnishings in your church compare with those suggested in this chapter?
What would you recommend to improve the provisions in your
church?

Notes

1. Bruce P. Powers, editor/compiler, *Christian Education Handbook* (Nashville: Broadman Press, 1981), p. 205.

2. Ibid., pp. 206-209, for further suggestions such as a literature handling schedule, a literature requisition form, and other helps regarding securing adequate curriculum materials.

3. See "Supervising Curriculum in the Local Church" in Howard P. Colson and Raymond M. Rigdon, *Understanding Your Church's Curriculum,* revised edition (Nashville: Broadman Press, 1981), pp. 126 ff.

4. For additional help regarding providing space and conserving energy see the books *Church Property and Building Guidebook,* compiled by T. Lee Anderton (Nashville: Convention Press, 1980); and *Church Energy Handbook: A Guide to Energy Conservation in Church Buildings,* compiled by Jerry A. Privette (Nashville: Convention Press, 1980).

17
Implementing and Evaluating

The potential of an effective educational ministry in a church is mammoth. It can encompass almost all that a church does. People are taught. They study, learn, and develop in Christian character. They are discipled, and they go about their lives and do the work of a church. In order to help in all of these and other aspects of a church's life and work, leaders must lead. They must lead in determining what the nature and purpose of a church is, what are needs of persons a church should attempt to meet and how a church might meet those needs, and then in how the work should be done.

The emphasis of this chapter is on how to do what needs to be done. To implement a church's ministry plans means to accomplish them, to complete them with appropriate action, to carry them out, to fulfill their intentions.

Several kinds of activity are required for implementing a church's ministry plans. The plans must be promoted. Teachers and leaders must be guided, supervised, and helped to succeed. Those involved need to know specifically what is happening and to whom, through records and reports. They must know how well the work is going, to how many, and what might be done to improve.

Essentials of Good Promotion

The ministry plans of a church deserve and need to be promoted. Promotion is what is done to advance something, to further it, to move it forward. Who could be opposed in a church to good promotion of the church's essential ministries? Wise leaders will not knowingly irritate the sensitivities of those whose support and participation they are trying to secure. They will ponder their own motivation and be ethical about avoiding manipulation. But they surely will promote, if anything is to happen!

285

Promotion in a church can be seen in at least two types of activity: (1) publicity and (2) enlistment. Publicity in this context is making known to people the information designed to advance the interests of a cause. The people are those in and out of the church to whom a church is trying to minister. The cause is the activity to which the church wishes those persons to relate. The information is the facts and truths about the activity which will convey to people what they need to know in order to decide about their participation.

Publicity is accomplished in many forms. In many churches, oral announcements at meetings is perhaps the most common way. Numerous, sometimes too many, announcements are made in classes, departments, and worship services. Some have deleted announcements entirely from worship services. This seems to be an extremely negative reaction. Few other occasions in the life of a church find as many of its congregation together at one time and place as does the worship services. An approach and a time for announcements in that setting (in good taste and effective) can be accomplished. In some churches it is done in the worship services at the beginning of the period, after all have arrived in the room. Perhaps a better time is at the end of the worship period, just prior to dismissal. This would seem most often to be an opportune time to focus attention to further activities of ministry, when the real expression of service is just beginning.

Announce only a very few items, three or four at most, in a session. Limit them to those which are of general interest to the particular group. For example, the announcement to the entire congregation of a committee meeting would rarely be warranted, unless the purpose is to inform the congregation of a vital meeting of general interest. If the concern is to get committee members to attend, contact them individually, not by general announcement. Furthermore, leaders should not be expected to announce to the congregation just any note someone hands or whispers to them as they are on the way to the platform.

Posters, church bulletin articles, bulletin boards, advertising in the media, dramatic skits, and other means can be useful in publicizing a church's ministries. Apply to announcements and to other publicity means the suggestions which follow in this section.

Enlistment often can be more effective when preceded and accompanied by good publicity. Enlistment is securing the participation, support, or help of persons. A church enlists teachers and leaders. It enlists members to attend and to support and to participate. It enlists persons outside the church membership in activities in keeping with the church's purposes. It begins with some presentation of the cause, moves to a decision or commitment of persons to participate, and is actually realized when the persons follow through on their decision or commitment.

Enlistment sometimes is accomplished through appeals to groups, with a response called for at the time of the appeal. Some enlistment is best done by one-to-one contact. The nature of the cause and the time available for enlisting are among the factors which help to determine whether the appeal should be to groups of persons or to individuals by one-to-one contact. Sometimes persons are asked to register their decision or commitment on a card or other form. There are times when such an active response is helpful both to firm up the decision and for follow-up purposes.

These suggestions about promotion, whether publicity or enlistment, should be the kinds of considerations leaders would use in trying to be effective as promoters.

(1) Determine the basic facts about the activity: why it is offered (focus on needs and benefits), what is it, for whom is it, when is it (date, day, and time), where is it, who will lead it, costs (if any direct costs to participants), how a person should respond if interested (either in more information or in making a commitment—sign a card or roster, buy a ticket, tell their teacher), preparation a person might need to make (if any), and the deadline for deciding and committing (if needed).

(2) Identify the target audience for whom the promotion should proceed.

(3) Decide what means of publicity will be used and who will do each part. Make clear assignments to those who will do the publicizing. Consider using the leaders who are responsible for leading the activity in the publicity. Too often one person attempts to do all the public announcements, and one result is that the announcer loses impact on the audience over a period of time. Inject a variety of promotional personnel.

(4) Plan for the best ways to enlist persons and for those who will do this best. Make clear assignments to these persons. In events or activities which involve a series of sessions, consider seeking

commitment from persons for the entire series in one decision. This could help the persons avoid having to decide whether or not to participate in each session. Make it clear how persons indicate their participation.

One of the major concerns of many churches is how to attract persons, both irregular attenders who are members and nonmembers, to basic educational activities such as Bible study (Sunday School) and discipleship training. There are many on the membership rolls of these organizations and others who are as unreached in terms of participation as those who have not been reached for enrollment. They could hardly be driven away, because they are already away. Then there are the multitudes who have never been members for whom a church is concerned. Good publicity can get through effectively to only a few of these hard to reach persons. Special enlistment techniques can help to attract some. Some might never participate as hoped; still a church must try.

For those difficult to attract persons, the first approach recommended is to use the regular organizational structure in efforts to reach them. In Sunday School this is the teacher, along with the outreach leader and group leaders. They should plan and carry out a systematic approach to contacting the nonattenders who are members or nonmembers. In the course of a quarter they can make some contact weekly, such as a visit by the teacher to deliver a Sunday School lesson periodical, a phone call, a visit by the outreach leader, a letter, a visit by the group leader, a church service bulletin in the mail with a personal note, a visit again by the teacher and a class member, another phone call, a visit by the group leader, a second letter, another visit by the outreach leader, and another visit to deliver the next quarter's lesson periodical.

Still another sometimes productive plan is to determine who in all of the church has some possibility of building a bridge of friendship over an extended period of contacts with the unreached or irregularly attending person. Ask a person who lives in the same neighborhood, works at the same location, has a mutual acquaintance, or has some other point of contact with the person about whom you are concerned to spend six months getting to know and to relate to that person. They could visit their homes, share a work break, go shopping together, celebrate birthdays or other special occasions, attend some community activities or church activities together, or other good occasions, which would allow a genuine bond to be established and a concern to be expressed. Some will respond and be blessed by such an effort. Of course, the interest should not disappear after the person is reached, lest it reflect a superficiality which should not exist.

Sometimes members who have not been attending for a long period might be invited to a meeting with the pastor. It could be a fellowship-dinner meeting, either at a home or at the church. At this gathering with a small number of persons at a time, the pastor could explore with them what kinds of Bible study or other organizational activities they might desire. Consider planning to arrange for what they would like, if possible. This approach has been especially effective with husband-wife nonparticipating members in activating their interest in discipleship training.

In any event, it is important that the people of the church not give up in seeking ways to promote the cause of the church, to reach persons for Christ for the sake of all concerned. In the words of Paul, "Love never ends" (1 Cor. 13:8). It is not always acknowledged, but it remains. If love is demonstrated even after all the methods have failed, some will respond. Ours is not the burden of winning but of being faithful to witness. God does the winning. We try to be useful to him in the process.

Supervision

It is the work of some to direct the work of others, to the end that the total work is accomplished and the workers are supported in terms of personal growth and development. This is the meaning of supervision.

Some confuse supervisory responsibility with quality of personhood. They mistake assignment to certain tasks to be primarily an indication of personal status, and are hindered by feelings of superior-inferior in personal terms. They do not understand the body analogies of the Scriptures. This is unfortunate when it happens in any setting; it is out of place in a church. Of all places and institutions, persons must be treated equally as persons in a church. This was a chief delight of the early church. When it has been violated, the church has assumed a character different from a church, though it retains the name. There are different levels of responsibility due to the nature of different tasks, but the persons are no more or no less persons because they have the different tasks. The church body gives the responsibility and the freedom to act (the authority, if you please) commensurate with the responsibility. Still, the assignment is task related, and not indicative of personal power over others.

Actually, supervision is a biblical concept. *Supervisor* is an English word which came directly from Latin *super,* meaning over, and *visor,* meaning one who sees. The Latin word matches the Greek word of the New Testament, *episcopas,* a combination of *epi,* meaning over, and *scopas,* meaning seer. *Episcopas* is the term from which the word *bishop* is derived. The educational ministries of a church need many *episcopoi!* They are the pastor, heads of organizations, division directors, department directors, teachers of classes, leaders of groups of many kinds. Each has as part of his/her work assignment the responsibility of leading others in performing their work as it relates to the total work of a church. This requires supervision.

In church ministries, a supervisor leads those who work with him in an assignment area to determine how they should do their work. The supervisor works as an enabler of others. He or she tries to see that workers have what they need in the way of encouragement, information, directions, feedback opportunities, organization, training, time, materials, money, space, equipment, furnishings, planning, preparation, evaluation, and other resources essential to getting the job done well. Followers have some responsibilities for these resources, too, but the supervisor has primary responsibility for taking the initiative.

In the April 1977 issue of *Church Administration,* I wrote a decalogue for supervisors entitled "Be a Better Supervisor." (1) Thou shalt establish and maintain adequate communication. (2) Thou shalt set clear and reasonable deadlines. (3) Thou shalt check appropriately on progress. (4) Thou shalt make needed help available. (5) Thou shalt encourage workers to seek help. (6) Thou shalt develop solution-minded workers. (7) Thou shalt attack problems, not people. (8) Thou shalt time guidance for optimum good. (9) Thou shalt avoid trivia. (10) Thou shalt learn from mistakes. Blessed is a church whose supervisors know and practice such guidelines. Such a supervisor is truly a "chief among equals" and deserves the esteem and cooperation of those on the team.

Recording and Reporting

The work of the educational ministries of a church requires records and reports in order to keep leaders and members adequately informed of the activities and progress of the ministries. A second reason is for historical purposes. Through records and reports, trends and needs appear which inform leaders and others so that they can know better how to proceed and what adjustments might be made to help improve the work.

Each unit and each organization should keep certain records of their activities and report regularly to the next larger unit in the church's organization. All church ministries should report regularly to the church itself. The reports of a church's major programs usually come in monthly or quarterly business meetings, with a summary report on an annual basis.

Many record systems have already been established, and the materials for them are easily available. The catalogs of denominational suppliers and others in the business should give church leaders the choices of record and reporting materials they need. Some churches have found computer services useful for assistance in various areas of record keeping and reporting. Most churches still rely on handwritten record systems. Leaders should choose and/or design the records they feel they need, and diligently advocate their proper use.

There are some well-designed, denominationally supplied record systems for the various educational ministries of a church. They help to focus not only on quantity—how many are in attendance or on the roll—but also on quality—who made certain preparation for the sessions or who rendered certain ministries to others. The information from such records should cause leaders to respond to certain needs the records reflect, and to try to improve or otherwise modify their efforts and the results.

It is helpful to train those who secure the records to help insure that full and adequate information is obtained. Annual training sessions of the records keepers, often called secretaries (of classes or departments), are recommended.

It is usually wise to keep all church organization records in the church office when they are not in use during meetings at the church. It is also important to have systematic ways of modifying the records, such as adding to the roll, transferring members, or dropping them from the roll. For example, a single multiple-use form can serve all of these purposes. Such a form should be completed in the class or elsewhere and returned through the regular channels to the organizational secretary who is authorized, in keeping with approved procedures, to record the information on the official records. To do this otherwise is to have records which are inaccurate and which do not consistently help implement the purposes for which records are needed.

Evaluating Quality and Quantity

Evaluation involves accurately analyzing what is occurring or what has occurred, comparing that with the intent or hope, observing the reasons for any differences between happenings and intentions, learning from the experience what might be done to improve or to increase (or both) the victories in the future, and celebrating the victories achieved. There are many degrees of intensity in evaluation, ranging from an informal "Wasn't that great!" to a detailed accounting and analysis of facts and figures, their meanings, suggested changes, and how to get the changes into the system.

Evaluation of a church's educational activities usually deserves more than the informal appraisal suggested by a passing comment. A form such as that in Figure 14 might be useful to the church council and to organizational councils in evaluating each of the major tasks and the activities related to them.

It is important to evaluate quality and quantity. A church cannot afford to neglect one in pursuit of the other. It is possible to have poor quality with small numbers, or any other combination of these elements. The absence or presence of one does not assure the other. It is a worthy ambition for a church to want to do as well as it can with as may as it can.

Use this form in the church council and/or organizational councils to evaluate tasks and related activities either at termination of each activity or at year's end. Use this rating scale: (1) *excellent;* very adequate; (2) *good,* but needs a few improvements; (3) *fair,* but needs major improvements; (4) *poor,* not at all adequate.

TASK: EQUIP CHURCH MEMBERS FOR DISCIPLESHIP AND PERSONAL MINISTRY

Activity List	Organiza- tional adequacy	Leaders		Resources			Promo- tion Effec- tiveness	Overall Effec- tiveness	Other
		Number	Effective- ness	Materials, supplies	Space, Equip- ment	Funds	(Public- ity, en- listment)		
1.									
2.									
3.									
4.									
5.									
6.									
7.									
8.									
9.									
10.									

After evaluating, transfer ratings on each activity to a simple listing and give copies to other persons who might be helped by this information. Include comments related to how to improve each activity in the future. Interpret sensitively.

Figure 14

Other aspects of the educational ministries should be evaluated. Teacher training and preparation and experiences of learners are illustrative of other areas which need to be appraised from time to time. Standards of excellence for classes, departments, and entire organizations can be useful tools for comprehensively evaluating the work of each of those units.

There are many possible principles of evaluating which might help church leaders. Several of these were identified in *Working Together Through the Church Council.*[1] They apply particularly to the evaluating work of a church council related to the ministry activities: (1) planners and implementers evaluate; (2) develop evaluation criteria before implementing plans; (3) evaluate qualitatively and quantitatively. (4) time evaluation to get maximum benefit; (5) evaluate processes and results, not personalities; (6) evaluate objectively and subjectively; and (7) communicate evaluation findings. These and other guidelines can help to improve and to increase the effectiveness of the educational ministries of a church.

Conclusion

A church has a mission to accomplish. It engages in educational and other ministries to accomplish that mission. Leaders must lead in this implementation. There are numerous elements involved. Among them is promotion—the publicity and the enlistment required to bring people and ministry plans together. There is supervision—directing the work of others to accomplish the work and to support the workers and those whom they serve.

Records and reports are also important parts of implementation. They serve to keep leaders, members, and others informed so that the ministries can be improved and increased. Evaluation is also an essential part of effective leadership. It is important to know what was accomplished, how well, for how many, and what the lessons of the past experiences can teach for the present and the future.

Concerns for Further Study

Consider these questions as you continue to reflect upon a church implementing and evaluating its educational ministries.

1. Think of the most effectively promoted event or activity you

have observed in a church's educational ministry. What were the key elements in the promotion? What might have been done even better?

2. Can you distinguish for yourself the quality of personhood from tasks to be performed (1) with you as supervisor; and (2) with you as the supervisee?

3. Do you agree that both quality and quantity are essential in the ministries of a church? Why or why not?

Note

1. Charles A. Tidwell, *Working Together Through the Church Council* (Nashville: Convention Press, 1968), pp. 64-68.

Appendix

Basic Church Programs

Six major church programs have been discussed in this volume. Each program has several tasks that are important to the total work of a church. For the convenience of the reader, these programs and tasks are outlined on this page.

Bible Teaching
1. Reach persons for Bible study.
2. Teach the Bible.
3. Witness to persons about Christ and lead persons into church membership.
4. Minister to Sunday School members and nonmembers.
5. Lead members to worship.
6. Interpret and undergird the work of the church and the denomination.

Church Training
1. Equip church members for discipleship and personal ministry.
2. Teach Christian theology and Baptist doctrine, Christian ethics, Christian history, and church polity and organization.
3. Equip church leaders for service.
4. Interpret and undergird the work of the church and the denomination.

Music Ministry
1. Provide musical experiences in congregational services.
2. Develop musical skills, attitudes, and understandings.
3. Witness and minister through music.
4. Interpret and undergird the work of the church and the denomination.

Brotherhood
1. Engage in missions activities.
2. Teach missions.
3. Pray for and give to missions.
4. Develop personal ministry.
5. Interpret and undergird the work of the church and the denomination.

Woman's Missionary Union
1. Teach missions.
2. Engage in mission action and personal witnessing.
3. Support missions.
4. Interpret and undergird the work of the church and the denomination.

Pastoral Ministries
1. Lead the church in the accomplishment of its mission.
2. Proclaim the gospel to believers and unbelievers.
3. Care for the church's members and other persons in the community.
4. Interpret and undergird the work of the church and the denomination.

Bibliography

Bibliography

Adams, Arthur M. *Effective Leadership for Today's Church.* Philadelphia: Westminster Press, 1978.

Adams, Ernest R., and Fitch, James E. *Reaching People Through the Sunday School.* Nashville: Convention Press, 1979.

Adams, Ernest R., and Allen, Mavis. *How to Improve Bible Teaching and Learning in Sunday School.* Nashville: Convention Press, 1976.

Belew, Wendell. *The Purpose and Plan of Baptist Brotherhood.* Memphis: Brotherhood Commission, 1979.

Benson, Clarence H. *A Popular History of Christian Education.* Chicago: Moody Press, 1943.

Bowman, Locke E., Jr. *Teaching Today.* Philadelphia: Westminster Press, 1980.

Byrne, H. W. *Improving Church Education.* Birmingham: Religious Education Press. 1979.

Coleman, Lucien E., Jr. *How to Teach the Bible.* Nashville: Broadman Press, 1979.

Colson, Howard P., and Rigdon, Raymond M. *Understanding Your Church's Curriculum.* Revised Edition. Nashville: Broadman Press, 1981.

Craig, Floyd. *Christian Communicator's Handbook.* rev. ed. Nashville: Broadman Press, 1977.

Edgemon, Roy T., compiler. *Equipping Disciples Through Church Training.* Nashville: Convention Press, 1981.

Ford, LeRoy. *Design for Teaching and Training.* Nashville: Broadman Press, 1978.

Groome, Thomas H. *Christian Religious Education.* San Francisco: Harper and Row, 1980.

Grubbs, Bruce, editor. *Helping a Small Church Grow.* Nashville: Convention Press, 1980.

Hendricks, William L. *A Theology for Children.* Nashville: Broadman Press, 1980.

Hinkle, Joseph W., and Cook, Melva. *How to Minister to Families in Your Church.* Nashville: Broadman Press, 1978.

Hinson, E. Glenn. *The Integrity of the Church.* Nashville: Broadman Press, 1978.

Kerr, Horace. *How to Minister to Senior Adults in Your Church.* Nashville: Broadman Press, 1980.

Leas, Speed, and Kittlaus, Paul. *Church Fights: Managing Conflict in the Local Church.* Philadelphia: Westminster Press, 1973.

Lindaman, Edward B. *Thinking in the Future Tense.* Nashville: Broadman Press, 1978.

Lindgren, Alvin. *Foundations for Purposeful Church Administration.* Nashville: Abingdon, 1965.

McDonough, Reginald M., compiler. *A Church on Mission.* Nashville: Convention Press, 1980.

McDonough, Reginald M. *Keys to Effective Motivation.* Nashville: Broadman Press, 1979.

McDonough, Reginald. *Working with Volunteer Leaders in the Church.* Nashville: Broadman Press, 1976.

McSwain, Larry, and Treadwell, William C., Jr. *Conflict Ministry in the Church.* Nashville: Broadman Press, 1981.

Madsen, Paul. *The Small Church: Valid, Vital, Victorious.* Valley Forge: Judson Press, 1975.

Miller, Randolph Crump. *Education for Christian Living.* Englewood Cliffs: Prentice-Hall, 1956.

Mosley, Ernest E. *Priorities in Ministry.* Nashville: Convention Press, 1978.

Piland, Harry. *Basic Sunday School Work.* Nashville: Convention Press, 1980.

Powers, Bruce P., editor/compiler. *Christian Education Handbook.* Nashville: Broadman Press, 1981.

Powers, Bruce P. *Christian Leadership.* Nashville: Broadman Press, 1979.

Reynolds, William J., compiler. *Building an Effective Music Ministry.* Nashville: Convention Press, 1980.

Richards, Lawrence O. *Creative Bible Teaching.* Chicago: Moody Press, 1970.

Richards, Lawrence O. *A Theology of Christian Education.* Grand Rapids: Zondervan Publishing House, 1975.

Schaller, Lyle E., and Tidwell, Charles A. *Creative Church Administration.* Nashville: Abingdon Press, 1975.

Sherrill, Lewis Joseph. *The Rise of Christian Education.* New York: The Macmillan Company, 1944.

Sisemore, John T., compiler. *The Ministry of Religious Education.* Nashville: Broadman Press, 1978.

Smart, James. *The Teaching Ministry of the Church.* Philadelphia: Westminster Press, 1954.

Sorrill, Bobbie. *WMU—A Church Missions Organization.* Birmingham: Woman's Missionary Union, 1981.

Taylor, Marvin J., editor. *An Introduction to Christian Education.* Nashville: Abingdon Press, 1966.

This, Leslie E. *A Guide to Effective Management.* London: Addison-Wesley Publishing Co., 1974.

Tidwell, Charles A. *Training Potential Sunday School Workers.* Nashville: Convention Press, 1976.

Tidwell, Charles A. *Working Together Through the Church Council.* Nashville: Convention Press, 1968.

Westerhoff, John. *Will Our Children Have Faith?* New York: Seabury Press, 1976.

Wyckoff, D. Campbell. *How to Evaluate Your Christian Education Program.* Philadelphia: Westminster Press, 1962.